# Contents

WP

# USA

# Top **25** attractions

**1** **Times Square** The 'crossroads of the world' blazes with neon, and is energized by new development and a revamped Great White Way *(see p.68)*

**2** **National Mall** The heart of the nation's capital is punctuated by venerable museums and iconic monuments *(see p.109)*

**3** **Hike the Grand Canyon** One of the world's greatest natural wonders – see it and you might still not believe its grandeur *(see p.187)*

**4** **San Francisco's Golden Gate Park**
A much-loved green space, with great
gardens and museums *(see p.238)*

**5** **Walt Disney World Resort** The
ultimate getaway, where 'imagineers'
anticipate every fantasy *(see p.139)*

**7** **Yellowstone National Park**
A geological wonder, where thermal
springs bubble and spout *(see p.207)*

**6** **Statue of Liberty** The beacon for
American liberty graces the New
York harbor *(see p.64)*

**8** **Freedom Trail** Follow in the Founding
Fathers' footsteps on this historic
route through Boston *(see p.75)*

**9** **The Strip** Viva Las Vegas! Sin City's main drag hums with over-the-top casinos and resorts *(see p.199)*

**10** **Chicago's Loop** Turn-of-the-20th-century high-rises, and Pop sculpture on every corner *(see p.161)*

**12** **Beale Street** The birthplace of the blues can be found in Memphis, Tennessee *(see p.134)*

**11** **Hollywood** The dream is alive in Tinseltown, where movie hopefuls tread the Walk of Fame *(see p.226)*

**13** **Metropolitan Museum of Art** New York City's premier museum is full of masterpieces *(see p.69)*

**18** **French Quarter** The feisty spirit of jazz music infuses every block of this historic district of New Orleans (see p.146)

**19** **Pike Place Market** Fishmongers sell the local catch, locals slurp oysters, and shoppers buy flowers at Seattle's famous market (see p.259)

**20** **The Everglades** Coursing through Florida is a 'river of grass,' a unique ecosystem swarming with rare wildlife (see p.142)

**21 Art Deco District** Miami Beach's South Beach neighborhood has oodles of retro style (*see p.138*)

**22 Liberty Bell** Philadelphia's pride is is represented by this icon of independence (*see p.99*)

**23 Blue Ridge Parkway** Enjoy a scenic drive through the Great Smoky Mountains (*see p.128*)

**25 San Antonio's River Walk** This waterfront walkway has café areas and shady arbors (*see p.183*)

**24 Arches National Park** Hike through the world's largest group of natural sandstone arches (*see p.204*)

# USA fact file

The contiguous US still feels much like the 'New World,' especially during your first trip. There's a vigorous energy and super-size grandeur in the landscape, from Alpine tundra in the Rocky Mountains to the swampy Everglades of Florida to the parched deserts of the Southwest. The historic eastern cities, such as New York and Philadelphia, have huge populations, while younger hubs, such as Los Angeles, sprawl far and wide into metropolitan areas.

## BASICS
**Population:** 311 million
**Area:** 3,794,100 sq miles
(9,826,675 sq km)
**Official language(s):** none
**No. of states:** 50 + Washington, DC
**State religion:** none
**Capital city:** Washington, DC
**President:** Barack Obama
**National anthem:** *The Star-Spangled Banner*
**National symbols:** bald eagle, Liberty Bell, Statue of Liberty, Uncle Sam
**National sports:** American football, baseball

## CURRENCY
US dollar ($). $1 = 100 cents (¢)
The following figures are approximate:
£1 = $1.62
€1 = $1.38

## TIME ZONES
GMT -5 for EST, -8 for PST
**In January:**
  New York: noon
  Washington, DC: noon
  London: 5pm
  Sydney: 2am the following day
  Auckland: 4am the following day
**In July:**
  New York: noon
  Washington, DC: noon
  London: 5pm
  Sydney: 1am the following day
  Auckland: 2am the following day

## SMOKING

Smoking bans are authorized by state and local jurisdictions. Most of the largest cities in the US, including New York City, Chicago, and Los Angeles, do not allow smoking in restaurants or bars. Some states enforce a no-smoking law for any type of enclosed workspace; some cities are starting to ban smoking in public parks

## ELECTRICITY

110 volts, 60 hertz
Flat 2- or 3-pin plug, American style

## OPENING HOURS

**Banks:** Mon–Fri 8am–5pm, Sat 9am–1pm
**Shops:** Mon–Fri 9am–6pm, Sat 10am–6pm, Sun noon–5pm; in major cities, stores often stay open late one weeknight (often Thursday or Friday); in large malls, shops tend to stay open until 8pm or 9pm
**Museums:** Hours vary considerably, but often museums close on Monday and stay open late on Friday or Saturday evenings

## POSTAL SERVICE

United States Postal Service (USPS)
**Post offices:** Mon–Fri 8am–6pm, Sat 9am–3pm; major cities have one main 24-hour branch
**Postboxes:** dark blue with rounded tops
**Standard post:** 44¢ for first-class letters
**Airmail:** 98¢ for first-class letters to the UK and the rest of Europe; 80¢ for first-class letters to Canada

# Trip planner

## WHEN TO GO

### Climate

Summers in the US are generally warm, except in northern New England and northern Oregon. Coastal areas of California, including Los Angeles and San Francisco, experience 'June gloom,' when it stays overcast in early summer.

In southern California and the Southwest, summer months tend to be dry and intensely hot, but in the South, Mid-Atlantic, and Midwest, June through August can be muggy. The Atlantic Coast, Florida, and the Gulf Coast face the threat of hurricanes from June through November.

New England is particularly beautiful in autumn, when the leaves turn gold and crimson. The weather is usually crisp yet pleasant at this time of year in northern California and the Pacific Northwest.

In winter, New England and the Heartland receive a covering of snow; the Mid-Atlantic states also experience a freeze. In the desert areas of the Southwest, temperatures drop precipitously at night. Heavy snowfalls can close roads in high mountains, such as the Rockies – though winter-sports fans eagerly hit the slopes. Snowbirds (those people looking to avoid the winter chill) usually head south for the winter to the relative warmth of Florida and Arizona.

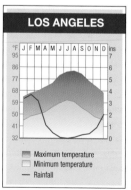

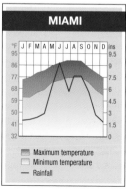

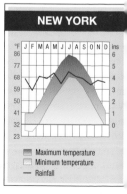

The sun sets over Sentinel Peak Park in Arizona

## High/low season

High season varies across the US but, broadly speaking, summer is the peak season for the Pacific Northwest, for beach towns in New England and California, and for national and theme parks – largely because of the school-holiday schedule. However, summer is part of hurricane season in the Gulf and along the southern Atlantic coasts. Cities such as Miami and New Orleans therefore hit high year only in the winter.

Autumn counts as high season for New England's 'leaf-peeping' zone and wine regions across the country. Winter sends hordes to the mountain resorts, from the east coast to the Rocky Mountains. Visitors should be aware that high-season hotel rates in popular vacation spots can climb by 30 to 50 percent.

### Public holidays

| | |
|---|---|
| **January 1** | New Year's Day |
| **Third Mon in Jan** | Martin Luther King, Jr. Day |
| **Third Mon in Feb** | Presidents' Day |
| **Last Mon in May** | Memorial Day |
| **July 4** | Independence Day |
| **First Mon in Sept** | Labor Day |
| **Second Mon in Oct** | Columbus Day |
| **November 11** | Veterans Day |
| **Fourth Thur in Nov** | Thanksgiving |
| **December 25** | Christmas |

*In addition to the above, there is often a holiday on Easter (variable year by year in March or April, depending on the Gregorian calendar). While Halloween (October 31) is not an official holiday, it is a very popular celebration. On federal holidays, post offices, banks, and many other businesses are closed.*

# ESSENTIAL EVENTS

Gasparilla Pirate Festival in Tampa, Florida

with firecrackers and a giant golden dragon snaking through the streets. **Houston Livestock Show and Rodeo**, late February and early March, Houston. Cowboy boots galore at the world's biggest rodeo, which packs in country singers, roping demonstrations, and bucking broncos.
**Mardi Gras**, Tuesday before Ash Wednesday, New Orleans. The streets fill with parades, floats, extravagantly costumed people throwing trinkets, and tipsy revelers.

## March

**National Cherry Blossom Festival**, starting on the last Saturday of March, Washington, DC. A two-week celebration of spring under the pink and white puffs of the Japanese cherry trees in the nation's capital.
**South by Southwest (SXSW)**, early March, Austin. A global magnet for music, film, and new-media lovers.

## April

**New Orleans Jazz & Heritage Festival**, last weekend of April and first weekend of May, New Orleans. Dozens of outdoor performances of jazz, blues, and Cajun music.

## May

**Bay to Breakers 12K Foot Race**, third Sunday in May, San Francisco. Cities such as New York and Boston hold famous marathons, but this century-old race is renowned as a fun run, with costumed racers and a finish-line party.

## January

**The Gasparilla Pirate Festival**, third weekend of January, Tampa. Offering a good opportunity to practice your pirateology, as pirates storm the city.
**Award Season**, January and February, Los Angeles. Stars grace the red carpets of Hollywood for the Golden Globes and Academy Awards.

## February

**Chinese New Year**, late January or early February, San Francisco. A clanging parade in Chinatown,

## June

**CMA Music Festival**, early June, Nashville. Country music's biggest and buzziest festival.

**San Francisco Pride**, late June, San Francisco. The country's biggest LGBT pride party, with parades and music.

## July

**National Independence Day**, July 4, Washington, DC, as well as communities across the country. The capital celebrates with parades, music, and tremendous firework displays.

## August

**Elvis Week**, Graceland, Memphis, Tennessee. Culminating on the anniversary of Elvis's death, this festival features the world's largest gathering of Elvis impersonators.

## September

**Burning Man**, one week in early September, Black Rock Desert in northern Nevada. Artists, provocateurs, and radicals engage in an experiment in community, self-expression, and self-reliance.

## October

**Halloween**, October 31. San Francisco and New York City are home to the country's best-supported, most elaborate, and most highly-spirited annual costume parades for this devilish festival.

## November

**Macy's Thanksgiving Day Parade**, fourth Thursday of November, New York City. Floats of giant inflated balloons, flanked by marching bands, cruise the streets of New York.

## December

**New Year's Eve**, night of December 31. In New York City, thousands crowd into Times Square for the country's biggest midnight countdown.

Trip planner

The ghoulish Halloween parade in New York City

# ITINERARIES

You would need at least a month for even a whistle-stop tour of the whole of the US, so it's much better to concentrate on just a few regions and do them justice. However, if you have just one week to spare, choose a particular city or state to explore; to focus your itinerary further, you could decide on your favored mode of transportation and/or devise a theme for the trip.

## One week California road trip

*Days 1–2:* **Los Angeles.** Start your trip in the capital of car culture by getting acclimatized to California's freeways. Swoop along Sunset Boulevard to the Santa Monica beaches and drive up the Pacific Coast Highway to Malibu. Consider visiting one of the Getty museums or catch a movie in Hollywood.

*Days 3–5:* **Big Sur.** Take the Pacific Coast Highway northward. Visit the lavish Hearst Castle for the morning, then stop overnight at the stunning seaside hamlet of Big Sur.

*Days 6–7:* **San Francisco.** Make an early start to see the morning light on the 17-Mile Drive, a breathtaking stretch of toll road. Give yourself a couple of hours at the Monterey Aquarium, then continue on the Pacific Coast Highway, twisting up to San Francisco. In the City by the Bay, park your car (all those one-way streets can be a hassle) and stretch your legs in Golden Gate Park. Alternatively, rent a bicycle and ride across the Golden Gate Bridge, then cycle down to Sausalito, where you can catch the ferry back to the city.

Sightseeing on four wheels in sunny California

Autumn, when the leaves turn to gold, is the best season to visit New England

## One week for music lovers

**Days 1–2: Nashville.** Rev yourself up at the spiritual home of country music, paying your respects at the Grand Ole Opry, Ryman Auditorium, and some of the Broadway clubs.

**Days 3–5: Memphis.** Drive southwest to the cradle of rock'n'roll, starting with a stop at Graceland, the home of Elvis Presley. During the day, feel the vibrations at Sun Studio; at night, prowl the Beale Street venues for the latest acts to take the stage.

**Days 6–7: New Orleans.** Nearly every block of this city hums with music. Fortify yourself with brunch, then savor the Delta blues on Bourbon Street, and thumping Cajun beats in off-the-beaten-track clubs. Keep an eye out for a New Orleans funeral, when jazz bands parade down the street to celebrate a life well lived.

## Ten days in classic New England

**Days 1–2: Boston.** Walk through the 18th-century streets along the Freedom Trail, visiting historic churches, and the homes of patriot Paul Revere and other notable citizens. Don't forget to stop by Faneuil Hall for a bite to eat, and go for a boat ride on the Charles River.

**Days 3–5: Berkshires or Cape Cod.** Drive inland to the rolling hills of the Berkshires, stopping at the postcard-perfect town of Stockbridge. If you crave a day on the beach instead, drive out along the arm of Cape Cod, settling in for a couple of days to enjoy the dunes and lobster rolls.

**Days 6–8: Vermont or New Hampshire.** Dip into one of these states on a major highway, and you'll see thickly forested hills punctuated by white colonial church steeples, but get off the main roads to really enjoy the scenery and the small-town charms. This is the best part of the country to enjoy the autumn foliage, which shimmers with gorgeous golds, reds, and auburns.

**Days 9–10: Portland.** Coastal Maine's biggest city has an atmospheric Old Port area and rugged beaches nearby. Try the local seafood for a real taste of life in the Lobster State.

# BEFORE YOU LEAVE

### Visas and entry requirements

Visitors coming to the United States must have a valid passport, visa, or other accepted documentation. However, in an effort to attract more tourists, the US initiated the Visa Waiver Program for those coming on vacation for a maximum of 90 days. With 36 countries participating, the program allows for select travelers to enter the US with only a machine readable passport. Recent increased security now requires all VWP participants to apply with the Electronic System for Travel Authorization. Done on-line, authorization does not take much time and can occur at any point before entry into the US.

### Embassies

**UK:** 3100 Massachusetts Avenue, NW, Washington, DC; tel: 202-588-6500; http://ukinusa.fco.gov.uk
**Canada:** 501 Pennsylvania Avenue, NW, Washington, DC; tel: 202-682-1740; www.canadainternational.gc.ca/washington
**Australia:** 1601 Massachusetts Avenue, NW, Washington, DC;

| Citizens | Visa required |
|---|---|
| UK | ✗ |
| Canada | ✗ |
| Australia | ✗ |
| New Zealand | ✗ |
| Ireland | ✗ |
| South Africa | ✓ |

tel: 202-797-3000; www.usa.embassy.gov.au
**New Zealand:** 37 Observatory Circle, NW, Washington, DC; tel: 202-328-4800; www.nzembassy.com/united-states-of-america
**Ireland:** 2234 Massachusetts Avenue, NW, Washington, DC; tel: 202-462-3939; www.embassyofireland.org
**South Africa:** 3051 Massachusetts Avenue, NW, Washington, DC; tel: 202-232-4400; www.saembassy.org

### Booking in advance

If you are attending one of the major festivals – such as Mardi Gras – described on pages 14–15, you should book a hotel room several months in advance. The lodging choices in popular national parks,

El Tovar Hotel, Grand Canyon

Keeping cool at Slide Rock State Park in Sedona, Arizona

such as the Grand Canyon, also fill up months ahead. If you have your heart set on one of the classic lodges, try to reserve at least six months in advance. Hotels in the top ski resorts also get booked up early.

## Tourist information
**Discover America,** www.discover america.com. There is no central US tourism authority with offices abroad. Instead, individual states are responsible for promoting themselves; unfortunately coverage is sporadic. Popular destinations (such as California) sometimes have their own tourist offices in foreign countries.

## Maps
The Rand McNally series of maps and driving atlases is quite reliable and should be readily available at major bookstores. Michelin's detailed fold-out maps can also widely be found. The American Automobile Association (AAA) has regional offices across the country and publishes its own maps.

## Websites
**http://eater.com** A cluster of sites covering the restaurant scenes of several major cities. Its sibling website, http://racked.com, gives the same treatment to shopping.
**http://nymag.com** *New York Magazine*'s website provides some of the smartest and most thorough coverage of the Big Apple.
**www.familytravelnetwork.com** Easy searches for child-friendly vacation spots.
**www.nps.gov** The National Park Service's comprehensive site has all sorts of park background, natural-history information, and travel tips.
**www.outtraveler.com** City guides and helpful recommendations for gay and lesbian travelers.
**www.petswelcome.com** Lists pet-friendly lodgings and activities.

### Books to get you in the mood
- *Here is New York.* E.B. White's poignant observations are both particular and universal.
- *On the Road.* Jack Kerouac's Beat classic about the American road trip.
- *Roadfood.* Jane and Michael Stern travel all over America's smaller back roads to report on the best regional home cooking.
- *Travels with Charley.* John Steinbeck's travelogue of his 1960s cross-country journey.
- *Walden.* Henry David Thoreau's memoir of rural Massachusetts in the mid-19th century.

# UNIQUE EXPERIENCES

# The American road trip

There's no better way to experience the US than by taking to the open road and exploring the country's varied landscapes, vibrant cities, and quaint small towns. A network of highways and back roads crisscross the nation like an elaborate web, leading to endless possibilities for adventure and discovery.

The United States is a nation of pioneers and explorers, immigrants, and adventurers. The country's history is built on movement, from the Native Americans who migrated across the country to the Pilgrims who first crossed the seas seeking religious freedom, to Meriwether Lewis and William Clark's great voyage of discovery across the continent, to the homesteaders and gold miners who opened up the West.

As a country, the US is founded on the principles of freedom, democracy, and individualism. These ideals, which are so fundamental to the nation's character and are a vital part of the national mindset, are also reflected in Americans' love of driving and the open road. On a road trip, the possibilities are endless. Driving is an individual pursuit, one that allows for spontaneous decisions, without being limited by the restrictions of other forms of travel (such as trains and airplanes). There are no security checks or boarding queues, no transfers or waiting rooms. If you want to stop somewhere along the way, you stop. If you want to leave, you get in your car and hit the road. And best of all, if you don't like where you're going, you can change direction at any time. It's the recreational version of the American dream.

No traffic jams, no schedules – just the freedom of the open road

The quintessential American road trip can best be described as 'meandering with a purpose.' Although you probably have your start and end points figured out, how you get to your destination and what you do en route are entirely up to you. Just be prepared that a road trip can easily take you off the beaten path, either by design or accident. Detours are expected – in fact, they often prove to be the most memorable part of the entire experience.

## Road trip basics

The United States is a big country. That may seem obvious, but many people don't quite realize the distances involved. From north to south, the state of California is roughly equal to the distance from Antwerp to Rome. The distance from Boston to Washington, DC is similar to traveling from Munich to Marseilles. And the state of Texas is larger than the whole of France.

It's important, therefore, not to bite off more than you can chew – it's better to see some of the country well than to see a lot of it in a hurry. Be realistic about the number of miles or hours you can drive in any given day, and always leave a little spare room in the schedule for the unexpected.

It's a good idea to stop at local grocery stores or truck stops to pick up

San Juan Skyway Scenic Byway in Colorado

some snacks to keep your stomach from growling while you're roaming, or buy some picnic items from a local produce stand and find a scenic spot to enjoy lunch with a view. One note of caution: if you see a sign that says, 'Last gas for 100 miles', take it seriously. Don't risk getting stuck

### Roadside attractions

The highways of the US are lined with roadside attractions, from the mildly odd to the extremely bizarre. It's impossible to drive along the I-90 (Interstate highway, see p.24) across South Dakota without being bombarded with advertisements for **Wall Drug** (510 Main Street, Wall, SD; tel: 605-279-2175; www.walldrug.com), a shopping mall with a cowboy theme. Down the highway is the **Corn Palace** (604 North Main Street, Mitchell, SD; tel: 605-996-5031; www.cornpalace.org), a Moorish-domed tourist attraction and event venue covered in murals and designs made entirely of corn and other grains.

Communities throughout the country take great pride in unusual – and often wacky – claims to fame, ranging from the World's Largest Spinach Can (in Alma, Arkansas) to the World's Largest Thermometer (in Baker, California) to the World's Largest Fake Nose and Glasses (in Michigan City, Indiana).

Other roadside oddities include a giant gorilla holding a Volkswagen Bug (Beetle) along US Route 7 in Leicester, Vermont; a half-sized replica of the Leaning Tower of Pisa (in Niles, Illinois); and a house covered in more than 50,000 beer cans (at 222 Malone Street, Houston, Texas).

The backbone of the US road network, Interstate highways cover nearly 42,800 miles (68,800km) of road. You could drive across the country from Seattle to Boston on I-90, or from Los Angeles to Jacksonville, Florida, on I-10. Interstate 95 runs down the east coast from northern Maine to Miami, while I-5 goes all the way from Mexico to Canada. Note that odd-numbered routes run north–south, while even-numbered routes go east–west.

Around the country, some 150 smaller routes are officially designated as National Scenic Byways (for full information, see www.byways.org). From the West Cascades Scenic Byway in Oregon to the Great River Road along the Mississippi River in Iowa to the Florida Keys Scenic Highway, these roads take in incomparable landscapes and vistas. There's also plenty of history and cultural heritage, from Kentucky's Country Music Highway to the Southwest's Trail of the Ancients to the Journey through Hallowed Ground Byway in Pennsylvania, Maryland, and Virginia.

in the middle of nowhere with an empty fuel tank or, arguably equally important, an empty stomach.

## From cities to scenic byways

As far as the major cities are concerned, there's a classic American joke that applies to just about every one: there are only two seasons: winter and road construction. In other words, be prepared for delays and detours wherever you may be traveling.

Outside of the main cities, options for crossing the country include Interstate highways and other such major roads (see box above) – marvels of infrastructure that will take you to many wonderful destinations. However, you'll be doing yourself a disservice if you limit yourself exclusively to these larger roads. Venturing onto the scenic byways and rural routes will give you a totally different view of the country, at a much slower pace than if you just blow by at highway speeds of 65 or 70mph (104–112kmph). Many of these roads are famous in their own rights, from

Along the legendary Route 66

A road trip through California affords the opportunity to stop at excellent wineries – although note that the drunk driving rules in the US are very strict, so drink responsibly

the historic Route 66 (sometimes dubbed the 'Main Street of America') to California's stunning Pacific Coast Highway. It's a good idea to pick up a detailed local map (*see p.19* for cartography recommendations) to help you on your way, and take the exit ramp to a slower-paced adventure.

Whatever route you choose, make sure that your daily schedule allows time to enjoy the serendipitous encounters that the highways and byways offer up. It may be that you happen upon a small-town festival, or decide to follow an intriguing roadside sign advertising an attraction such as the World's Biggest Ball of Twine (which, just for the record, is located in Cawker City, Kansas).

If you don't have a plan at all, that's just fine, too. There's nothing like simply getting in the car and driving, only stopping to explore when you see something interesting. One of the biggest benefits of a road trip is the freedom to explore as the fancy takes you.

## Themed tours

Picking a theme for your road trip can be a fun way to plan your route. There is a multitude of options, from following in the footsteps of Meriwether Lewis and William Clark (who led the first expedition from Washington, DC to the Pacific Coast) or exploring the ghost towns of the Wild West. Or what about visiting great baseball stadiums, or sampling your way through California's wine country? You may want to visit the national parks of the Southwest, trace musical history from Nashville to New Orleans, or just meander along the back roads of New England to see the spectacular foliage displays in autumn.

## Renting a vehicle

If you don't have your own vehicle, never fear: rental cars are easy to come by in the US, provided you meet certain basic requirements. The most popular companies include **Budget** (www.budget.com), **Enterprise** (www.enterprise.com), **Avis** (www.avis.com), **Dollar** (www.dollar.com), **Thrifty** (www.thrifty.com), and **Hertz** (www.hertz.com). It's worth checking several companies as well as general online travel booking agencies to find the best deal. Most companies require a credit or debit card deposit to reserve and rent a vehicle, although in some cases you also have the option to pay cash when you return the car.

The minimum age to rent a car at most places in the US is 21; however, special surcharges and restrictions typically apply to drivers under the age of 25. Most rental agencies will charge an additional fee if more than one person will be driving, so be sure to provide license information for all potential drivers.

One-way rentals are usually available, though the price may be higher than for round-trip rentals. There are usually no restrictions on taking rental cars across state lines, but bringing rental vehicles into Canada or Mexico generally requires special permission for insurance reasons. No matter where you travel, be sure to check whether your rental includes unlimited mileage or a fixed distance per day.

International visitors can use their home-country driver's license in the US. However, if your license is not in English, it may be worth obtaining an International Driving Permit before arrival. This document provides translations of the information on your license into several languages and supplements your original license. It helps US police to recognize that your driver's license is legitimate and unexpired in the event that you are stopped or involved in an accident. Since the International Driving Permit is a supplement and not a replacement for your licence, it is essential that you keep your original license with you at all times to avoid unnecessary headaches.

When it comes to your choice of vehicle, if you want to feel the wind in your hair as you drive through the countryside, consider renting a convertible – or, at the very least, a car with a sunroof.

If you are comfortable driving large vehicles, you may want to rent an RV (recreational vehicle), essentially a camper van. Major RV rental companies include **Cruise America** (tel: 1-800-671-8042; www.cruiseamerica.com), **El Monte RV** (tel: 1-888-337-2214; www.elmonterv.

Driving across the country in a convertible is a memorable experience

com), **Moturis and Camping World** (tel: 1-877-297-3687; www.moturis.com), and **Compass Campers** (tel: 1-866-425-0307; www.compasscampers.com). Most RVs don't require any special license, although you should be familiar with the ins and outs of maneuvering a large vehicle before you take one of these on a small, winding, country road.

Finally, don't forget to bring some music to enjoy on your road trip, otherwise you'll be spending a lot of time spinning the dial on the radio, searching for stations as you cross from one broadcast area to another. In less-populated parts of the country, such as Texas, Iowa or Nebraska, you often won't find any radio stations at all.

Motels are usually affordable and conveniently located by the roadside

The American road trip

## Road stories

For as long as Americans have been taking to the road, they've been telling stories about it. The most famous road book of them all, Jack Kerouac's *On the Road*, published in 1957, defined the post-war Beat Generation, while Nobel Prize-winner John Steinbeck's work included his classic *Travels with Charley: In Search of America*, published in 1962. William Least Heat-Moon documented his wanderings along America's back roads in his early 1980s' *Blue Highways*, while journalist Charles Kuralt brought stories of life across America to generations of viewers during his quarter-century 'On the Road' segments for CBS Television from the late 1960s.

Similarly, generations of American singers have extolled the joys of travel, from the folk harmonies of Simon and Garfunkel's *America* to Willie Nelson's country classic *On the Road Again* to Bruce Springsteen's rousing rock anthem, *Born to Run*.

The American love of travel has also prompted an entire genre of road movies. In Ridley Scott's 1991 *Thelma and Louise*, two women escaping from their constrained lives cross the country in an unplanned crime spree. A cocky young man finds family and redemption on a cross-country jaunt with his autistic older brother in Barry Levinson's 1988 film *Rain Man*. In *Smoke Signals* (1998), two young Native American men journey from Idaho to Arizona to retrieve a relative's ashes. A week-long road trip through California's wine country is the focus of *Sideways*, while in *Little Miss Sunshine* (2006) a dysfunctional family drives an equally dysfunctional Wolkswagon bus across the Southwest to a children's beauty pageant.

## Where to stay

The most challenging part of any road trip – apart from choosing which of the many roads to take – is figuring out where to lay your head at night. Fortunately, you'll find various types of lodging available in just about any populated part of the country, from luxury hotels to independent motels and to reliable mid-range chains such as Holiday Inn, Best Western, or Hampton Inn.

If your route is fairly fixed or you have specific needs (or simply want to stay at the best hotels), booking ahead is a good idea. However, if you prefer to leave yourself open to going where the mood takes you, it's generally not too difficult to find a decent motel room as you go along, provided you're able to be somewhat flexible about location and amenities.

It's worth noting that youth hostels are rare in the US. They can be found in the major cities, and if you're on a tight budget and are looking for a backpacking-style vacation, it's a good idea to join the Youth Hostel Association, as many hostels offer beds to members only.

If you're camping, you'll find the opposite – there'll be a range of developed campgrounds just about everywhere you go. Most campgrounds have electricity and water hookups for RVs and camper vans, as well as sites for more traditional tent camping. Restroom and shower facilities are generally located in a central building, and laundry rooms and a convenience store may also be available, along with recreational facilities such as pools or games rooms. Some campgrounds also have rustic cabins, although you will need to provide your own bedding, and sometimes even your own mattress. If you're planning a longer trip, consider joining Kampgrounds of America (KOA), whose low annual membership fee provides discounts at member campgrounds all over the country, along with other benefits.

Campgrounds, both developed and basic ones, can also be found in many national parks *(see p.40)*, national forests (www.forestcamping.com), state parks, and other public lands. For these sites, you may have to reserve a pitch in advance. Contact the Parks Service for more information.

## Eating across America

A big part of the road-trip experience is sampling all the regional foods you'll encounter along the way. America might be the country of hamburgers and fries, but if you're

Hiring an RV solves the problem of where to lay your head at night

Gas stations can be few and far between, so don't leave it to the last minute to refuel

willing to experiment a little and avoid the infamous golden arches, you'll be able to chow down on some of the country's most unique cuisines.

Philadelphia is known for the Philly cheesesteak, a sandwich made with thinly sliced steak and melted cheese in a long bread roll. When ordering, be sure to specify whether you want your sandwich 'with' or 'without'. (Locals know that this refers to fried onions.) New York City is the place to go for pizza, and, if you order a slice in Brooklyn, be sure to fold it in half, longways. New Orleans has its southern specialties such as gumbo (a type of meat or fish stew) and beignets (like square donuts, without the hole), while San Francisco is the birthplace of sourdough bread. You can't visit Maine without tasting lobster, and the Pacific Northwest revels in Dungeness crab and other seafood.

If you're driving across the emptier stretches of the country, your choices will probably be more limited. No matter where you go, you're likely to become well acquainted with that all-American staple of life on the road: the truck stop. These roadside facilities typically include a restaurant or food court, fueling station, restrooms, and a convenience store with snacks and essentials. Many also have shower facilities for the long-haul truck drivers who stop for rest and refreshment. If you feel like you could use a rest, don't be afraid of using these facilities. It is far safer to stop for a nap than to keep driving when tired.

Another American icon is the diner, a prefabricated restaurant, traditionally with a layer of stainless steel covering the outside of the building. Diners are casual establishments serving a wide range of grilled and fried food such as burgers, sandwiches, French fries, eggs, bacon, waffles, and pancakes. Customers can dine in booths or on stools at the counter. Nowadays the word 'diner' is often used for any restaurant serving typical diner food, whether or not it is a true diner in the traditional sense.

In addition to local establishments, you're sure to find unexciting but reliable chain restaurants such as Denny's, Applebee's, and Cracker Barrel across the country.

## Coming home

Last but not least, don't forget to document your trip with photographs, postcards, maps, etc. Your own stories of this or that quirky festival, or a tiny town with the best hotdog, may just inspire someone else to go on their own American road trip.

# Civil War battlefields

The Civil War of the 1860s was the bloodiest conflict in US history. It tore the country apart, and its scars on the American psyche remain to this day. The war not only ended slavery but also reaffirmed the sanctity of the Union and the place of the states within it.

The Civil War lasted four years, leaving at least 620,000 Americans dead and hundreds of thousands wounded.

The conflict arose out of two increasingly different ways of life: the immigration-fueled industrialized society of the North and the slave-based agricultural economy of the South. Tension escalated when South Carolina seceded from the Union, followed by six other southern states. They formed their own government, the Confederate States of America, a move the North rejected as illegal.

The first shots were fired in April 1861, when Confederate soldiers captured Fort Sumter (www.nps.gov/fosu) in Charleston, South Carolina. Soon afterward, four additional states joined the Confederacy, bringing the total number of rebel states to 11.

Four years after the war began – almost to the day – the South's hopes came to an end when Confederate General Robert E. Lee finally surrendered his army to Union General Ulysses S. Grant at the Appomattox Court House in Virginia.

A century and a half later, echoes of the Civil War – though fading – still linger. Battlefields are viewed as sacred ground, places where the past is very much alive, a reminder of the huge cost of liberty and national unity.

A cannon overlooks the land where the Battle of Malvern Hill raged on July 1, 1862

## Major battlefields

The National Park System preserves dozens of Civil War sites, including forts, battlefields, and a variety of historic buildings. Most have excellent visitor centers with museum exhibits, orientation films, bookstores, as well as ranger-led walks and interpretive programs. Frequent living-history events bring the past to life, and self-guided driving routes and hiking trails are also available.

Virginia, the closest Confederate state to the Union capital, Washington, DC, took the brunt of much of the fighting. The Confederacy won two early victories at **Manassas** (www.nps.gov/mana), while the area around **Fredericksburg** and **Spotsylvania** (www.nps.gov/frsp) saw four major battles within a 17-mile (27km) radius. Conflict swirled around the Confederate capital, Richmond (www.nps.gov/rich), home to the South's primary munitions factory, the Tredegar Iron Works.

The Confederate Army strove to move the eastern theater of war out of Virginia by invading the North. In September 1962, Confederate troops captured the Union arsenal at **Harpers Ferry**, Maryland (www.nps.gov/hafe). A few days later, the bloodiest single-day battle of the war took place at **Antietam** (www.nps.gov/anti), halting the invasion and forcing General Lee's army to retreat back

Virginia's Manassas National Battlefield Park, the site of two Civil War battles

across the Potomac River to Virginia. The following July, Lee invaded the North again. Even bloodier than Antietam, the ensuing three-day battle of **Gettysburg**, Pennsylvania, resulted in around 50,000 casualties, and ended the Confederacy's efforts to bring the war to Union soil once and for all.

Civil War battlefields

## Abraham Lincoln's assassination

On the night of April 14 1865, President Abraham Lincoln and his wife Mary were attending a performance at Ford's Theatre in Washington, DC, when John Wilkes Booth, a well-known actor with Southern sympathies, entered the presidential box and shot Lincoln. The president died some nine hours later, sending the Union into deep mourning. Even the South was shocked by the assassination, which cast a shadow over its hopes of a peaceful reconciliation.

Visit **Ford's Theatre National Historic Site** (511 10th Street NW, Washington,

DC; tel: 202-426-6924; www.nps.gov/foth) for a dramatic retelling of the assassination and a look at such artifacts as Booth's revolver and the clothes Lincoln was wearing when he was shot.

At the west end of the National Mall, the **Lincoln Memorial** contains Daniel Chester French's magnificent sculpture of the slain president. Excerpts from Lincoln's famous Gettysburg Address and his Second Inaugural Address are carved into the walls of the memorial. The president is buried at Oak Ridge Cemetery in Springfield, Illinois.

Further west, the Union sought to cut off the Confederacy's supply of arms and other equipment, capturing **Fort Donelson** (www.nps.gov/fodo) on the Cumberland River in Tennessee in 1862 and **Vicksburg**, Mississippi (www.nps.gov/vick), in 1863. The latter gave the North control of the Mississippi River, effectively splitting the South in two. Another significant Union victory, at **Pea Ridge**, Arkansas (www.nps.gov/peri), thwarted Southern efforts to bring Missouri into the Confederacy.

The beginning of the end came when Lee was forced to abandon Richmond and Petersburg, Virginia, after a lengthy siege by Grant's Union Army. Lee's final stand at **Appomattox Court House** (www.nps.gov/apco) ended with his surrender to Grant on April 9, 1865.

## The great generals

General Robert E. Lee lived for 30 years at Arlington House (www.nps.gov/arho), the family home of his wife, Mary Custis Lee, overlooking Washington, DC. A reluctant secessionist, Lee nevertheless resigned his US Army commission to fight for his home state when Virginia joined the Confederacy. During the war, Union troops occupied the house and began burying their dead on the property. The land is now Arlington National Cemetery, while the house is maintained as the Robert E. Lee Memorial. Lee himself is buried in the chapel at Washington and Lee University in Lexington, Virginia, where he served as president following the war.

Thomas 'Stonewall' Jackson, a Southern general, was declared a hero of the Confederacy when he led the assault on Harpers Ferry. Jackson was accidentally shot by his own men during the battle of Chancellorsville, Virginia in 1863. The building where he died eight days later is now the Stonewall Jackson Shrine at Fredericksburg and Spotsylvania County Battlefields Memorial Park.

On the Union side, Ulysses S. Grant rose from relative obscurity to become the most successful general for the North. (He also later became president of the United States.) The Ulysses S. Grant National Historic Site in St Louis, Missouri (www.nps.gov/ulsg) preserves the home where Grant lived for many years with his wife, Julia. His remains lie in an imposing tomb at the General Grant National Memorial in New York City (www.usps.gov/gegr).

Depicting the Battle of Gettysburg, fought in Pennsylvania on July 1–3, 1863

Modern-day Confederate soldiers fire their guns during a Civil War re-enactment, some 150 years after the conflict tore the US apart

# Civil War events and re-enactments

It's now 150 years since the Civil War ravaged North America, and hundreds of sesquicentennial events and exhibitions are planned throughout the country through 2015. See www.civilwar150.org and www.nps.gov/civilwar150 for details.

The Battle of Gettysburg is re-enacted each year from July 1–3 on the Pennsylvania site on which the 1993 movie *Gettysburg* was filmed (www.gettysburgreenactment.org). In addition, numerous other re-enactments and Civil War events take place annually across the country – often in places that never saw any fighting during the war itself.

In addition to the Gettysburg re-enactment, Pennsylvania has annual events at Neshaminy State Park and Pennypacker Mills. New York has its annual Brickhouse Re-enactment in September, while the entire town of Keokuk, Iowa, goes back to Civil War times for two days each April. Two of the Midwest's biggest events take place every summer in Wauconda, Illinois, and Boscobel, Wisconsin. Even California gets in on the act, with major re-enactments in places such as Fresno and Moorpark in the fall. For details on upcoming events, see www.reenactmenthq.com

## African-Americans in the Civil War

Approximately 185,000 African-Americans fought for the North during the Civil War, making up more than 10 percent of the Union Army and a significant portion of the Union Navy.

The most famous battle fought by African-American soldiers was the assault on Fort Wagner, South Carolina, by the 54th Massachusetts, one of the first black regiments, on July 18, 1863. The battle was commemorated in the 1989 movie *Glory*, starring Denzel Washington, Matthew Broderick, Morgan Freeman, and Cary Elwes.

Black slaves were frequently used by the Confederacy to provide physical labor for the army, but were not usually given arms to fight.

# Gambling

Drop in a coin, say a prayer, and pull the lever. The wheels begin to spin. One by one, they come to a stop, and suddenly a siren clangs. Coins come tumbling out in a mad rush. It's every gambler's dream: winning the jackpot. The United States abounds with places to test your luck, and, even if you don't win big, you're bound to have a good time trying.

Although glittering Las Vegas may be the first place that comes to mind when people think of casinos, there are opportunities to gamble in just about every corner of the US. Over the last few decades, gaming has grown into a multi-billion-dollar industry that includes everything from riverboat and racetrack casinos to gaming operations on Native American tribal lands. The only two US states without any legalized gambling of any kind are Utah and Hawaii, but the other 48 states will find a way to make your spirits (and pockets) lighter.

## A potted history

The modern US gaming industry was born in 1931, when Nevada officially legalized casino gaming. In 1947, mobster Bugsy Siegel opened the **Flamingo** (3555 Las Vegas Boulevard South, Las Vegas, NV; tel: 888-902-9929; www.flamingolasvegas.com) in Las Vegas, setting off that city's transformation into a gambling mecca.

The industry grew quickly, despite concerns about criminal influence, as more people discovered the flashing lights and hypnotic daze that a day of gambling involves. In the late 1960s, billionaire Howard Hughes purchased several casino properties in

Waitstaff, bellhops, and dealers in casinos depend heavily on tips to make a living

Nevada, signaling that there was legal and legitimate money to be made in this desert locale. A new era of casino resorts dawned in 1989 with the opening of the **Mirage Hotel and Casino Resort** (3400 Las Vegas Boulevard South, Las Vegas, NV; tel: 702-791-7111; www.mirage.com).

New Jersey was the second state to legalize casino gaming, and opened its first casino in Atlantic City in

1978, turning the Jersey shore into the gambling capital of the East Coast. Currently, the charms of Atlantic City sparkle the brightest at **The Borgata** (1 Borgata Way, Atlantic City, NJ; tel: 609-317-1000; www.theborgata.com).

## Gambling cities

The biggest gambling destination of them all, **Las Vegas,** needs little introduction. From the glitzy casinos of the Las Vegas Strip to the less flashy establishments scattered throughout other parts of the city, Las Vegas thrives on the ringing slot machines and spinning roulette wheels.

Exploring the themed casinos is an adventure in itself. Walking the Las Vegas Strip is like meandering through a make-believe microcosm of the world. There are gondolas plying indoor canals through **The Venetian** (3355 Las Vegas Boulevard South, Las Vegas, NV; tel: 702-414-1000; www.venetian.com), and Egyptian landmarks at **Luxor** (3900 Las Vegas Boulevard South, Las Vegas, NV; tel: 702-262-4444; www.luxor.com).

Steps from the Eiffel Tower replica at **Paris** (3655 Las Vegas Boulevard South, Las Vegas, NV; tel: 702-946-7000; www.parislasvegas.com) you'll find **New York, New York** (3790 Las Vegas Boulevard South, Las Vegas, NV; tel: 1-800-689-1797; www.newyorknewyork.com), with copies of the Brooklyn Bridge and Coney Island roller-coaster. Pirates battle at **Treasure Island** (3300 Las Vegas Boulevard South; Las Vegas, NV; tel: 702-894-7111; www.treasureisland.com) and knights joust at **Excalibur**'s medieval-style castle (3850 Las Vegas

Fortunes are made or lost on the flip of a card

Boulevard South, Las Vegas, NV; tel: 702-597-7777; www.excalibur.com), while at **Circus Circus** (2880 Las Vegas Boulevard South, Las Vegas, NV; tel: 702-734-0410; www.circuscircus.com) trapeze artists and acrobats perform dazzling feats of skill and agility. At the **Bellagio** (600 Las Vegas Boulevard South, Las Vegas, NV; tel: 888-987-6667; www.bellagio.com), the fountain-and-light shows captivate audiences on a nightly basis.

Roughly 450 miles (724km) to the northwest, **Reno, Nevada**, is often called the 'Biggest Little City in the World'. More laid-back than Las Vegas, Reno has a lingering feeling of the old West and a passion for outdoor activities, making it a good option for families. In addition to the table games and slot machines, there are also entertainment and dining opportunities similar to those in Las Vegas, but with rather less glitz.

## Indian casinos

Considered sovereign entities under US law, Native American tribes are permitted to operate casinos on their land, even in states where gambling is otherwise illegal. According to the 2010 American Gaming Association (AGA) Survey of Casino Entertainment, 233 tribes in 29 states operate 456 Indian gaming facilities, most of them full-scale casinos. Nearly a quarter of these are in Oklahoma. Indian gaming, as it is commonly known, is also widespread in California, Minnesota, Washington, Wisconsin, Arizona, and New Mexico.

**Milwaukee**, **Wisconsin**, is home to the largest Native American casino of them all: **Potawatomi Bingo Casino** (1721 West Canal Street, Milwaukee, WI; tel: 800-729-7244; www.paysbig. com). It boasts 3,100 slot machines, plus blackjack, craps, roulette, poker, baccarat, bingo, and off-track race betting. San Diego, California, has the largest concentration of Native American tribes in the country and a correspondingly high number of casinos. California's largest are the **Pechanga Resort & Casino** (45000 Pechanga Parkway, Temecula CA; tel: 951-693-1819; www.pechanga.com), and the ranch-style **Barona Resort and Casino** (1932 Wildcat Canyon Road, Lakeside, CA; tel: 619-443-2300; www.barona.com).

In eastern and southern states, where casinos are few and far between, gamblers and tourists travel substantial distances to establishments such as Florida's Seminole-owned **Hard Rock Casino** (1 Seminole Way, Hollywood, FL; tel: 866-502-7529; www.seminolehardrockhollywood. com) or Connecticut's **Foxwoods Resort Casino** (350 Trolley Line Boulevard, Mashantucket, CT; tel: 800-369-9663; www.foxwoods.com), owned by the Mashantucket Pequot tribe, and **Mohegan Sun** (1 Mohegan Sun Boulevard, Uncasville, CT; tel: 888-226-7711; www.mohegansun. com), owned by the Mohegan tribe.

## Colorado mountain towns

In 1859, prospectors struck gold in the mountains of Colorado, setting off a gold rush that lasted until the mid-1860s. These days, there's a new kind of gold-seeker coming to these hills, drawn by the limited-stakes gambling that was made legal in three historic communities in 1991.

The Venetian in Las Vegas mirrors the City of Bridges, with canals and gondoliers

Once known as the 'richest square mile on Earth', two of the towns, Black Hawk and Central City, are located just a mile (1.6km) apart, about 34 miles (55km) west of Denver. With 21 casinos, Black Hawk is the booming capital of Colorado gaming. Here you'll find large, flashy casinos reminiscent of Las Vegas, with plenty of card tables and hundreds of slots and video poker – nearly 1,400 of them in the largest casino, the tropical-themed **Isle of Capri** (401 Main Street, Black Hawk, CO; tel: 303-998-7777; http://black-hawk.isleof capricasinos.com).

Central City is much quieter, with five casinos that are generally less crowded and more intimate than those down the road. The **Doc Holliday Casino** (131 Main Street, Central City, CO; tel: 303-582-1400; www.dochol lidaycasino.net) is full of charm, even though it's not historic. If you need a break from the tables, Central City also hosts an abundance of music and arts events. The world-famous **Central City Opera** (124 Eureka Street, Central City, CO; tel: 303-292-

The Famous Bonanza Casino in Colorado's Central City maintains an historic front

6700; www.centralcityopera.org) is a great treat in the summer months.

Cripple Creek, 48 miles (77km) southwest of Colorado Springs, was once called the World's Greatest Gold Camp. Saloons and historic buildings from the 19th century line the streets, and a narrow-gauge railroad takes visitors into gold-mining country. There

---

### Beyond gambling: entertainment and dining

Although it's often the hope of a big payout that lures people in, casino games are by no means the only draw. Dining and entertainment have also become key parts of the casino experience. Larger establishments typically offer an array of dining establishments, many of them world class.

If quantity is as important as quality, the all-you-can-eat buffets of Las Vegas and beyond are a good option, though the standard certainly varies from one place to another. The most popular buffets on the Strip include those at the **Bellagio** (tel: 702-693-7111; www. bellagio.com), **Paris** (tel: 702-946-7000 www.parislasvegas.com), **Rio** (www.rio lasvegas.com), and **Wynn** (tel: 702-770-7000; www.wynnlasvegas.com). You'll find less expensive buffets at off-Strip hotels. Elsewhere in the country, casinos generally have at least one restaurant.

Slot machines were invented by a San Franciscan mechanic in the late 19th century

are 16 casinos here, and entertainment includes the fifth-oldest opera company in the United States.

## Racetrack casinos

The traditional style of racetrack betting, in which winners divide the total amount bet in proportion to the amount wagered, is known as pari-mutuel gaming. You'll find this sort of gambling in many states, including some that don't have any other gaming operations. Betting ranges from horse racing to greyhound racing to jai alai. Only seven states – Alaska, Georgia, Hawaii, Mississippi, North Carolina, South Carolina, and Utah – do not allow some form of pari-mutuel betting.

### Gambling revenue for good causes

An increasing number of states, tribes, and communities have jumped on the casino bandwagon, recognizing the potential for tax revenues and other income to fund social programs, create jobs, and stimulate local economies. In 2009, states and communities earned nearly $5.59 billion in direct gaming taxes on commercial casinos. Gambling revenue funds youth programs, education, infrastructure, historic preservation, property tax relief, and health-care services, among other programs.

In Connecticut, each of the state's 169 municipalities receives a portion of the revenue from slot machines, which is used to fund everything from nursing homes to schools to public-safety programs.

Atlantic City gambling laws require casinos to reinvest 1.5 percent of their profits into New Jersey economic development and community programs including infrastructure, neighborhood revitalization efforts, and social services.

In Iowa, a small portion of the state's gaming-tax revenue goes to special foundations in each of the counties without commercial casinos. A quarter of these funds must be kept in a permanent endowment, while the remaining 75 percent is given to local charitable projects.

Revenue from Native American casinos is mostly used for tribal economic development and community programs. However, there is some debate about the effectiveness of Indian Gaming, as many tribal lands are far from cities or tourist attractions, making it hard for Indian-run casinos to attract players. For the few successful tribes (such as Florida's Seminole, who run Tampa's Seminole Hard Rock Hotel and Casino), there are dozens of others left with little to show for their efforts.

More recently, an increasing number of states have opened racetrack casinos, which combine pari-mutuel betting with casino gaming (typically slot machines only). The first 'racino' opened in Rhode Island in 1992. **Empire City** (810 Yonkers Avenue, Yonkers, NY; tel: 914-968-4200; www.yonkersraceway.com), just north of New York City, is the top racetrack casino market in the US.

## Ways to play

Slot machines are by far the most popular form of gambling, so it's not surprising that you'll find more electronic games than anything else in casinos across the US. In fact, there are nearly 833,000 electronic gaming machines scattered throughout the country. Well over a third of these are located in three states: Nevada, California, and Oklahoma.

Still, it's not all about one-armed bandits and video poker. Many casinos offer a variety of table games, with blackjack by far the most popular. Poker – varieties include Crazy 4, Pai Gow (or double-hand) poker, Let It Ride Stud, 3-Card, and Texas Hold 'em – comes in second, followed by roulette and craps. You're also likely to find baccarat, Casino War, and Big Six. In some places you'll also find off-track race betting or betting on other sporting events.

Casinos are specially designed to keep you gambling. There are often no clocks and no windows anywhere on the gaming floor, so it's easy to lose track of time. The buildings are deliberately maze-like, making it hard to find the exit (or the cashier, to retrieve your winnings). Machines ring constantly, calling to you to wager your money. Even the garish carpets are designed to keep gamblers alert and playing.

In Las Vegas, casino designers are experienced at manipulating gamblers on the most subtle level: each casino on the Strip has a custom-designed scent. Researchers have suggested that the nose can remember smells and bring back memories more effectively than sight or sound, so the casinos are hoping visitors will remember the smell of success and return to play another day.

In the end, no matter what type of gaming establishment you visit or what game you choose to play, the key is to have fun and gamble responsibly. It's wise to set a daily limit and keep track of your losses, because everything in a casino is designed to keep you gambling away your hard-earned money.

Popular table games include blackjack, poker, roulette, and craps

# National parks

Famously called 'America's best idea' by the writer Wallace Stegner, the 394 units of the national park system are the pride and joy of the United States, attracting more than 280 million visitors each year with their scenic beauty, diverse wildlife, and historic attractions.

America's national parks are a reflection of the human need for wild places that feed the spirit and nourish the soul. Within their borders are vast deserts and humid wetlands, primeval forests and treeless prairies, rushing rivers and placid lakes, pristine beaches and rocky shorelines, active volcanoes, and ancient mountains.

Look a little closer, and you'll find a wealth of wildlife, from birds and small mammals to iconic species such as bears, moose, alligators, and whales. Equally varied, the flora includes everything from delicate wild flowers to giant moss-draped trees to fuzzy-looking cacti. Then there are the historical parks, which preserve sites from the prehistoric to the 19th century and up to today.

The world's first national park was Yellowstone, and was set aside by Congress and President Ulysses S. Grant in 1871. Over the next century, many more national parks and monuments were created throughout the US. Most were initially carved out of the wilderness areas of the west, but some areas were eventually designated in the more populous east.

In 1980, President Jimmy Carter more than doubled the land within the National Park System when he signed into law the Alaska National Interest Lands Conservation Act,

The parks are a popular destination, but it's possible to find your own bit of heaven

which established 10 new national parks and expanded three existing parks in Alaska. The state also has more than 70 state parks and 24 wildlife sanctuaries.

The National Park System now preserves more than 84 million acres (34 million hectares) in the 50 states, District of Columbia, and US island territories. In addition to 58 national parks, the system includes 123 parks or historic sites, 74 monuments,

25 battlefields or military parks, 18 preserves, 18 recreation areas, 10 seashores, four parkways, four lakeshores, and two reserves, all administered by the National Park Service, a division of the Department of the Interior. Delaware is the only state in the union without a national park, although there have been proposals to protect some coastal regions of the state in a national park.

## Mountain landscapes

The grande dame of the park system is **Yellowstone National Park**, which encompasses mountains, lakes, the amber-hued Grand Canyon of the Yellowstone, and diverse wildlife – including bison, moose, bears, and wolves – as well as a geothermal wonderland of geysers, hot springs, fumaroles, and mudpots. The most famous geyser, Old Faithful, erupts an average of 17 to 20 times per day, usually every 90 minutes or so.

The adjacent **Grand Teton National Park** is a classic Rocky Mountain landscape of towering peaks rising above the meandering Snake River. Much of Grand Teton is Alpine back country, with park roads providing views from the plains. For road access to higher elevations, **Rocky Mountain National Park** and **Glacier National Park** are spectacular alternatives. Hiking, backpacking, cross-country skiing, snowshoeing, and wildlife viewing are popular activities in these parks.

In Alaska, **Katmai National Park and Preserve** is famous for its rugged volcanic landscape and its population of brown bears. **Denali National**

A Roosevelt elk stag in Redwood National and State Park, California

National parks

**Park** is also known for abundant wildlife, as well as for Mount McKinley, the highest mountain in North America (20,320ft/6,194m), a magnet for mountaineers. Well-prepared adventurers can explore some of the continent's last remaining

### Taking to the air

For a different perspective, sign up for one of the 'flightseeing' excursions offered at parks such as Grand Canyon, Yellowstone, and Glacier. Heli-hiking (helicopter drop-offs and pick-ups with hiking in between) is available at Denali National Park.

Hot-air ballooning is another popular experience offered at several national parks, including Yosemite, Grand Teton, Glacier, Zion, and Rocky Mountain. These excursions usually take place just outside the park boundaries.

true wilderness at undeveloped **Gates of the Arctic National Park and Preserve** in the Brooks Range.

The highest peak in the contiguous United States is California's Mount Whitney (14,505ft/4,421m), lying partly within **Sequoia National Park**. Together with Kings Canyon and Yosemite National Parks, this park preserves the big trees and stunning Sierra Nevada scenery that inspired the 19th-century naturalist John Muir, one of the founders of the American conservation movement. **Yosemite National Park** is also noted for Yosemite Falls, the highest waterfalls in North America (2,425ft/739m), together with dramatic granite formations such as Half Dome and El Capitan, which attract a steady stream of photographers and rock climbers.

Forming the spine of the Pacific Northwest, the Cascade mountain range is riddled with volcanoes, none more imposing than Washington's Mount Rainier (14,411ft/4,392m), the fifth-highest peak in the lower 48 and the centerpiece of **Mount Rainier National Park**. Popular with hikers, mountaineers, and snowshoers, Mount Rainier boasts 27 active glaciers, more than any other US peak outside Alaska, and often serves as a training ground for Himalayan expeditions. If you can conquer Mount Rainier, you might also have luck on Everest or K2.

To the west, the snow-capped Olympic Mountains rise almost directly from the sea in **Olympic National Park**, creating a rain-shadow effect with various distinct

Rock climbing is popular in national parks including Mount Rainier and Denali

climatic zones, including the only temperate rainforest in the lower 48 states. The interior of the park is a road-free wilderness, making it a popular destination for back country trips. If you decide to explore this region, be sure to notify the park rangers of your travel plans. Every year there are a few hardy souls who have to be rescued in adverse weather conditions.

The **Pacific Crest National Scenic Trail** hiking route passes through 25 national forests and seven national parks in California, Oregon, and Washington on its 2,650-mile (4,265km) route from Mexico to Canada.

The region's volcanic past is visible up close at **Mount St Helens National Volcanic Monument**, site of a devastating eruption on May 18 1980. Various stages of natural recovery can be seen in the different zones. The Johnson Ridge Observatory, named in honor of volcanologist David Johnson, who died in the 1980 explosion, is an excellent place to learn more about the volcano and its modern rumblings. For an older comparison, a catastrophic eruption created the centerpiece of Oregon's **Crater Lake National Park** approximately 7,700 years ago. Over the millennia, the resulting caldera filled with water; it is now the deepest freshwater lake in the United States.

In California, the cinder cones and numerous geothermal features of **Lassen Volcanic National Park** – site of a dramatic 1915 eruption – are yet another reminder of the volatile geology of the Pacific Rim.

*Walking in California's arid Joshua Tree National Park (see page 44)*

To experience ongoing volcanic activity, you will need to visit **Hawai'i Volcanoes National Park**, where you can drive or hike to the crater rim of Kilauea, explore recent lava flows, and – depending on current conditions – see lava bubbling in a vent or flowing from the volcano to the ocean.

In the eastern US, much older and more eroded mountains attract millions of visitors each year with their scenic beauty, waterfalls, hiking trails, and glorious autumn foliage. The 2,000-mile (3,219km) Appalachian Trail traverses North Carolina's **Great Smoky Mountains National Park** and Virginia's **Shenandoah National Park**. Hikers typically travel south-to-north, and while some do attempt to hike the entire thing, it's a popular day activity to hike just a short section.

## Desertscapes

The desert landscapes of the Southwest have long fascinated visitors, and there are many national parks spread amongst its canyons, mountains, and plateaus or mesas. The most famous, **Grand Canyon National Park**, slices across northwestern Arizona in a mile-deep gash of colorful rock layers. Where the Grand Canyon dazzles with its sheer size and splendor, the red-rock spires of Utah's **Bryce Canyon National Park** offers a more delicate display of the magic that wind and water can work on stone.

Rock climbers and hikers also flock to the sheer cliffs and narrow slot canyons of other desert national parks such as Zion, Arches, Canyonlands, Death Valley, and Capitol Reef.

Epitomizing both the romance of the wilderness and a dedication to conservation and public service, national-park rangers are instantly identifiable by their distinctive uniforms of gray shirts, forest-green trousers, and wide-brimmed hats. The human face of the national parks for nearly a century, the rangers are jacks of all trades, whose duties include everything from traffic management, law enforcement, firefighting, and search-and-rescue to scientific research and wildlife management.

In addition, park rangers are naturalists and historians, providing visitor information, guided walks, and other interpretive programs to the millions of people who visit the national parks every year. Rangers typically take great pride in being both stewards and ambassadors of the natural and cultural heritage of the areas in which they work.

The intriguing flora of the Southwest runs the gamut from brilliant spring wild flowers to the towering multi-armed cacti of **Saguaro National Park** in the Sonoran Desert and the bizarrely shaped namesake yuccas of **Joshua Tree National Park** in the Mojave. In a remote corner of Texas, **Big Bend National Park** protects a large expanse of Chihuahuan Desert mountains and canyons, where more bird species have been sighted than in any other US national park.

## Water worlds

Sea kayakers find heaven amongst the tidewater glaciers and abundant marine life of Alaska's **Glacier Bay**, **Kenai Fjords,** and **Wrangell-St Elias National Parks**; along the rugged Atlantic shore of **Acadia National Park**; and in the island lagoons and caves of **Channel Islands National Park** – dubbed North America's Galapagos for the extraordinary abundance of its wildlife.

For wilderness canoeing, head to the remote Midwestern lakes of **Voyageurs and Isle Royale national parks**, or to the wildlife-rich wet-lands of Florida's **Everglades**. Also in Florida, the coral reefs, man-groves, and numerous small islands of **Biscayne National Park** attract snorkeling and diving enthusiasts.

Free entrance for those under 16 and Junior Ranger programs help to engage children

The tidal pools of Acadia, Olympic, and other coastal parks are wonderful places to search for starfish, urchins, and other creatures at low tide.

White-water rafting is a popular activity in many national parks throughout the west. For the experience of a lifetime, book a multi-day rafting trip on the Colorado River through the Grand Canyon. Many operators offer these kind of adventures, but spaces generally fill up well in advance, so plan ahead.

## Underground caves

Wonders underground await at New Mexico's impressive **Carlsbad Caverns** and Kentucky's **Mammoth Cave National Park**, the longest known cave system in the world. Although some self-guided exploration is permitted, it is not recommended. Guided tours give access to more of the caves than you would be able to see on your own, and they are far safer; pre-booking is recommended (tel: 1-877-444-6777 or 518-885-3639; www.recreation.gov).

## Other natural highlights

South Dakota's rugged **Badlands** and the cathedral-like groves of California's **Redwood National Park** are just a few of the many other outstanding national-park landscapes. Don't forget the national monuments; highlights include the snowy gypsum dunes of New Mexico's **White Sands** and the dramatic monolith known as **Devil's Tower**, rising from the Wyoming plains. Some of these sites are remote from civilization, so plan a few extra days for the journey.

The Giant Forest Museum and sequoia trees at California's Sequoia National Park

National parks

## History and prehistory

Remnants of pre-European civilization, including ancient cliff dwellings and pueblos dating back 700 to 1,200 years, can be seen at **Mesa Verde National Park**, **Canyon de Chelly National Monument**, and other sites in the Southwest. Even older signs of habitation are visible in paintings and etchings on canyon walls, as well as at the remains of campsites that are up to 4,500 years old.

The more recent past comes alive at Virginia's **Colonial National Park**, which includes Jamestown, the first permanent English settlement in North America, and Yorktown Battlefield, site of a major Revolutionary War victory. Trace the events leading up to the war at **Boston National Historical Park** in Massachusetts and visit the scenes of the first battles at nearby

**Minute Man National Historical Park. Independence National Park** in Philadelphia contains the world-famous Liberty Bell, as well as Independence Hall, where the Declaration of Independence and US Constitution were signed.

The National Park System also preserves dozens of historic battlefields and other sites from the American Civil War *(see pages 30–3).*

During the 1890s, the Klondike Gold Rush lured countless prospectors to the goldfields of Alaska and made a boom town of Seattle, Washington, the major gateway to the region. **Klondike Gold Rush National Park** has units in Seattle and Skagway, Alaska.

America's heritage as a melting-pot of ethnicities is best explored at New York City's **Statue of Liberty National Monument**, which includes the immigration station at Ellis Island, the point of entry for approximately 12 million people from 1892 through 1954. You'll stand in the entrance hall, where immigrants once stood clutching their suitcases and paperwork, hoping to pass the literacy and health examinations to gain entrance to the US.

## Practical information

National-park entrance fees range from free to around $25 per private vehicle at the most popular parks. Tickets are typically valid for repeat entries over a seven-day period. Per-person fees apply to visitors entering by other means and for all visitors in certain parks. Children under 16 enter the parks for free.

If you plan to visit several parks while you're in the United States, consider purchasing an **America the Beautiful Pass**, which covers admission to national parks and a wide variety of other federally protected areas. Available at most national-park fee stations, the pass admits the holder and accompanying passengers in a non-commercial vehicle, or the holder and up to three additional adults where per-person fees apply. The price is $80 for an annual pass, or just $10 for a lifetime pass for US citizens or permanent residents aged 62 and over.

In recent years, the National Park Service has waived park fees on certain days at all parks. Check www.nps.gov/findapark/feefreeparks.htm for the latest information.

A permit is required for back-country camping in the parks

Popular parks, including Zion, Bryce, Yosemite, Grand Canyon, and Mount Rainier, often provide a free shuttle bus to reduce traffic on park roads. Be sure to stop by the visitor center to find out about free ranger-led programs, a great way to learn about a park's natural and human history. Many parks offer special activities for children, including a popular Junior Ranger program.

**Camping** is permitted in designated campgrounds, some of which can be reserved in advance (www.nps.gov/pub_aff/plan_your_visit/lodging.htm). Larger parks often have several developed campgrounds, while smaller units may have only primitive facilities. Many larger parks also have historic lodges or small hotels within their boundaries. Motels can usually be found in nearby communities. Back-country (wilderness) camping in parks requires a permit, available at visitor centers on a first-come, first-served basis. It's always a good idea to check with park rangers for the latest

Before hiking, be sure to supply yourself with enough water and emergency materials

conditions before heading into the back country, and be sure to let someone know your travel plans in case of an emergency. Never travel alone in remote areas, and always bring adequate supplies, including water and warm blankets.

## Volunteering and working in national parks

If you've got the time and the inclination, one of the best ways to get to know a national park is to become a volunteer through the Volunteers in Parks program (www.nps.gov/getinvolved/volunteer.htm). Opportunities available throughout the National Park Service include joining both short-term work crews and long-term projects. Volunteers from outside the US are welcome as long as they meet visa requirements. See the NPS International Volunteers in Parks Program website (www.nps.gov/oia/topics/ivip/ivip.htm)

for details. The Student Conservation Association (www.thesca.org/serve/internships) also offers internship and volunteer opportunities, some of which are in national parks.

Paid seasonal jobs and internships are also available. Xanterra Parks & Resorts (www.xanterra.com) operates lodges and gift shops in many parks and hires seasonal staff from the US and other countries. International applicants must be students and obtain a J-1 Exchange Visitor Visa.

# The great game of baseball

The United States is a sport-loving country, and no other athletic endeavor holds quite the same place in the nation's collective heart as baseball. For a truly American experience – complete with crowd sing-alongs and obligatory fast-food snacks – attend a home game at one of the country's great ballparks.

Known as America's favorite pastime, baseball has been around longer than any other professional sport in the US. Played under modern rules since 1845 and professionally since 1869, baseball has weathered racism, scandals, strikes, world wars, owner-player feuds, and the changes wrought by television broadcasting and soaring player salaries.

The American obsession with baseball is typically passed down from generation to generation. Parents take their kids to the local ballpark, play catch in the backyard, and cheer on their miniature sluggers at Little League games. Kids across America dream of playing in the Major Leagues, and throughout the country, devoted fans live and die with their teams' successes and failures.

Baseball can be fairly slow or extremely exciting, depending on the pitching and hitting quality on any given day, as well as on the charisma of individual players and the reputations of the teams. Some teams, such as the Boston Red Sox and the New York Yankees, have a national following, attracting nearly as many fans on the road as the teams they play against. Others are lucky to fill their home stadiums – although often the underdog is the secret favorite.

The catcher is the only player who can see the whole field, he often directs the play

## The basics

The baseball season runs from April to September, with a series of play-offs in October that lead to the World Series. There are two leagues: the National League and the American League; teams play 162 games within their own league during the regular season, only facing the opposing league during the play-offs and special events such as the All-Stars game.

Similar to English rounders, baseball is a ball-and-bat game, where players score points by hitting the ball and running around the bases. Players on the batting team rotate through the line-up to face the pitcher of the fielding team. The pitcher's goal is to throw a ball that is difficult to hit, but is still within a hitter's strike zone. If it's a good pitch, but the hitter fails to connect with the ball, it's called a strike.

After three strikes, the hitter is called out, and after three hitters are called out, the inning is over. There are typically nine innings per game, with each team getting a turn to bat and field once per inning. If the score is tied after nine innings, the game will continue until someone scores. (The longest baseball game in history lasted 33 innings – over 8 hours and 25 minutes!)

If the hitter connects with the ball, he immediately drops the bat and starts running around the bases. The goal of the runner is to touch each base around the diamond before returning to home plate, where he officially scores a point. The fielding team tries to touch the runner out with the ball, which is usually the most exciting part of the game. You'll probably see a few players slide into the bases, which is how the pristine uniforms, some with pinstripes, end up so dirty.

## Going to a game

Although the finer points of baseball can be mystifying, a general under-standing of the rules will infinitely enhance your enjoyment of the game. If you find yourself confused

The atmosphere of the crowd at a major league game can be electrifying

at any point, don't hesitate to ask someone sitting nearby. Baseball fans are usually more than willing to explain the game. In fact, going to a ball game often resembles a day in the park more than a sporting event. Except during the post-season or match-ups between great rivals, there's little of the intensity of many other professional sports such as American football or hockey.

A Major League ball game begins with the singing of the national anthem, followed by the ceremonial throwing out of the first pitch (usually by a local celebrity). Halfway through the seventh inning comes a break in play known as the seventh-inning stretch – a good time to stretch your legs and get some refreshments. Traditionally, at the start of the seventh-inning stretch the whole crowd stands and sings *Take*

The great game of baseball

*Me Out to the Ball Game*, a 1908 Tin Pan Alley song. Everyone is encouraged to sing along:

> *Take me out to the ball game,*
> *Take me out with the crowd.*
> *Buy me some peanuts and Cracker Jack,*
> *I don't care if I never get back,*
> *Let me root, root, root for the home team,*
> *If they don't win it's a shame.*
> *For it's one, two, three strikes, you're out,*
> *At the old ball game.*

Note that most singers replace the words 'home team' with the actual name of the home team. Since the terrorist attacks of September 11, 2001, *God Bless America* has also been sung during the seventh-inning stretch. It is considered a sign of respect to remove your hat and place your right hand over your heart.

## Best ballparks

Baseball revels in its history, legends, and statistics. Although many old stadiums have been replaced with larger, more modern facilities, at least two ballparks steeped in baseball lore remain. **Fenway Park** (4 Yawkey Way, Boston, MA; tel: 877-733-7699; www.redsox.com), the home of the Boston Red Sox, opened on April 20 1912, just five days after the sinking of the *Titanic*. **Wrigley Field** (1060 West Addison Street, Chicago, IL; tel: 800-843-2827 for in-state calls, 866-652-2827 for out-of-state calls; www.cubs.com), home of the Chicago Cubs, opened two years later. Smaller than most Major League ballparks, both are intimate, quirky, and regarded as baseball's cathedrals.

At the other end of the spectrum are the new stadiums, which dazzle with their architecture, scale, and views. Among the most lauded are **PNC Park** (115 Federal Street, Pittsburgh, PA; tel: 412-321-2827; www.pirates.com), the waterfront **AT&T Park** (24 Willie Mays Plaza, San Francisco, CA; tel: 415-972-2000; www.sfgiants.com), **Oriole Park at Camden Yards** (333 West Camden Street, Baltimore, MD; tel: 888-848-2473; www.orioles.com), and **Safeco Field** (1250 First Avenue South, Seattle, WA; tel: 206-346-4000; www.mariners.com).

## The complete experience

Food is a big part of the ballpark experience. Roaming vendors sell snacks and drinks (including Cracker Jack – peanuts and caramel-coated popcorn), while concession stands

Scoreboards often show the status of games being played in other cities

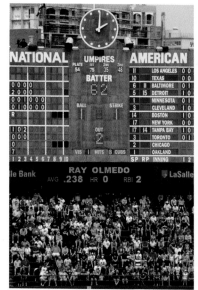

Snacks, from Cracker Jack to hot dogs to sushi, are a key part of the experience

com), bratwurst (Miller Park, 1 Brewers Way, Milwaukee, WI; tel: 414-902-4000; www.brewers.com), and pirogi (Progressive Field, 2401 Ontario Street, Cleveland, OH; tel: 216-420-4487; www.indians.com). San Francisco's Gilroy garlic fries earn plaudits, as does Seattle's sushi roll, the Ichiroll, named for star player Ichiro Suzuki.

Whole vacations – even honeymoons – have been designed around visiting baseball stadiums. For those who don't want to make arrangements on their own, there are organized trips such as **Jay Buckley's Baseball Tours** (tel: 608-788-9600; www.jaybuckley.com) and **Around the Horn Baseball Tours** (tel: 888-648-0052; www.aroundthehorn-baseballtours.com). Facility tours are also available directly at most ballparks.

serve up local and themed specialties such as Philly cheesesteak (Citizen's Bank Park, One Citizens Bank Way, Philadelphia, PA; tel: 215-463-1000; www.phillies.com), Texas-style barbecue stuffed baked potato (Minute Maid Park, 501 Crawford Street, Houston, Texas; tel: 713-259-8000; www.astros.

## Great rivalries

Baseball produces some of the most intense rivalries in American sport,

---

### Baseball lingo

Baseball has a language all of its own, and learning the lingo is part of the fun. Here are some key terms you should know:

- *Strike:* A well-thrown pitch counted against the batter. After three strikes, the batter is out.
- *Ball:* A poorly thrown pitch counted against the pitcher. Four balls give the batter an automatic walk to first base.
- *Full Count:* When a pitcher has thrown two strikes and three balls in a single at-bat (time at bat). One more strike makes an out; one more ball 'walks' the batter.

- *Home Run:* A hit that allows the batter to circle all the bases on a single play.
- *Grand Slam:* A home run hit with all bases occupied, thus scoring four runs.
- *Batting Average:* A player's total hits divided by his number of times at bat.
- *RBI (Runs Batted In):* The total number of runs resulting from a player's at-bats.
- *ERA (Earned Run Average):* The number of runs a pitcher has given up per nine innings pitched, not including runs scored through defensive errors.
- *Double Play:* When fielders manage to get two players out on a single turn.

Stadiums range from the vintage (Boston's Fenway Park and Chicago's Wrigley Field) to the huge and state-of-the-art (New York's Yankee Stadium and Citi Field)

and tickets to games between major rivals typically command higher prices. Fan enthusiasm also tends to be at its peak at these games, making them the ideal occasions for experiencing the American passion for the sport.

Among the most famous rivalries is between the Boston Red Sox and the New York Yankees, which dates back to the trade of Babe Ruth – often called the best player in baseball history – from Boston to New York in 1919. The move touched off the Yankees' era of greatness (27 World Series titles as of 2010), while Boston went without a championship for 86 years until 2004, when they staged a dramatic comeback to beat the Yankees in the American League Championship Series en route to sweeping the St Louis Cardinals in the World Series.

Another baseball rivalry is between the San Francisco Giants and the Los Angeles Dodgers. This feud dates back to the late 1800s, when both teams were based in New York City, and it has continued unabated since they moved to California in the late 1950s.

New York now boasts two teams, the Yankees and the Mets. For most of the regular season, teams play others in the same league, but during interleague play, the two teams meet in what's known as the Subway Series, a classic New York event.

## Special baseball experiences

Baseball offers many special experiences beyond regular-season games. To check out the sport at closer range and in a more casual setting than the Major League ballparks, consider attending the pre-season **Spring Training camps** in Arizona and Florida starting in February or early March.

The **All-Star Game,** between the National and American Leagues, is usually held on the second Tuesday in July (in a different location each year). The winning league earns home-team advantage in the World Series in October. Among the greatest advantages of attending an All-Star Game is the opportunity to see many of the best players in baseball from different teams at the same time.

## Baseball in the movies

Over the years, film-makers have found in baseball a rich source of cinematic material, from *Pride of the Yankees* (1942), the triumphant and tragic story of the great player Lou Gehrig, to the film adaptation of the Broadway musical *Damn Yankees* (1958), to *A League of Their Own* (1992), the story of the first professional women's baseball league.

The best baseball movies are about much more than runs, strikes, and outs. Themes of father-and-son relationships and second chances resonate through many films, including perennial favorite *Field of Dreams* (1989), starring Kevin Costner as an Iowa farmer who obeys a mysterious voice and builds a baseball field in his cornfield. *The Natural* (1984) features Robert Redford as a brilliant player who gets a second chance at baseball glory 16 years after a tragic mistake derails his budding career. In *The Rookie* (2002), Dennis Quaid plays a high-school teacher and baseball coach who becomes the oldest rookie in Major League history.

Costner also stars as a Minor League catcher in the much-loved *Bull Durham* (1988), with Tim Robbins as a cocky young pitcher and his future long-term partner (they split up in 2009) Susan Sarandon as a team groupie. Other popular films include *Major League* (1989), starring Tom Berenger, *The Bad News Bears* (1976) with Walter Matthau, *Eight Men Out* (1988) with John Cusack, and a third Costner film, *For Love of the Game* (1999).

If you happen to be in the home of one of the leading teams in October, try to snag tickets to a **play-off game**. It's an exciting opportunity to see the best players battle it out for the ultimate honor.

You don't have to go to a Major League game to have a great baseball experience. Watching a **Minor League** game in a small-town ballpark can be very enjoyable; some teams, such as North Carolina's Durham Bulls, are quite well known – and you may just catch a glimpse of the next great player before he becomes a star.

For true baseball fans – or anyone who simply wants to understand the sport's place in US culture and history – the **National Baseball Hall of Fame** (5 Main Street, Cooperstown, NY; tel: 888-425-5633 or 607-547-7200; www.baseballhall.org) is another unmissable experience. Exhibits explore the history, the records, the great players, and the memorable moments of the sport.

At the end of the game, most players are willing to sign autographs for the fans

# Spas and springs

For soothing the aches and pains of everyday life – or even the stresses of a demanding travel schedule – there's nothing quite like a relaxing massage or a soak in a thermal pool. Spa vacations have, in recent years, become increasingly popular across the US, with a diverse array of facilities and treatments available.

From California to New York and from Idaho to West Virginia, the United States is peppered with hot springs, a natural bounty that gave rise to a 19th-century spa culture that has continued to evolve to the present day.

For Native Americans across the continent, hot springs were typically considered neutral ground, where different tribes could come for relaxation, healing, and ceremonies. European settlers soon discovered the springs and their therapeutic properties, and from the late 1700s onward established many spa towns.

With the introduction of additional treatments, spas have proliferated far beyond hot-springs areas, and you'll now find spa resorts all across America, as well as day spas in most major cities. While some spas focus on meeting therapeutic goals in a beautiful and often luxurious setting, spa vacations have also become popular for relaxation, pampering, and enjoyment.

## Historic spa towns and hot springs

America's first spa town, tiny Berkeley Springs, West Virginia, was established in 1776. Its historic Roman-style baths at **Berkeley Springs State Park** (2 South Washington Road, Berkeley

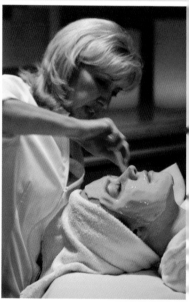

Restorative facials are a popular service at many spas in the US

Springs, WV; tel: 304-258-2711; www.berkeleyspringssp.com) and four other full-service spas continue to attract visitors to this day.

Under federal protection as early as 1832, Hot Springs, Arkansas, became a national park in 1921. The traditional **Buckstaff Bathhouse** (509 Central Avenue, Hot Springs National Park, AR; tel: 501-623-2308; www.buckstaffbaths.com), on historic Bathhouse Row, has been in continuous operation for a century, while down the street, the **Quapaw Baths & Spa** (413 Central Avenue, Hot Springs National Park, AR; tel: 501-609-9822; http://quapawbaths. com) has four modern communal soaking pools.

Saratoga Springs, New York, was visited by so many celebrities during the Victorian era that it became known as the 'Queen of Spas.' Visitors can enjoy mineral baths at **Crystal Spa** (120 South Broadway, Saratoga Springs, NY; tel: 518-584-2556; www. thecrystalspa.net) and the **Roosevelt Baths and Spa at the Gideon Putnam Resort** (39 Roosevelt Drive, Saratoga Springs, NY; tel: 1-800-452-7275; www.gideonputnam.com/spa. aspx). Drinking fountains throughout the city provide a taste of the area's 17 distinctly flavored mineral springs.

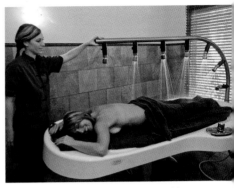

Unwind and enjoy: a deluxe and thoroughly 21st-century hydro massage

At the northern end of Napa Valley's wine country, California's premier hot springs destination, Calistoga Springs, boasts an abundance of spa choices, including the state's oldest spa facility, the 150-year-old **Indian Hot Springs Resort and Spa** (1712 Lincoln Avenue, Calistoga,

## Popular treatments

- **Swedish massage:** A gentle massage that stimulates blood circulation and promotes relaxation.
- **Deep-tissue massage:** A massage targeting deeper layers of muscle and tissue to ease tension and knotting.
- **Hot-stone massage:** Placing heated smooth stones on the body for sore muscle relief and relaxation.
- **Thai massage:** A combination of massage and yoga-like muscle manipulation.
- **Aromatherapy:** The use of botanical oils and essences for gentle healing and relaxation.
- **Reflexology:** The application of pressure to specific points on the feet (and also the hands, although manipulation of the feet is more typical) to restore energy flow through the body.
- **Facial:** Rejuvenating the face through exfoliation, cleansing, massage, and moisturizing.
- **Body wrap:** Enveloping the body in a therapeutic cocoon for detoxification or slimming.
- **Body scrub:** Rubbing a slightly abrasive substance into the skin all over the body for exfoliation and rejuvenation.
- **Hydrotherapy:** Any therapy using water, from mineral baths to hot tubs to underwater massage.
- **Spa salon services:** Beauty services, such as manicures and pedicures.

Glenwood Springs is a natural hotspring pool in the mountains of Colorado

CA; tel: 707-942-4913; http://indian springscalistoga.com), and newer resorts such as **Solage Calistoga** (755 Silverado Trail, Calistoga, CA; tel: 866-942-7442; http://solagecalistoga.com).

Another state rich in hot springs is Colorado, where the most famous spa resort is **Glenwood Hot Springs** (401 North River Street, Glenwood Springs, CO; tel: 970-945-6571). Its principal attraction is the world's largest outdoor geothermal pool (405ft by 100ft/123m by 30m).

In southwestern New Mexico, the historic hot-springs town of Truth or Consequences is unusual in that its 10 bathhouse spas include not only the luxurious **Sierra Grande Lodge & Spa** (501 Mcadoo Street, Truth or Consequences, NM; tel: 575-894-6976; www.sierragrandelodge.com), but also budget motels and an RV park.

## Luxury spa resorts

The ultimate vacation getaway, spa resorts combine top-notch spa services and facilities with luxurious hotel rooms, gourmet dining, and a wide range of leisure activities. Spa resorts can be found throughout the US, from desert ranches in Arizona to ocean-side retreats in Florida to mountain lodges in Montana.

In the Allegheny Mountains, **The Greenbrier** (300 West Main Street, White Sulphur Springs, WV; tel: 304-536-1110; www.greenbrier.com) luxury resort has hosted many famous visitors since it was established in 1778. Outdoor recreation complements the wide range of spa services.

**French Lick Resort** (8670 West State Road 56, French Lick, IN; tel: 888-936-9360, www.frenchlick.com) is a scenic 3,000-acre (1,200-hectare) property with two historic hotels offering mineral-spring baths and other spa treatments, as well as three golf courses and other facilities.

Located in a historic Connecticut country house, the **Mayflower Inn and Spa** (118 Woodbury Road, Route 47, Washington, CT; tel: 860-868-9466; www.mayflowerinn.com) combines New England charm with spa treatments and wellness activities.

**Tips for a great spa experience**

- Drink plenty of water before and after your treatment.
- Eat lightly and cut back on caffeine, sugar, and alcohol beforehand.
- Ask questions about what's going on to ensure you understand and feel comfortable with your treatment.
- Schedule your treatment with plenty of relaxation time before and after.
- Be on time to ensure you receive your full treatment.
- Let the spa know in advance if you have any specific preferences.
- Speak up if you are uncomfortable with anything during your treatment.

The **Lake Austin Spa Resort** (1705 South Quinlan Park Road, Austin, TX; tel: 512-372-7300; www.lakeaustin. com) is a luxurious lakeside retreat in the Texas Hill Country.

## Destination spas

Destination spas are resorts that emphasize healthy living, typically offering a menu of spa services, healthy meals, physical-fitness activities, and educational programs designed to promote weight loss, detoxification, or general wellbeing.

The beautiful Arizona desert provides a backdrop for numerous destination spa resorts, including **Mii Amo at Enchantment Resort** (525 Boynton Canyon Road, Sedona, AZ; tel: 928-203-8500; www.miiamo. com) and **Canyon Ranch** (8600 East Rockcliff Road, Tucson, AZ;

Many resort spas offer therapy sessions to assist in lifestyle changes

tel: 520-749-900; www.canyonranch. com), which also has a branch in the Berkshire Hills of Massachusetts (165 Kemble Street, Lenox, MA; tel: 413-637-4100.)

Other well-known destination spas include California's **Golden Door Escondido** (777 Deer Springs Road, Escondido, CA; tel: 760-744-5777; www.goldendoor.com) and **Cal-a-Vie** (29402 Spa Havens Way, Vista, CA; tel: 760-842-6831; www.cal-a-vie.com.)

## Day spas

You don't have to go to a spa town or resort to pamper yourself. A variety of day spas are available in most cities, from upscale facilities such as the luxurious **Le Petite Retreat** (331 North Larchmont Boulevard, Los Angeles, CA; tel: 323-466-1028; www.lprday-spa.com) to more budget-friendly options such as **Healing Arts Day Spa** (1845 South Dobson Road, Suite 110, Mesa, AZ; tel: 480-897-2146; www.thehealingartsdayspa.com), which offers standard treatments at affordable prices.

# PLACES

# Getting your bearings

The United States is a vast nation with a complex geography. The eastern shores range from Florida's beaches past the genteel cities of the South, through the historic regions of the Founding Fathers and into the rough coastline of Maine.

**THE PACIFIC NORTHWEST**
Pages 258 – 273

**THE WEST**
Pages 198 – 221

**CALIFORNIA**
Pages 222 – 257

**TEXAS AND THE SOUTHWEST**
Pages 176 – 197

PACIFIC OCEAN

MEXICO

Along the western seaboard, California stretches along the coast. The Rocky Mountains traverse the country, extending up into Canada. The central states make up the Heartland of the nation, where a visitor can experience the true taste of America.

For ease of reference when using this guide, each region of the USA is covered by a dedicated chapter, color-coded for quick navigation. Regional maps are found at the beginning of each chapter, and detailed city maps can be found within each region.

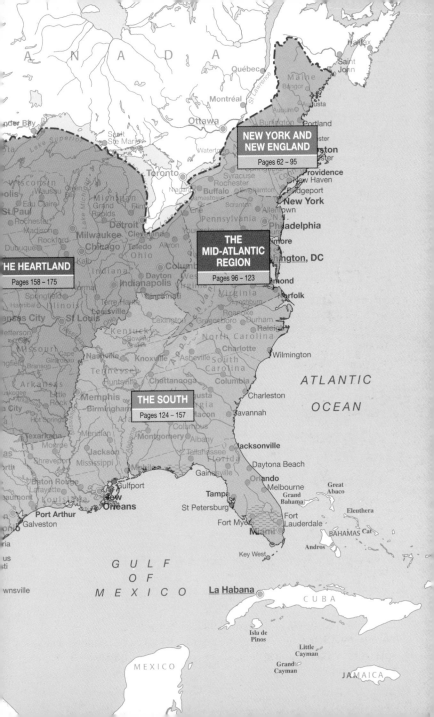

**NEW YORK AND NEW ENGLAND**
Pages 62 – 95

**THE MID-ATLANTIC REGION**
Pages 96 – 123

**HE HEARTLAND**
Pages 158 – 175

**THE SOUTH**
Pages 124 – 157

# New York and New England

Taken together, New York and New England form America's frenetic 'front office', as well as the country's treasure-stuffed 'attic'. In the northern states, you'll find the landmarks of the 18th-century American Revolution, while in New York City, you'll feel the fast-beating pulse of a 21st-century metropolis.

## New York City, Boston, Burlington, and Portland

 **Population:** New York City 8.4 million; Boston 618,000

 **Local dialing codes:** New York City 212, 718, and 646; Boston 617; Burlington 802; Portland 207

 **Local tourist offices:** New York City: 810 7th Avenue; tel: 212-484-1200; www.nycgo.com. Boston: 2 Copley Place; tel: 617-536-4100; www.bostonusa.com. Burlington: 60 Main Street; tel: 877-686-5253; www.vermont.org. Portland: 94 Commercial Street; tel: 207-772-5800; www.visitportland.com

 **Main police stations:** New York City: 306 West 54th Street; tel: 212-767-8400. Boston: 1 Schroder Plaza; tel: 617-343-4633. Burlington: 1 North Avenue; tel: 802-658-2704. Portland: 109 Middle Street; tel: 207-874-8479

 **Main post office:** New York City: 421 8th Avenue; Boston: 25 Dorchester Avenue; Burlington: 11 Elmwood Avenue; Portland: 125 Forest Avenue

 **Hospitals:** New York City: Lenox Hill Hospital, 100 E. 77th Street; tel: 212-434-2000. Boston: Massachusetts General Hospital, 55 Fruit Street; tel: 617-726-2000. Burlington: Fletcher Allen Health Care, 111 Colchester Avenue; tel: 802-847-0000. Portland: Maine Medical Center, 22 Bramhill Street; tel: 207-662-0111

 **Local newspapers/listings magazines:** *The New York Times*, *Boston Globe*, *Burlington Free Press*, and the *Portland Press Herald* are the main daily newspapers. In New York City, the weekly magazines *New York* and *Time Out New York* do entertainment listings

 **Time zone:** EST

In New York and New England, you'll get a slice of America old and new. In Massachusetts, Maine, Vermont, and New Hampshire, you're never far from the country's colonial past or landmarks of the Revolutionary War. In New York City, you'll see the greatest example of America's melting-pot ethos – a world-renowned cultural and business capital shaped by centuries of immigration.

The region's two main cities form a stark contrast. Boston is steeped in colonial history, with maze-like streets and a hearty reverence for its colonial past. As New York City's core, Manhattan hungers for anything new and spectacular. The grid of avenues bristle with skyscrapers reaching for the sky. Where Boston is brick and cobblestone, New York is steel and glass. One looks to the past, the other focuses on the future. But they also have key elements in common: they're both wonderful walking cities and are rich in cultural activities and have outstanding museums.

Beyond the cities, you'll find historic towns and stunning scenery, from the windswept beaches of Cape Cod to the Vermont ski slopes. Maine is loved for its rugged coastline, while up at the Canadian border, Niagara Falls thunders night and day.

## New York City

Although the roots of **New York City** ❶ reach deep into America's past, there's a constant feeling of newness about the place. Of the city's five boroughs, the island of Manhattan burns the brightest: the hub of finance and fashion, a hotbed of internet entrepreneurs and cultural innovators. Although changed irrevocably by the attacks of September 11, 2001,

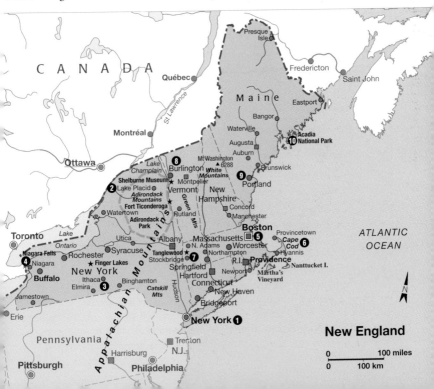

**Airports:** JFK International Airport (JFK); tel: 718-244-4444; **www.panynj.gov/airports/jfk.html**; 15 miles (24km) from midtown Manhattan. AirTrain JFK: about an hour to midtown Manhattan by connecting with subways, $7.25 including subway fare, runs 24 hours daily. Taxi: roughly an hour to midtown Manhattan, $45.

LaGuardia Airport (LGA); tel: 718-533-3400; www.panynj.gov/airports/laguardia.html; 8 miles (13km) from midtown Manhattan. NYCAirporter shuttle bus: about an hour to midtown Manhattan, $12.75, every 30 minutes 6am to 11pm. Taxi: roughly 45 minutes to midtown Manhattan, $30

 **Subway:** New York's subways are run by the Metropolitan Transit Authority (MTA), tel: 718-330-1234; **www.mta.info**. The 22 lines run 24 hours a day throughout the city; during high-traffic times, taking the subway is not only cheaper but also quicker than taking a taxi. Single rides cost $2.25; a 7-day unlimited pass costs $29. Buy a MetroCard at any station or at some convenience stores; you'll need to swipe the card at turnstiles at each station. Each MetroCard ride also allows you one free transfer to a bus. On weekends, subway services are often changed or interrupted, so check the MTA site or announcements posted in stations

 **Buses:** The bus system is also run by the Metropolitan Transit Authority (MTA), tel: 718-330-1234; **www.mta.info**. Dozens of bus lines reach even further into the city than the subways. Technically, most buses run 24 hours a day, but late-night services are infrequent. During rush hour, bus services can slow to a crawl. Buses also use MetroCards for payment, but you must purchase your card at a subway station or from another vendor, not from the bus driver. As with the subway, single rides cost $2.25, and a 7-day unlimited pass costs $29

 **Taxis:** You'll see the iconic yellow cabs all over New York City as they troll for fares. You can hail taxis anywhere on the street. Available cabs have their central roof light illuminated. If the light is off, the taxi is occupied; if only the end roof lights are lit, the taxi is off duty. Taxis cost $2.50 for entry, then 40 cents for each unit (measured in distance and time). Most taxis accept credit cards as well as cash. When giving your destination, it's best to give a cross street rather than a street number. To report any issues, contact the New York City Taxi & Limousine Commission; www.nyc.gov

 **Car Hire:** Carmel Car and Limousine Service: 1-866-666-6666; **www.carmellimo.com**

New York is one of the most popular destinations in the world.

### Lower Manhattan

Lower Manhattan is the original New York, where winding streets once led to bustling docks and clippers. Dutch colonists first settled here in 1624, claiming the island of Mannahatta from a local Algonquin tribe after trading for tools and trinkets. Today, the area goes from high-powered firms in the Financial District to the glossy shopping streets of Soho to the boho charms of the West Village.

Perhaps the best place to start exploring is the monument that's considered the gateway to America: the **Statue of Liberty** (tel: 212-363-3200; www.nps.gov/stli; daily 9am–5.15pm;

Looking south over Manhattan from the Top of the Rock at Rockefeller Center

charge for ferry). This statue, with its upraised torch, became an inspiring symbol of freedom as it greeted boatloads of immigrants from its perch in New York's harbor. Formally called *Liberty Enlightening the World*, the 151ft (46m) sculpture was a gift from France to the US, unveiled in 1886. Access to the crown is limited, but even if you only reach the pedestal, it's thrilling to gaze up at the sternly beautiful figure.

The true gateway for millions of immigrants was a small neighboring outpost, Ellis Island. At the **Ellis Island Immigration Museum** (tel: 212-363-3200; www.nps.gov/elis; daily 9am–5.15pm; charge for ferry) you can get a glimpse of what new arrivals encountered at this station, which operated from 1892 to 1954. The Great Hall was packed with hundreds of steerage passengers per day, all hoping to pass the tests that would allow them entry to the US. Now you can do genealogical research in the Ellis Island records and read the names of thousands of immigrants on a memorial wall.

Visiting the Statue of Liberty and Ellis Island takes careful planning. **Statue Cruises** (tel: 1-877-523-9849; www.statuecruises.com) operates the ferries that visit both islands. Boats leave Battery Park, at the tip of Manhattan, every half-hour until 3pm. Be prepared for long ferry lines. To visit the Statue of Liberty's pedestal or crown, you'll need a free Monument Pass, reserved at least two weeks in advance online or by phone. There are strict security checks at both the ferry and the Statue of Liberty; large bags are not allowed.

Downtown Manhattan's other defining monument takes the form of painful absence. The **World Trade Center Site** marks the original location of the World Trade Center. In the attacks of September 11, 2011, terrorists hijacked two jets and crashed them into the WTC's twin towers. A memorial was completed just before the 10th anniversary of the attacks, and consists of a field of trees and two reflecting pools in the size and shape of the base of the original towers. There is also a

memorial wall listing the names of those who lost their lives that day. The memorial, called Reflecting Absence, was designed by Peter Walker and Michael Arad.

Heading north along Broadway, you'll skirt two long-standing ethnic communities: Chinatown (growing) and Little Italy (shrinking). On the streets west of Broadway, north of Canal Street, you'll see the distinctive cast-iron facades of **Soho** (short for 'south of Houston'). Once industrial sweatshops, then artists' lofts, and now basically an outdoor mall, these buildings are some of the most prized addresses in Manhattan. Mega-chains, upscale brands, and a few tenacious galleries make this a popular place to window-shop and people-watch.

Just east of Soho is another busy boutique neighborhood, in an area called **Nolita** (*no*rth of *Li*ttle *Ita*ly),

along Mott and Elizabeth streets, between Spring and Houston streets. For yet more stylish shopping, head northwest of Soho into **Greenwich Village** (aka the **West Village**) and prepare to get lost. Even longtime New Yorkers get confused in this lovely neighborhood, where the usual grid system becomes scrambled. Bleecker Street is a classic route; you'll pass artisanal food shops, tempting clothing stores, and bookshops. **Washington Square Park**, which marks the bottom of Fifth Avenue, is winding up a long renovation project; its Beaux Arts marble arch gleams freshly white.

Locals consider **14th Street** as the dividing line between downtown and, well, everything else. **Union Square**, where 14th Street meets Broadway, hosts the city's biggest greenmarket four days a week. The far west end of this busy thoroughfare pours into

Walking along the popular High Line, a park reclaimed from an abandoned elevated railway

the **Meatpacking District**. The meat markets here are now of the club and bar variety, but one unmissable sight is the **High Line** (tel: 212-500-6035; http://thehighline.org; daily Apr–Nov 7am–10pm, Dec–Mar 7am–8pm; free). This park atop an old elevated rail line gives a wonderful perspective on the neighborhood's architecture, with glimpses of the Hudson River.

### Midtown

With its square-shouldered profile and changing spectrum of lights, the **Empire State Building** (tel: 212-736-3100; www.esbnyc.com; daily 8am–2am; charge) is one of New York's most celebrated landmarks. When it was completed in 1931, it was the tallest building in the world and the fastest-built skyscraper, taking just 13 months to climb 103 stories high. You'll get a breathtaking view of the city from the two observation decks.

Sunset is the best time to visit, as the city lights twinkle below.

Further north, where Broadway intersects with West 42nd Street, the skyscrapers blaze around **Times Square**. Now flanked by giant, family-friendly stores and chain restaurants,

Times Square has a newly established pedestrian zone perfect for people-watching

Fri 10.30am–8pm, with exceptions; charge), a few blocks north of the Rockefeller Center. There are masterpieces around nearly every corner in the cool white galleries. Highlights include Picasso's *Les Demoiselles d'Avignon*, Van Gogh's *The Starry Night*, Monet's *Water Lilies*, Jackson Pollock's drip paintings, and contemporary photography. It's worth stopping in the central garden, an oasis studded with sculptures.

New York's backyard claims the middle of Manhattan: the 843 acres (341 hectares) of **Central Park** (www.centralparknyc.org; daily 6am–1am; free) stretch from 59th to 110th streets. In the mid-19th century, Frederick Law Olmsted and Calvert Vaux transformed a former swamp into a graceful sweep of lawns, playgrounds, rocky outcrops, ponds, and looping roads. Sheep Meadow and the Great Lawn are ideal for sunbathing, while kids make a beeline for the small zoo in the southeast corner. The elegant, elm-lined Mall leads to the angel-topped Bethesda Fountain.

### Upper Manhattan

Where Fifth Avenue zips up the east side of Central Park, there is a concentration of fine museums in a stretch known as **Museum Mile**. It begins at East 70th Street, with the **Frick Collection** (tel: 212-288-0700; www.frick.org; Tue–Sat 10am–6pm, Sun 11am–5pm; charge). Once the home of a turn-of-the-20th-century robber baron, it now displays

Times Square epitomizes a certain kind of New York gentrification, where peep shows have been replaced by Toys R Us. Since the area is so clogged with sightseers, locals tend to avoid it whenever possible – with the exception of going to a Broadway theater for a show. Most of the Great White Way theaters are between 42nd and 47th streets.

Fifth Avenue is the spine of midtown Manhattan, lined with department stores and glossy flagship boutiques as it nears Central Park. Between 48th and 51st streets, the Art Deco **Rockefeller Center** stretches along the west side of Fifth Avenue. In winter, its gilded statue of Prometheus watches over a petite ice rink. The **Top of the Rock** observation center (tel: 212-698-2000; www.topoftherocknyc.com; daily 8am–midnight; charge) vies with the Empire State Building for the best skyline views.

For a dose of culture instead of commerce, turn to the **Museum of Modern Art** (MoMA; tel: 212-708-9400; www.moma.org; Sat–Mon and Wed–Thur 10.30am–5.30pm,

New York and New England

The American Museum of Natural History offers a one-hour Highlights tour

paintings by Vermeer, Rembrandt, and Boucher.

Up by East 82nd Street, one of New York's most famous cultural institutions overflows into Central Park: the **Metropolitan Museum of Art** (tel: 212-535-7710; www.metmuseum.org; Tue–Thur and Sun 9.30am–5.30pm, Fri–Sat 9.30am–9pm, with exceptions; donation). Like a crash course in global art through the ages, the Met can feel a bit overwhelming, so you may want to choose a few collections to visit rather than attempting to cram everything into one session. The Met's wonders range from the Egyptian Temple of Dendur to the Greek and Roman galleries, and Old Masters galore. Spectacular traveling exhibits also regularly feature.

A few blocks further north coils the Frank Lloyd Wright-designed **Solomon R. Guggenheim Museum** (tel: 212-423-3500; www.guggenheim.org; Sun–Wed and Fri 10am–5.45pm, Sat 10am–7.45pm; charge). It's worth visiting for the architecture alone; inside, a ramp spirals past modern artworks. Visitors are meant to start at the top and walk down.

On the west side of Central Park, at West 79th Street, stands the **American Museum of Natural History** (tel: 212-769-5100; www.amnh.org; daily 10am–5.45pm; charge). It's the largest such museum in the world, with soaring dinosaur skeletons, tableaux of mounted mammals, a butterfly conservatory, and an awe-inspiring model of a blue whale that has become iconic in the minds of many New Yorkers. The Rose Center for Earth & Space is a modern marvel attached to the main building, with the Hayden Sphere hovering inside a glass cube.

### The outer boroughs

Mesmerizing as Manhattan is, there's far more to New York City than

---

**Central Park special events**

In summer, Central Park buzzes with all sorts of events – concerts, dance, live theater, and film screenings – most of which are free. **SummerStage** (www.summerstage.org) mounts shows by high-profile rock, jazz, and other international musicians. The Public Theater hosts **Shakespeare in the Park** (http://shakespeareinthepark.org), luring star-studded casts to perform the Bard's plays in an amphitheater. Thousands crowd the Great Lawn twice a summer to hear the **New York Philharmonic** outdoor concerts (http://nyphil.org/attend/summer).

just this one borough. Brooklyn has become increasingly influential, while the Bronx claims a pair of the city's best outdoor attractions.

Crossing the East River to Brooklyn by walking over the **Brooklyn Bridge** is a memorable experience. A pedestrian walkway starts on the Manhattan side across from City Hall, stretching through the cathedral-like stone towers. Once on the Brooklyn side, historic brownstones line the quiet residential streets of **Brooklyn Heights**, southwest of the bridge. From Orange to Remsen streets, the **Brooklyn Heights Promenade** looks across to the postcard-favorite Manhattan skyline view. Down on the waterfront, the new **Brooklyn Bridge Park** (tel: 718-802-0603; www.brooklyn bridgepark.org; daily 6am–1am; free) takes shape, with sloping lawns and playgrounds.

On the far side of Brooklyn is the nostalgic beach boardwalk of **Coney Island**, New York's 'poor man's Riviera' for over a century. Strolling along the boardwalk, trying a Nathan's hot dog, and braving the rickety wooden Cyclone coaster (though not necessarily in that order) are classic summer moments for New Yorkers.

The Bronx, north of Manhattan, still has more than its share of rough neighborhoods, but it also has two remarkable getaways. The **Bronx Zoo** (tel: 718-220-5100; www.bronx-zoo.com; Apr–early Nov Mon–Fri 10am–5pm, Sat–Sun 10am–5.30pm, mid-Nov–Mar daily 10am–4.30pm; charge) is the biggest city zoo in the US, complete with big cats and a re-created rainforest with gorillas. Across the Bronx-Pelham Parkway from the zoo, the **New York Botanical Garden** (tel: 718-817-8700; www.nybg.org; Tue–Sun 10am–6pm; charge) spreads over 250 acres (100 hectares), with a vast rose garden and a grand, Victorian-style conservatory.

Just west of the zoo is New York's last true Italian community, far more authentic than Manhattan's Little Italy. **Arthur Avenue**, the main drag of the Bronx, is crammed with butchers, bakeries, and bustling restaurants. Just try to resist the fresh *cannoli* (a Sicilian pastry dessert).

Traversing the iconic Brooklyn Bridge by bike

Lake Placid hosted the Winter Olympics in 1932 and 1980

## New York State

New York City may be the Big Apple, but there's a greater orchard of attractions across the Empire State. Upstate, to the north and west of the city, there are the Olympic winter-sports facilities tucked up in the Adirondack Mountains, as well as recently established wineries around the Finger Lakes, and the majestic Niagara Falls at the state's border with Canada.

### Adirondacks

The Adirondack Mountains thrust up through the northeast corner of the state. The region, threaded with rivers and speckled with lakes, inspired several public figures in the late 1800s to campaign for its protection. In an early example of land conservation, approximately 6 million acres (2.4 million hecatares) were preserved as the **Adirondack Park** (tel: 518-891-4050; www.apa.state.ny.us).

To get a taste of Olympic glory, head to **Lake Placid ❷** in the High Peaks area of the park. This Alpine village was America's first winter-sports playground; it went on to host two Winter Olympics, in 1932 and 1980. Much of the action happens at **Whiteface Mountain** (www.whiteface.com), where you can ride the Cloudsplitter Gondola for soaring views or watch while ski-jumpers train their muscles and muster their courage.

In the southern Adirondacks, **Lake Champlain and Lake George** trickle down New York State's northeast border. Both are ideal for kayaking or sightseeing cruises. Meanwhile, history buffs gravitate to Lake Champlain's **Fort Ticonderoga** (tel: 518-585-2821; www.fort-ticonderoga.org; late May–late Oct daily 9.30am–5pm; charge), the site of the first colonial victory of the American Revolutionary War, in 1775. It is now a living-history museum, featuring interpretive exhibits, parades, and re-renacted military drills.

## The Finger Lakes

Reaching from Syracuse in the east to Rochester in the west, the Finger Lakes region encompasses skinny glacial lakes, craggy gorges, progressive cities, and increasingly prestigious vineyards. Summer and fall are the best seasons to drive through this scenic area.

The university town of **Ithaca ❸**, at the southern tip of Cayuga Lake (the longest finger of the Finger Lakes, at 38 miles/61km), makes a fairly central base for exploring the area. The town's **Cornell University** has a picturesque campus with ivy-clad buildings, and is well worth a visit.

Taking Route 96 north from Ithaca will start you on the **Cayuga Lake Wine Trail**, one of three lake-circling routes that connect dozens of family-owned wineries. The **Finger Lakes Wine Country** tourism organization (tel: 800-813-2958; www.finger-lakeswinecountry.com) provides detailed maps and listings.

## Niagara Falls

One of the world's most famous cascades provides a roaring border between the US and Canada, in the northwest corner of New York. The **Niagara Falls ❹** moniker refers to both the natural wonder and the less-than-wonderful tourist town along-side. The Canadian side of the falls is typically less touristic and more pleas-ant, plus there are better views.

Spilling over a ledge 180ft (55m) high, the Falls are actually three waterfalls in one. The American and Bridal Veil falls on the American side are the stars of the **Niagara Falls**

The thundering waters of Niagara Falls from above

## Boston transportation

 **Airport**: Boston Logan International Airport (BOS); tel: 1-800-235-6426; **www.massport.com/logan-airport**; 4 miles (6km) from downtown Boston. Free shuttle buses run to the Blue Line of the subway (the T). The T into the city costs $1.70 and takes about 20 minutes; trains run from about 5.15am to 12.30am. Silver Line 1 (part of the T): $1.70 to South Station, Boston's bus and commuter rail hub, roughly 20 minutes. Taxi: at least 20 minutes to downtown, $25

 **Subway**: The country's oldest subway system is managed by the Massachusetts Bay Transportation Authority (MBTA), tel: 617-222-3200; **www.mbta.com**. Five color-coded lines run roughly from 5am to 12.30am daily. Single rides cost $1.70 using a CharlieCard, which includes a free transfer to a local bus. A day-long LinkPass costs $9 while a weekly LinkPass costs $15. These LinkPasses allow unlimited travel on public transit. Cards can be purchased at kiosks in subway stations or online

 **Taxis:** Getting a taxi in Boston involves calling a dispatcher, finding a cab stand, or just luck. The best places to catch a cab are near major hotels, at the transit hubs of South Station or Back Bay station, or in Harvard Square. The first one-seventh of a mile costs $2.60 and every one-seventh of a mile following is 40 cents. For dispatchers, contact Boston Cab Association, tel: 617-536-3200; or City Cab Association, tel: 617-536-5100. To report any issues, contact the Hackney Unit of the Boston Police Department, tel: 617-343-4475

# Boston

**Map legend**

0 — 500 yds
0 — 500 m

CAMBRIDGE · DONNELLY FIELD · AHERN FIELD · EAST CAMBRIDGE · CambridgeSide Galleria · Cambridge St · Lechmere · Salem · CHARLESTOWN · Charlestown Navy Yard · Boston Inner Harbor · PAOPOLO PARK · GOPP'S HILL BURYING GROUND · Old North Church · St Stephen · Binney Street · Land Boulevard · Cambridge Parkway · Museum of Science · Hayden Planetarium · Science Park · WEST END · North Station · North Station · Causeway St · Keany Square · NORTH END · St Stephen · Atlantic Ave · Main Street · Broadway · CHARLESBANK PARK · Massachusetts General Hospital · Merrimac St · Old West Church · Cambridge St · Haymarket · New England Holocaust Memorial · WATERFRONT · Paul Revere's House · COLUMBUS PARK · Kendall/MIT · Massachusetts Institute of Technology (MIT) · Main St · Longfellow Bridge · Charles/MGH · Bowdoin · City Hall · Government Center · Faneuil Hall · Quincy Market · Aquarium · MIT Chapel · Charles River Yacht Club · MIT Sailing Pavilion · Charles St Meeting House · BEACON HILL · Nichols House Museum · Mass. State House · Old City Hall · State · New England Aquarium · Memorial Drive · Harvard Bridge · Charles · Hatch Shell · Boston Athenaeum · FINANCIAL DISTRICT · Gibson House Museum · Storrow Drive · Beacon Street · Arlington St · Charles St · Beacon Street · Park Street · BOSTON COMMON · Downtown Crossing · Storrow Drive · Clarendon St · Berkeley St · Boylston · Macy's · Boston Tea Party Ship & Museum (Beaver II) · Massachusetts Ave · Marlborough Street · Commonwealth Ave · Newbury St · Park Street · Chinatown · Institute of Contemporary Art · Ames Mansion · Newbury St · BACK BAY · Boylston Street · Arlington · Stuart St · South Station · South Station · Summer St · Kenmore · Hynes · Copley · Copley Square · John Hancock Tower · Back Bay Station · NE Medical Center · CHINATOWN · Ted Williams Tunnel · Fenway Park · Prudential Center · Prudential Tower · Copley Place · SOUTH END · Shawmut Ave · Washington St · Harrison Ave · A Street · Logan International Airport · Storrow Drive · BACK BAY FENS · Museum of Fine Arts, Isabella Stewart Gardner Museum · Prudential · Boston Center for the Arts · Columbus Ave · Kennedy Library · FENWAY

Boston's historic Faneuil Hall was built in the first half of the 18th century

from several prestigious universities, the city exudes both the seriousness and the exuberance of ambitious up-and-comers. It is vaunted as the birthplace of the American Revolution due to the powder-keg events of the 1770s. With its tangle of streets, it's a wonderful place to explore on foot and find historic neighborhoods, great museums, and dazzling new architecture.

### The Freedom Trail

Following the **Freedom Trail** (tel: 617-357-8300; www.thefreedomtrail. org; free, charge for guided tour) is an ideal way to discover Boston's Revolutionary history. This 2.5-mile (4km) route, marked on pavements in red, can be done as a self-guided walk or as a tour with a guide in 18th-century dress. It connects 16 sights related to the colonial fight for independence.

**Boston Common**, America's oldest public park, marks one end of the Freedom Trail, bounded by Tremont, Park, Beacon, Charles, and Boylston streets. From here, you can look up the slope of Beacon Hill to the gilded dome of the 1798 **State House**. Just across Charles Street lies the **Public Garden**, a more formally landscaped park with a pond where swan-shaped boats glide in summer.

The Trail winds roughly northeast to **Faneuil Hall**. The hall itself, on Dock Square, was called the 'Cradle of Liberty' for the fiery speeches given by Samuel Adams and other

**State Park** (tel: 716-278-1796; www. niagarafallsstatepark.com), while Horseshoe Falls is on the Canadian side and is arguably more impressive. The Cave of the Winds tour goes to the base of Bridal Veil; for an aerial view, ride an elevator up the observation tower beside the American Falls. The *Maid of the Mist* sightseeing boat cruises to the base of both falls, where passengers (who are provided with waterproof ponchos) are bathed in spray and deafened by the sound.

## Boston

No city in America blends its game-changing past with its thriving present as seamlessly as **Boston 5**. Flush with biotech companies and students

# STROLLING IN NEWPORT, RI

Newport, Rhode Island was transformed in the 19th-century Gilded Age by millionaires who, in the search for privacy, built extravagant mansions here. Now those plutocrats' palaces are popular destinations for day trips from Boston or long weekends from New York City.

Downtown Newport has a wealth of 17th- and 18th-century buildings, which are well worth seeing before moving on to the gilded excess of the 19th-century mansions. Begin at the **Gateway Visitor Center** (23 America's Cup Avenue; tel: 1-800-976-5122; www.gonewport.com), then walk south along America's Cup Avenue to the **Museum of Newport History** (127 Thames Street; tel: 401-846-0813; http://newporthistorical.org; Tue–Sun

10am–5pm; donation), on the left in the restored 1762 Brick Market building. The exhibits touch on the early settlers as well as the colorful, wealthy families who built massive homes here in the late 1800s.

Next, walk south down Spring Street to Queen Anne Square, home to the white clapboard **Trinity Episcopal Church** (tel: 401-846-0660; www.trinitynewport.org), built in 1725–6 and said to be based on the designs of Sir Christopher Wren. Walk a block west to Newport Harbor to lunch at the **Black Pearl** (Bannister's Wharf; tel: 401-846-5264; www.blackpearlnewport.com), which is popular with the yachting set.

To get close to the water, take one of the popular afternoon sails from Bowen's Wharf. The **Adirondack II** (Bowen's Wharf; tel: 401-847-0000; www.sail-newport.com) offers several packages, including a Morning Mimosa sail for those up bright and early, and a Dark and Stormy sail in the early evening.

## Tips

- Distance: 3 miles (5km)
- Time: A full day
- Start: Gateway Visitor Center
- End: Marble House
- Examine the backyards of the mansions from the **Cliff Walk**, a 3.5-mile (5.5km) path hugging the cliffs along the Rhode Island Sound. Take at least half a day to admire the views, but be sure to plan how you'll get back, as it can me a long walk in the dark.

Trinity Episcopal Church

The Italian Renaissance-style Breakers, built for Cornelius Vanderbilt II

Bellevue Avenue is the town's main thoroughfare. From here, it's best to head south towards the real lure – the over-the-top mansions that their millionaire owners referred to as 'summer cottages'. Don't be fooled by the ironic nomenclature; these are nothing like cottages. If you plan to tour several mansions, the **Preservation Society of Newport** (242 Bellevue Avenue; tel: 401-847-1000; www.newportmansions.org) sells various tickets for admission and offers tours; check its website, as seasons and hours at the properties vary greatly. Spend at least a few hours at each mansion, and don't forget to tour the gardens, as most of the 'cottages' have amazing sea views.

Heading south, **The Elms** (367 Bellevue Avenue; charge) will be the first mansion you'll reach. It's based on the French Château d'Asnières but also borrows from a range of styles, including Chinese and Venetian. Sign up for the behind-the-scenes tour to see the mansion from the servants' point of view, as well as to go up on the roof. Save some time to stroll the beautiful formal gardens.

**The Breakers** (44 Ochre Point; charge) is considered the most magnificent of the Newport 'cottages'. This Italian Renaissance-style palace, designed by Richard Morris Hunt, was completed in 1895 for Cornelius Vanderbilt II of the railroad fortune. Its rooms are adorned with marble, alabaster, gilt, mosaic, crystal, and stained glass. The mansion has 70 rooms, and the kitchen alone is the size of a small house.

Constructed in 1892 for William K. Vanderbilt and styled after the Grand and Petit Trianons of the palace of Versailles, **Marble House** (596 Bellevue Avenue; charge) upstages even The Breakers for ostentation, though it is smaller in size. Its extraordinary ballroom is awash with gold, and a Chinese tea-house stands in the grounds.

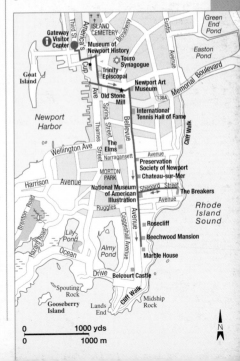

The Boston skyline includes the Prudential Building and the John Hancock Tower

Revolutionary orators. Faneuil is also shorthand for the market stalls and Quincy Market building facing the meetinghouse – a handy lunch spot.

One of the most scenic parts of the Trail runs through the **North End**, a picturesque Federal neighborhood that is now known for its Italian community (where you'll find plenty of espresso, gelato, and pasta). The **Paul Revere House** (tel: 617-523-2338; www.paulreverehouse.org; mid-Apr– Oct daily 9.30am–5.15pm, Nov–Dec and early Apr daily 9.30am–4.15pm, Jan–Mar Tue–Sun 9.30am–4.15pm; charge) gives a touching sense of the daily life of a Revolutionary hero, with period furnishings and examples from Revere's day job as a silversmith.

As a detour from the Freedom Trail, leap forward a few centuries by heading over to visit the waterfront **Institute of Contemporary Art** (tel: 617-478-3100; www.icaboston.org;

Sat–Sun and Tue–Wed 10am–5pm, Thur–Fri 10am–9pm; charge). The striking, translucent building cantilevers over the water's edge.

### Back Bay

Stretching west of the Public Garden are the handsome 19th-century rowhouses and less labyrinthine streets of the **Back Bay**. The broad, straight **Commonwealth Avenue**, known as Comm Ave, anchors this neighborhood. **Newbury Street**, running parallel, is the main commercial drag, with boutiques, galleries, and restaurants filling its converted town houses. Along the southern bank of the Charles River runs the green ribbon of the **Esplanade**, a favorite place for jogging or strolling. Shouldering its way into this genteel area is Boston's first skyscraper, the **Prudential Tower**, a 1964 slab with a host of stores and a convention center at its feet. It looms over Copley Square, at the intersection of Boylston and Dartmouth streets.

## Fenway

Say 'Fenway' to a baseball fan and they'll immediately think of **Fenway Park** (tel: 617-226-6666; http://boston. redsox.mlb.com), the legendary 1912 ballpark that's home to the Red Sox. But Fenway is more than a park, it's a neighborhood that is also home to shrines of another sort: a pair of outstanding museums with sizeable collections of European, Asian, and Egyptian art and artifacts.

The **Museum of Fine Arts** (MFA, tel: 617-267-9300; www.mfa.org; Sat–Tue 10am–4.45pm, Wed–Fri 10am–9.45pm; charge) skirts the Fens park, off Huntington Avenue. This already impressive museum became even grander with the opening of a new American art wing in 2010, where you can see classic paintings by John Singer Sargent and Winslow Homer. The MFA also boasts a fine collection of Impressionist paintings, particularly by Monet, as well as ancient Egyptian and Asian treasures.

A stone's throw from the MFA stands the much smaller but equally inspiring **Isabella Stewart Gardner Museum** (tel: 617-566-1401; www. gardnermuseum.org; Tue–Sun 11am–5pm; charge). This 1903 neo-Venetian palazzo with a dreamy interior courtyard was built by Boston's most flamboyant grande dame.

Gardner may have scandalized Boston's society but she also had excellent taste in art. During the 1890s, she collected masterpieces by Titian, Rembrandt, Vermeer, and Sargent, and then oversaw the creation of her fantasy palace. It still feels intensely personal, although an adjacent new building by Renzo Piano is scheduled to open in 2012.

## Cambridge

Elizabeth Hardwick once described Boston and Cambridge as two ends of the same mustache. The Charles River

Boston's Museum of Fine Arts has 53 galleries to enjoy

may divide Cambridge from Boston, but the two cities are inseparable.

Just across Harvard Bridge is the **Massachusetts Institute of Technology** (MIT), a leader in the world of science. Further inland beats the heart of Cambridge, **Harvard Square**, with bookstores, cafés, and shops. **Harvard University's Harvard Yard**, with its tree-shaded walkways and colonial buildings, lies behind the walls along one edge of the Square.

## Massachusetts

Like its capital, Boston, the state of Massachusetts is full to the brim of early American historic landmarks and stellar cultural attractions – and that's to say nothing of its beautiful scenery. From the windswept dunes of Cape Cod to the lush hills of Berkshire County, each region has potent artistic or literary connections.

### Cape Cod

Shaped like a bodybuilder's flexed arm, **Cape Cod 6** reaches 31 miles (50km) eastward into the Atlantic Ocean, then another 31 miles (50km) north. The peninsula is edged with more than 310 miles (500km) of beaches, many of which are protected as part of the **Cape Cod National Seashore** (tel: 508-771-2144; www.nps.gov/caco). The crook of the arm forms Cape Cod Bay, where the waters are much calmer than the Atlantic. In summer, the Cape's clam shacks and bed and breakfasts are packed with vacationers.

Route 6 is usually the fastest way along the peninsula, with local roads peeling off to the atmospheric villages of Sandwich, Yarmouth, Port Chatham, Falmouth, and Wellfleet (famed for its oysters). **Hyannis** is the year-round commercial center, with a small airport and ferry points for

Harvard Square, in Cambridge (see p. 79)

*The Mayflower* landed at Provincetown in 1620

the nearby islands, Nantucket and Martha's Vineyard. Even in the most touristic centers, the sense of maritime history is palpable, with lighthouses forever standing guard.

At the very tip of the Cape clings **Provincetown**, where the Pilgrims first landed in 1620 and signed the Mayflower Compact, the new arrivals' initial governing document. The site became a fishing village; then, much later, in the early 1900s, it began to attract painters and other artists from New York. By the 1950s, it was a full-fledged art colony. Since the 1970s, the town has evolved into a major gay vacation spot, with rowdy bars joining the galleries and kitsch curio shops on the main drag, Commercial Street.

---

## Massachusetts' literary lights

In the 19th century, a literary golden era, writers in New England produced dozens of novels and essays that are now considered American classics. Below are a few seminal works whose inspirational settings can still be visited today.

- *The House of Seven Gables* (1851), written by Nathaniel Hawthorn. The namesake home described in this spooky novel is in Salem and was owned by Hawthorn's cousin. It's now part of a larger Hawthorn-centric historic site.

- *Walden* (1854), written by Henry David Thoreau while on Walden Pond. A transcendentalist chronicle of the author's experiment with simple living close to nature. Walden Pond is now a state reservation, considered the cradle of the conservation movement.

- *Little Women* (1868), written by Louisa May Alcott in Concord. Alcott based her much-loved novel on her own family (she had three sisters), and worked on it at their home, Orchard House.

Brant Point Lighthouse on Nantucket Island

### Nantucket

To experience an exquisitely preserved whaling town, hop on a ferry to the island of **Nantucket**, 30 miles (48km) off the coast of Hyannis. From 1800 to 1840, this was the base for the world's largest fleet of whaling vessels. (The classic novel *Moby Dick* was based on a whaler from Nantucket.) After the whale-oil market collapsed, Nantucket turned to its own natural beauty and has since relied on the tourist trade.

The north shore's harbor-front **Nantucket town** is the island's focal point and only commercial center. Despite the chic shops and restaurants, it can feel as if it's preserved in amber, with beautifully restored antebellum houses and cobblestone streets. Large swaths of the island's parkland and beaches are also protected.

### Berkshires and Pioneer Valley

For centuries, the valleys and rolling hills in western Massachusetts have inspired both outdoors and artistic types. The Massachusetts Turnpike (I-90) races west from Boston; at Springfield, the I-91 leads north into the Pioneer Valley. Here, the town of **Northampton** is a vibrant cultural nexus, with five top colleges, including Amherst and Smith, and the

### Whalewatching

Ships still seek out whales around Cape Cod, but these days the hunt is purely for sightseeing. Humpback whales migrate to the coast of Massachusetts each year between April and October. **Dolphin Fleet** (tel: 1-800-826-9300; www.whalewatch.com) sails from Provincetown several times a day in high season. **Explore Nantucket** (tel: 508-228-7037; www.explorenantucket.com) operates from Nantucket. Sightings are almost guaranteed and, with luck, you'll even see a whale breaching, or leaping from the water.

attendant cafés, bookstores, funky shops, and fizzing student energy.

Further west, the Berkshires' beauty lies in back roads and villages. The town of **Great Barrington**, south of the Turnpike on Route 7, has long been a visitors' hub. While it's not quite as picturesque as Stockbridge, it does have plenty of places to stay and eat.

The main street of **Stockbridge** ❼ may look familiar from the illustrations of Norman Rockwell. The all-American artist lived and worked here, using local people as his models. The **Norman Rockwell Museum** (tel: 413-298-4100; www.nrm.org; May–Oct daily 10am–5pm, Nov–Apr Mon–Fri 10am–4pm, Sat–Sun 10am–5pm; charge) displays his well-known images in a fine setting, as well as hosting visiting art exhibitions.

Music lovers gravitate north of the Turnpike to **Tanglewood**, home of the Berkshires' best-loved summer festival. The Boston Symphony Orchestra and popular guest musicians and singers perform here annually. Up in North Adams is the **Massachusetts Museum of Contemporary Art** (Mass MoCA, tel: 413-662-2111; www.massmoca. org; Sept–June Wed–Mon 11am–5pm, July–Aug daily 10am–6pm; charge). A huge, 19th-century factory complex now buzzes with modern and contemporary art. The industrial space provides the perfect setting for super-size works and installation.

## Vermont and New Hampshire

Imagine rural New England and you'll likely picture Vermont. Those wooded hills, red barns, and white-steepled churches epitomize the Green Mountain State. Both Vermont and its neighbor, New Hampshire, are characterized by a tough self-reliance that's a particularly Yankee trait. The mountain ranges make for great winter skiing and scenic drives in summer and fall.

### The White Mountains

New Hampshire's **White Mountain National Forest** (tel: 603-536-6100;

A view of classic Americana at the Norman Rockwell Museum in Stockbridge

## Leaf peeping

A scenic drive to enjoy crimson and gold fall leaves is a timeless New England tradition. Thousands of leaf peepers roam the countryside in October, when foliage is often at its brightest. Among the favorite drives are Vermont's Route 100, New Hampshire's Route 302, the Mohawk Trail in Massachusetts, and the Park Loop Road in Maine's Acadia National Park. Here are a few tips for expert peeping:

- **Track the leaves.** Dedicated websites and hotlines predict peak foliage times.

*Yankee* magazine runs a site, www.yankeefoliage.com, with peeper reports, maps, and other information.

- **Reserve early.** For a rural overnight stay, be sure to book a room several weeks in advance. Many small towns have limited lodgings and fill up fast.
- **Consider the interstate.** Although the back roads sound poetic, they can also get clogged with gawking drivers. Some highways, such as Vermont's I-91, have stunning views with lighter traffic.

---

www.fs.fed.us/r9/forests/white_mountain) covers almost 800,000 acres (323,700 hectares) in the northern part of the state, including the rugged Franconia and Presidential mountain ranges. While the scenery is dramatic, the 1,200-plus miles (1,900km) of hiking trails are quite accessible, with many summits within relatively easy reach. The heart of the park is **Mount Washington**, the highest peak east of the Mississippi at 6,288ft (1,197m). The 8-mile (13km) switchback Mount Washington Auto Road climbs to the top. To spare your car's brakes, there's also the 1869 **Mount Washington Cog Railway** (tel: 1-800-922-8825; http://thecog.com; May and Nov Sat–Sun at 10.30am and 1.30pm, June–Oct multiple daily departures; charge), which is located just off scenic Route 302.

The historic Mount Washington Cog Railway

A snowboarder weaves down the slopes at Stowe Mountain Resort in Vermont

the *Sound of Music* family. The **Stowe Mountain Resort** (tel: 1-800-253-4754; www.stowe.com) unveiled a major redevelopment in 2010, with new lodges and an arts center.

### Burlington

Situated on the waterfront of Lake Champlain, the historic town of **Burlington** ❽ has a youthful energy about it. It benefits from the University of Vermont campus, easy mountain access, and a revitalized lakefront with a bike path. Downtown's **Church Street Marketplace** (tel: 802-863-1648; www.churchstmarketplace.com) is a pedestrian zone set up as an open-air mall.

A few miles south of town along Route 7, the **Shelburne Museum** (tel: 802-985-3346; http://shelburnemuseum.org; mid-May–Oct Mon–Sat 10am–5pm, Sun noon–5pm; charge) displays American folk art and crafts, ranging from toys to quilts to paintings. The complex also includes several 18th- and 19th-century New England buildings, a covered bridge, and a steamboat.

## Maine

By New England standards, much of Maine is a mysterious wilderness. A land of jagged coastlines and vast pine forests, it's larger than the other New England states combined. While the southern coast and its lobster shacks are popular, inland and northern Maine remain off the beaten track (and locals would like to keep it that way).

### The Green Mountains

Vermont's Green Mountains are synonymous with skiing and snowboarding. The **Green Mountain National Forest** (tel: 802-747-6700; www.fs.fed.us/r9/forests/greenmountain), with over 400,000 acres (160,000 hectares), reaches from the top of the state down into its core. After World War II, several ski resorts were established here as the sport took off; it was here, in the 1960s, that a Stratton bartender invented the snowboard.

**Stratton** is a ski area towards the southern end of the Green Mountains. Further north, past the state capital of Montpelier, **Stowe** and the state's highest mountain, Mount Mansfield, form another popular getaway. The area is known for its inns, notably the Trapp Family Lodge established by

### The south coast

The best way to see Maine is to start at the southern tip and head northeast along the old coastal highway, US 1. (I-95 is faster, but far less scenic.)

The town of **Ogunquit** is aptly named; the word means 'beautiful place by the sea' in the language of the Abenaki tribe. **Marginal Way**, a cliff-top walk, offers spectacular views.

The neighboring communities of **Kennebunk and Kennebunkport** share a centuries-old shipbuilding heritage. Kennebunkport has an especially rich assemblage of historic buildings, with many Federal homes in the streets off the Dock Square.

### Portland

By far the biggest city in Maine, **Portland ❾** has taken its licks but made strong comebacks. It has been burnt to the ground three times, once in each of the 17th, 18th, and 19th centuries. Each time, a blank slate allowed for a new, well-planned urban center on a peninsula jutting into Casco Bay. Now it's known for a thriving cultural scene and a large number of excellent restaurants.

The atmospheric **Old Port** district, fronting Commercial Street, is both a working waterfront and a social hotspot. While the wharves stay busy, warehouses have been transformed into restaurants and shops. The **Arts District**, a few blocks in from the Old Port, is anchored by the I.M. Pei-designed **Portland Museum of Art** (PMA, tel: 207-775-6148; www. portlandmuseumofart.org; June–mid-Oct Mon–Thur and Sat–Sun 10am–5pm, Fri 10am–9pm, mid-Oct–June Tue–Thur and Sat–Sun 10am–5pm,

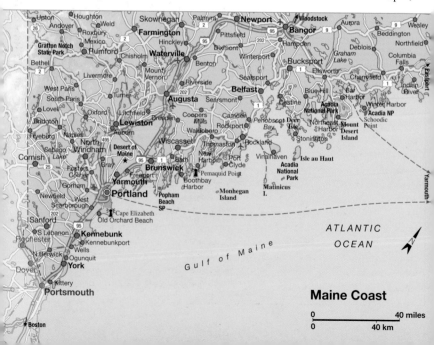

**Maine Coast**

0       40 miles
0       40 km

The colorful Old Port area in Portland, Maine's largest city

Fri 10am–9pm; charge). Its collection of American paintings is notable. The PMA also acquired Winslow Homer's last studio in nearby Prouts Neck and plans to open it to the public in 2012.

### Acadia National Park

Cobbled together with privately donated land, **Acadia National Park** ❿ (tel: 207-288-3338; www.nps.gov/ acad; charge May–Oct) pulls together craggy coastline and a large section of **Mount Desert Island**, just off the coast from the mainland town of Ellsworth. High society discovered this remote spot in the mid-1800s. Over the next 50 years, several wealthy philanthropists were moved to contribute land to what would eventually become the national park.

The one-way **Park Loop Road**, open from mid-April through November depending on weather, makes a circuit of the most scenic spots in the park. A highlight is **Cadillac Mountain**, at 1,530ft (459m) the highest point along the coast, with amazing views of Frenchman Bay.

**Bar Harbor** is Mount Desert Island's main town. It is perhaps overdeveloped, but has a pretty town green and tempting shops and restaurants. Sailing charters and whale-watching boats set off from the wharf.

## Maine's legendary lobsters

The sight of colorful lobster buoys dotting the coast is one of the classic images of Maine, as more lobster is fished here than in any other state. *Homarus americanus* is the real deal, with large, meaty front claws, unlike the crustaceans found in warmer water. Maine's lobsters account for about 80 percent of the nation's catch, but most lobsters are still caught by individual fishermen in small boats. Though lobstermen stay close to shore, it's dangerous work, and economic challenges have made it a difficult life.

Lobsters molt every year, shucking off their old shells and growing ever-larger ones. Molting happens when the water is warm, usually in June or July. New-shell lobsters can taste sweeter, while hard-shell lobsters are bigger. Every year, Rockland hosts the **Maine Lobster Festival** (tel: 1-800-562-2529; www. mainelobsterfestival.com), which the late author David Foster Wallace described as 'a deliberate collision, joyful and lucrative and loud.' The festival offers cooking contests, craft stalls, and live music.

# ACCOMMODATIONS

Manhattan is one of the toughest places in the country to get a deal on a hotel room – or indeed to get a room at any price – so book well in advance. Rooms tend to be smaller here than in other cities; a mere 250 sq ft (23 sq m) isn't uncommon. It's easier to get a room in Boston, but be aware of university-related peak periods, such as May graduations. In rural areas, historic country inns are a great option; remember that October is prime leaf-peeping season, so bed and breakfasts fill up fast. Some coastal hotels close in winter.

## New York City

### The Jane
113 Jane Street
*Tel: 212-924-6700*
**www.thejanenyc.com**
For a cheap yet chic crash pad, the Jane can't be beaten. Nautical standard and bunk-bed cabins have twin beds and share communal bathrooms down the hall. Captain's rooms are larger, with private baths. The lobby café and bar offer great people-watching – without the seasickness. **$–$$**

### Library Hotel
299 Madison Avenue
*Tel: 212-983-4500*
**www.libraryhotel.com**
Inspired by the nearby main public library, this hotel plays with the Dewey Decimal System. Rooms are stocked with themed books (biography, romantic novels) but the look is sleek rather than stuffy. **$$$$**

### The Standard
848 Washington Street
*Tel: 212-645-4646*
**www.standardhotels.com/new-york-city**
Straddling the High Line park, right off the Hudson River, the Standard feels both surreal and somewhat yacht-like. The views are outstanding (though just remember that park-goers can see you, too). This voyeuristic dimension sometimes draws a hedonistic crowd. The restaurant and bar attract plenty of hip locals. **$$$**

### St Regis
2 E. 55th Street
*Tel: 212-753-4500*
**www.starwoodhotels.com**
Among the best of New York's palatial hotels, the St Regis is in the sweet spot of Fifth Avenue, right around the corner from MoMA and the most glittering shops. The Beaux Arts design is authentic from 1904. Rooms contrast high-tech amenities with French antiques; the King Cole Bar is famed for its Maxfield Parrish murals. **$$$$**

## New York State

### The Giacomo
222 First Street, Niagara Falls
*Tel: 716-299-0200*
**www.thegiacomo.com**
Opened in 2010, the Giacomo stepped into a 1929 Art Deco former post office. It has more

A palatial room at NYC's St Regis

charm than the usual chains in town and is just a few minutes' walk from the falls. **$$**

### Lake Placid Lodge
144 Lodge Way, Lake Placid
*Tel: 518-523-2700*
**www.lakeplacidlodge.com**
Rebuilt in 2008, this lodge is the only one right on the lake. It balances rustic comfort and elegance with twig motifs, antiques, and fireplaces in the bedrooms. **$$$$**

### William Henry Miller Inn
303 North Aurora Street, Ithaca
*Tel: 607-256-4553*
**www.millerinn.com**
This lovely 1880 Victorian home was built by Cornell University's first architecture student. Period details are carefully preserved, while the large bathrooms have been modernized in chic style. **$$–$$$**

## Boston
### Charlesmark Hotel
655 Boylston Street
*Tel: 617-247-1212*
**http://charlesmarkhotel.com**
A classic Back Bay home on the outside, a modern boutique hotel on the inside. Rooms are small but comfortable, and offer plenty of storage. **$$**

### Four Seasons Boston
200 Boylston Street
*Tel: 617-338-4400*
**www.fourseasons.com/boston**
Usurping the Ritz as the city's best grand hotel, the Four Seasons overlooks the Public Garden. The best rooms have a view of the garden and the golden State House dome. The spacious modern suites are business- and family-friendly. **$$$$**

## Massachusetts
### The Orleans Inn
3 Old County Road, Orleans
*Tel: 508-255-2222*
**www.orleansinn.com**
Ask for a room overlooking the water in this 1875 inn; a back deck floats right above the

The exclusive Wauwinet

Town Cove. Rooms are homey; listen out for a bump in the night from one of the ghosts that haunt the inn. **$$$–$$$$**

### The Porches Inn
231 River Street, North Adams
*Tel: 413-664-0400*
**www.porches.com**
Right by Mass MoCA, this complex has a cheerful vibe with a touch of irony, as displayed in its colorful 'granny chic' decor. There are long porches with rocking chairs ready for a quiet evening. **$$–$$$**

### The Wauwinet
120 Wauwinet Road, Nantucket
*Tel: 508-228-0145*
**www.wauwinet.com**
Guests have access to private beaches on both the bay and ocean sides of the island; the property also backs on to a wildlife sanctuary. Bedrooms have pine furniture and bright chintzes. A spa, water-taxi service, and tennis are just a few of the amenities on offer. **$$$$**

## Vermont
### Willard Street Inn
349 S. Willard Street, Burlington
*Tel: 802-651-8710*
**www.willardstreetinn.com**
A grand 1881 home built for state senator Charles Woodhouse, the Willard Street Inn has kept many of its period details. **$$–$$$**

## Maine

**Bar Harbor Inn**
Newport Drive, Bar Harbor
*Tel: 207-288-3351*
**www.barharborinn.com**
This place has been a Mount Desert Island institution for over 125 years. The main building is more traditional in style, while two new buildings have a modern look. Most rooms have fireplaces and good views; some have private decks. **$$–$$$**

**Portland Regency Hotel & Spa**
20 Milk Street, Portland
*Tel: 207-774-4200*
**www.theregency.com**
Set in the Old Port neighborhood, this neo-classical building was originally built to be a home of Maine's National Guard. Today, it retains its traditional feel and furnishings, but it combines them with warm, appealing decor and modern facilities, including a spa for beauty and relaxation treatments. **$$$**

# RESTAURANTS

New York City claims several of the best restaurants in the country – and the world. (And of course, who could overlook the pizza?) Boston and Portland also have thriving culinary scenes, with the focus on locally sourced produce and seafood. Along the coast in Cape Cod and Maine, don't miss the fresh-from-the-sea shellfish.

90

### Restaurant price categories

Prices are for a main course meal for one, excluding alcoholic drinks:

**$** = less than $15
**$$** = $15–$25
**$$$** = $25–$50
**$$$$** = more than $50

## New York City

**Artichoke**
114 10th Avenue
*Tel: 212-792-9200*
**http://artichokepizza.com**
It may be a newcomer (for now), but Artichoke has already claimed the hearts of many a New York pizza lover. Of the various branches, this one, in the Chelsea area of town, is the biggest. Try the plain Sicilian-style slice or the super-creamy artichoke-spinach pie. **$–$$**

**Gramercy Tavern**
42 E. 20th Street
*Tel: 212-477-0777*
**http://gramercytavern.com**
Danny Meyer's hospitality is legendary; this formal restaurant in his empire is a gold standard. Sophisticated, seasonal American cooking is enhanced by reliable and friendly service. If you'd like a taste of Meyer's approach without a three-digit bill, look for one of his casual Shake Shack burger stands. **$$$$**

**Joe's Shanghai**
9 Pell Street
*Tel: 212-233-8888*
**www.joeshanghairestaurants.com**
The Chinatown branch of this growing Shanghai-style restaurant group always has a line for its plump soup dumplings, and pork or crab meatballs. **$$**

**Katz's Delicatessen**
205 E. Houston Street
*Tel: 212-254-2246*
**http://katzsdelicatessen.com**
This archetypal Jewish deli first opened in 1888, and is still the best place in New York for giant pastrami sandwiches. Diners also enjoy the vintage Americana on display on the walls. The restaurant became famous worldwide after it featured in the movie *When Harry Met Sally*. **$$**

**Lupa**
170 Thompson Street
*Tel: 212-982-5089*
**www.luparestaurant.com**

One of Mario Batali's early restaurants, Lupa echoes a Roman trattoria, with a rough-hewn look and expertly cooked, comforting Italian specialties. **$$$**

# New York State

**Moosewood Restaurant**
215 N. Cayuga Street, Ithaca
*Tel: 607-273-9610*
www.moosewoodrestaurant.com
Known for its bestselling vegetarian cookbooks, the restaurant that started it all keeps turning out straightforward but delicious meals prepared with only the best organic produce. **$$**

**The View**
77 Mirror Lake Drive, Lake Placid
*Tel: 518-523-2544*
www.mirrorlakeinn.com
This refined hotel restaurant makes good on the promise of its name, with wonderful views over Lake Placid. The kitchen lightens the formality by giving an experimental edge to its cooking. **$$$$**

# Boston

**Legal Sea Foods**
255 State Street
*Tel: 617-742-5300*
www.legalseafoods.com
Though a chain, Legal maintains top quality with its seafood, with regular options (bluefish, salmon) supplemented by daily catches. This branch keeps you close to the water. **$$$–$$$$**

Katz's Delicatessen in New York City

**Mamma Maria**
3 North Square
*Tel: 617-523-0077*
www.mammamaria.com
A quintessential North End spot, this beats the many other Italian restaurants in the neighborhood hands down. Terrific seasonal northern-Italian cooking (think osso buco and seafood risotto), plus a location across from Paul Revere's house. **$$$$**

**Myers + Chang**
1145 Washington Street
*Tel: 617-542-5200*
www.myersandchang.com
Based on Chinese and Southeast Asian street food, the small plates here are easy to share, ranging from pork belly buns to vegetarian fritters. **$$**

# Massachusetts

**The Clam Shack**
277 Clinton Avenue, Falmouth
*Tel: 508-540-7758*
At this classic, bare-bones waterfront shack, families pack on to picnic benches and gobble up fried full-belly clams and lobster rolls. Like many such spots, the shack is only open from Memorial Day through Labor Day. **$–$$**

**Eastside Grill**
19 Strong Avenue, Northampton
*Tel: 413-586-3347*
www.eastsidegrill.com
A popular (but not entirely collegiate) Cajun-influenced grill with plenty of surf'n'turf options. **$$**

# Vermont

**Boves**
68 Pearl Street, Burlington
*Tel: 802-864-6651*
http://boves.com
First opened in 1941, this Italian restaurant seems caught in a time warp, and that includes its prices. Dishes are of the no-fuss variety – the simple spaghetti with marinara sauce, for example. Everything is under $10. **$**

## Maine

### Fore Street
288 Fore Street, Portland
*Tel: 207-775-2717*
**www.forestreet.biz**
Fore Street devotes itself to locally sourced produce, meat, and scallops. Simple yet finessed cooking with these ultra-fresh ingredients is the common denominator. **$$$**

### Street and Co.
33 Wharf Street, Portland
*Tel: 207-775-0887*
**www.streetandcompany.net**
A relative old-timer in the fast-developing Old Port district of Portland, Street and Co. cooks local seafood with precision and flair, and with a Mediterranean twist. Fish in the pan is served on to the copper-topped tables. **$$$**

# NIGHTLIFE AND ENTERTAINMENT

New York City keeps a tight grip on its reputation for nonstop nightlife and outstanding cultural offerings. Whether you crave a night at the opera, a Broadway musical, or a gritty wee-hours rock club, New York comes through. Boston's performing-arts scene, meanwhile, usually outstrips its nightlife. The city is still influenced by Puritanical laws, so bars close at 2am.

## Bars

### The Field
20 Prospect Street, Cambridge
*Tel: 617-354-7345*
**www.thefieldpub.com**
Boston's Irish community ensures that the city has plenty of reliable pubs. This one, located over the river in Cambridge, hits all the right notes: Guinness, darts, grad students, and pub grub.

### Great Lost Bear
540 Forest Avenue, Portland
*Tel: 207-772-0300*
**www.greatlostbear.com**
A granddaddy of American microbrewing, the Bear serves some 50 Northeast craft beers on tap, including several from Maine.

### Pegu Club
77 W. Houston Street, New York City
*Tel: 212-473-7348*
**www.peguclub.com**
On the edge of Soho, this swanky haven offers cutting-edge mixology without the exclusive attitude of other cocktail dens.

### White Horse Tavern
567 Hudson Street, New York City
*Tel: 212-989-3956*

It's almost impossible in these parts not to be told the legend of Dylan Thomas, who drank himself to death at this famous pub. Sodden poets aside, it's a homey, low-key place for a pint and conversation.

## Dance club

### Cielo
18 Little W. 12th Street, New York
*Tel: 212-646-5700*
**www.cieloclub.com**
A rare creature: a long-running Meatpacking District club that still pulls in a good crowd and top house DJs.

The White Horse Tavern is where Dylan Thomas drank immediately before his death

The Boston Symphony Orchestra

## Live music

### Beacon Theatre
2124 Broadway, New York City
*Tel: 212-465-6500*
**www.beacontheatre.com**
An elegant, three-tier, Art Deco theater, the Beacon still rocks the house with acts such as Adele and Elvis Costello. The Allman Brothers roll through each spring.

### Bowery Ballroom
6 Delancey Street, New York City
*Tel: 212-533-2111*
**www.boweryballroom.com**
The acoustics may not be the best, but the indie line-ups at this mid-size venue are consistently good. Its bookers handle several other venues in the city, too, so check the website for options if the Bowery is sold out.

### Citi Performing Arts Center
270 Tremont Street, Boston
*Tel: 617-482-9393*
**www.citicenter.org**
Encompassing the Wang and Shubert theaters in Boston's Theater District, this group puts on musicals and concerts by mellow rockers such as Sheryl Crow.

## Opera and classical music

### Boston Symphony Orchestra
301 Massachusetts Avenue, Boston
*Tel: 617-266-1492*
**www.bso.org**

The BSO remains one of the top symphony orchestras in the US. The city's Symphony Hall also hosts the Boston Pops, devoted to American music.

### Carnegie Hall
881 7th Avenue, New York City
*Tel: 212-247-7800*
**www.carnegiehall.org**
The joke about getting here (practice, practice) takes on new meaning when you hear the impeccable acoustics and sense the history in this famous concert hall. Concerts feature some of the biggest names on the classical-music circuit, as well as luminaries in the fields of jazz and world music.

### Lincoln Center for the Performing Arts
Broadway, between W. 62nd and W. 66th streets, New York City
*Tel: 212-546-2656*
**http://new.lincolncenter.org/live**
A vast arts campus that's slowly undergoing expansion, Lincoln Center overflows with nearly every performing art you can imagine. Among its world-renowned offerings are the Metropolitan Opera, the New York Philharmonic, and the New York City Ballet. Theater companies, a jazz center, and a cinema come under its umbrella, too.

## Theater

### American Airlines Theatre
227 W. 42nd Street, New York
*Tel: 212-719-1300*
**www.roundabouttheatre.org**
One of 42nd Street's grand theaters, this space is the home of the Roundabout Theatre Company, which mounts revivals of classic plays and favorite musicals such as *Anything Goes*.

### Colonial Theatre
106 Boylston Street, Boston
*Tel: 617-426-9366*
**www.bostonscolonialtheatre.com**
Dating back to 1900, the Colonial is the oldest continuously operating theater in New England. It stays in the game with touring Broadway shows.

# SPORTS AND ACTIVITIES

New York City and Boston have several historic rivalries, but one of the most potent involves baseball. The Yankees and Red Sox have been mortal enemies since 1920, when legendary slugger Babe Ruth was traded by the 'BoSox' to the Yankees. Far from the stadiums, New York state's Adirondacks and Vermont's Green Mountains beckon with great opportunities for snow sports.

## Baseball

**Boston Red Sox**
4 Yawkey Way, Boston
*Tel: 1-877-733-7699*
**http://boston.redsox.mlb.com**
Fenway Park, the 1912 stadium, is known for the Green Monster, a wall in left field that's the highest in the major leagues.

**New York Yankees**
1 E. 161st Street, New York
*Tel: 718-293-6000*
**http://newyork.yankees.mlb.com**
In 2009, the Yankees moved from their original stadium, the House That Ruth Built, to a new stadium across the street.

## Skiing

New England and upstate New York offer some of the best skiing opportunities in the US. The season usually lasts from late November through mid-April.

**Stowe Mountain Resort**
Mountain Road, Stowe, VT
*Tel: 1-800-253-4754*
**www.stowe.com/mountain**
Hit the ski slopes of Vermont's highest mountain, Mount Mansfield – it measures 4,395ft (1,340m) –and its 'great 48' trails.

**Whiteface Lake Placid**
Route 86, Wilmington, NY
*Tel: 518-946-2223*
**www.whiteface.com**
Test your mettle at Lake Placid's Olympic Mountain, which has a whopping vertical drop. The resort area offers bobsled and gondola rides, curling, and there's an Olympic ice rink, too.

# TOURS

Since both Boston and New York are great walking cities, they offer, unsurprisingly, many excellent walking tours. (*See also Boston's Freedom Trail, p.75.*)

## Boat tours

**Boston Duck Tours**
Prudential Center, Boston
*Tel: 617-267-3825*
**www.bostonducktours.com**
Shrug off self-consciousness and climb on a World War II amphibious vehicle, which drives around many of Boston's biggest downtown sights and then splashes into the Charles River. Runs mid-March through November.

**Circle Line Sightseeing**
Pier 83, W. 42nd Street, New York
*Tel: 212-563-3200*

**www.circleline42.com**
These tour boats can teach even New Yorkers a thing or two about the sights of their city, with three-hour trips all around Manhattan and spectacular views.

## Food tours

**Maine Foodie Tours**
*Tel: 207-233-8818*
**www.mainefoodietours.com**
Bring an appetite for these Portland-based sessions: two walking tours, one on local food, one on beer, plus a culinary tour on an old-fashioned street trolley.

## Walking tours
### Big Onion Walking Tours
*Tel: 1-888-606-9255*
**www.bigonion.com**
With high-energy guides and a variety of themed tours, this company digs deep into New York. It runs lots of specialty food crawls and neighborhood history walks.

### Boston by Foot
*Tel: 617-367-2345*
**www.bostonbyfoot.org**
Most of Boston by Foot's walks focus on the architecture and history; there's also a children-specific short route. Regularly scheduled tours often run May through October, with private tours available year-round.

# FESTIVALS AND EVENTS

In cities with vibrant ethnic communities and regions with such eventful histories, hardly a week goes by without some kind of festival or special event. Summer brings a slew of festivals to coastal villages; in fall, rural towns throw harvest fairs. New York and Boston have a wealth of activities throughout the year.

## June
### NYC Pride
New York City
**www.hopinc.org**
One of the US's biggest LGBT pride events, with a rally, parade, and drag queens galore.

## July
### Newport Folk Festival
Newport, RI
**www.newportfolkfest.net**
Ever since Bob Dylan's 1963 performance, this has been a premier music event.

### Tanglewood
Berkshire Hills, MA
**www.bso.org**

Gay Pride parade in New York City

The Boston Symphony Orchestra and other musical guests enjoy a working holiday in the beautiful rural climes of the Berkshires.

## August
### Maine Lobster Festival
Rockland
**www.mainelobsterfestival.com**
Thousands of pounds of lobster, a lobster-crate race, and a crustacean-themed parade help to put this festival on the map.

## November
### Macy's Thanksgiving Day Parade
New York City
**http://social.macys.com**
Gargantuan floats make their way past Central Park and crowds of onlookers.

## December
### First Night
**New Year's Eve**
Boston, Portland, and other towns
**www.firstnight.org**
Boston initiated these family-friendly civic events, all with music and fireworks.

### Times Square New Year's Eve
Times Square, New York
**http://timessquarenyc.org/nye**
The country's biggest televised countdown.

# The Mid-Atlantic region

Philadelphia is noted for its monuments relating to the nation's Founding Fathers, Virginia has re-created some of the early colonial settlements, and Washington, DC, the capital city, is home to all the offices and symbols of the federal government that make the United States such a powerful model of democracy to this day.

## Philadelphia and Washington, DC

**Population:** Philadelphia: 1.55 million; Washington, DC: 600,000

**Local dialing codes:** Philadelphia: 215 and 267; Washington, DC: 202

**Local tourist office:** Philadelphia: 1700 Market Street; tel: 215-636-3300; www.philadelphiausa.travel. Washington, DC: 901 7th Street NW; tel: 202-789-7000; http://washington.org

**Main police station:** Philadelphia: 750 Race Street; tel: 311. Washington, DC: 300 Indiana Avenue NW; tel: 202-727-9099

**Main post office:** Philadelphia:

3000 Chestnut Street; Washington, DC: 900 Brentwood Road

**Hospitals:** Philadelphia: Hospital of the University of Pennsylvania, 3400 Spruce Street; tel: 215-662-4000. Washington, DC: Washington Hospital Center, 110 Irving Street; tel: 202-877-7000

**Local newspapers/listings magazines:** The *Philadelphia Inquirer* and *Washington Post* are the main city dailies. Both Philadelphia and DC have editions of the weekly *CityPaper*, which provides entertainment listings

**Time zone:** EST

If Boston is the birthplace of American liberty, Philadelphia could be considered its nursery. It was here that the country took it's first foudnering steps into nationahood. Benjamin Franklin grew into a statesman for the ages within this city, and it was here that Thomas Jefferson drafted the Declaration of Independence.

The City of Brotherly Love, as it is known, retains a great many sites of historical importance and was the new nation's temporary capital until 1800, when northern and southern states finally agreed on a site for the permanent capital. They chose, of course, Washington, DC, situated right on the boundary between the two regions.

For visitors today, a trip to Washington, DC and an excursion to see the colonial heritage of Virginia makes an interesting comparison between the businesslike north and the more leisurely south.

# Philadelphia

Over the past decade, the current cultural scene of Philadelphia ① has finally been getting the recognition it deserves – catching up with its storied past as a reason to visit. These days, locals and tourists alike are as eager to hit the Museum District or a hot new restaurant as they are to visit Independence Hall. Center City encompasses many of the stellar sights and cozy neighborhoods that make Philadelphia such a popular destination. While the city has a robust public transportation system, most areas of interest are easy to explore on foot.

## *Center City*

The grand **City Hall**, at the intersection of Market and Broad streets, anchors Center City. At 40 stories high, this was the tallest building in Philadelphia until the 1980s, when developers broke an informal gentleman's agreement and started constructing skyscrapers to the west. City Hall itself has walls that are nearly 22ft (6.7m) thick, built to support the great weight of the masonry that towers above.

From City Hall, the broad, museum-studded Benjamin Franklin Parkway stretches northwest. Over to the east lie Independence National Historical

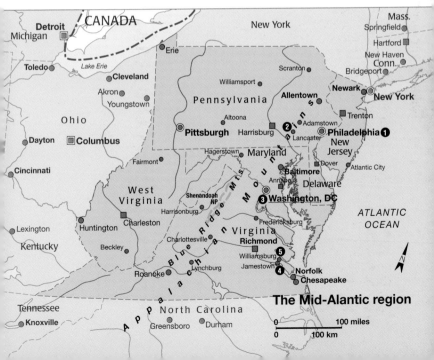

The Mid-Alantic region

## Philadelphia city transportation

 **Airport:** Philadelphia International Airport (PHL); tel: 215-937-6937; www.phl.org; 8 miles (13km) southwest of downtown. SEPTA train: about 20 minutes to Center City, $7, runs 5.30am to 11.30pm daily. Taxi: roughly half an hour to downtown, $28.50 flat rate

 **Subways:** The city's subway, elevated train, and trolley system is an integrated one; it is run by Southeastern Pennsylvania Transportation Authority (SEPTA), tel: 215-580-7800; www.septa.org. There are two main train lines, Broad Street (orange) and Market-Frankford (blue), running from around 5am to midnight daily. An on-site cash fare costs $2. Discounted tokens can also be bought, two or more at a time, at stations for the equivalent of $1.55 a ride. Independence Passes for unlimited one-day travel can be purchased at stations for $11

 **Taxis:** Taxis are usually easy to hail from the street in Center City. A cab ride costs $2.70 at flag drop, then $2.30 per mile. Taxis are technically equipped to accept credit cards but many drivers will request cash. To call ahead for a cab, try Olde City Taxi, tel: 215-247-7678, or Quaker City Cabs, tel: 215-726-6000. To report any issues, contact the Philadelphia Parking Authority, tel: 215-683-9440

Park and the Old City, which is (fittingly) home to Philadelphia's oldest landmarks, including the Betsy Ross House and Elfreth's Alley.

One of the loveliest Center City areas to wander round is **Rittenhouse Square**, at 18th and Walnut streets, where elegant homes, shops, and cafés surround a leafy park. The park has many benches, which are popular with lunch-time visitors.

The smell of soft pretzels lures hungry hordes to the **Reading Terminal Market** (tel: 215-922-2317; www.readingterminalmarket.org; Mon–Sat 8am–6pm, Sun 9am–5pm;

The Schuylkill River winds its way through Philadelphia

Philadelphia's City Hall was the world's tallest habitable building from 1901 to 1908

### The historic center

To immerse yourself in the early history of the United States, make a beeline for the **Independence National Historical Park** (tel: 215-597-8787; www.nps.gov/inde; most sites daily 9am–5pm; free). This central area accommodates dozens of buildings and exhibits that bring the birthplace of the nation to life.

**Independence Hall** is a linchpin in the historic parks system. It's quite a popular destination, so note that it has a timed entry system to help control the crowds. It was in these assembly- and courtrooms that George Washington became the commander of the Continental Army, the Declaration of Independence was signed, and the United States Constitution was hammered out and finalized. There are powerful mementoes of the nation's founding ideals around every corner. Independance Hall has a rarefied atmosphere that helps visitors to experience the history that was made here.

The **Liberty Bell**, an American icon, is suspended in a glass pavilion nearby. The 18th-century bell was inscribed with the words 'proclaim liberty throughout the land unto all the inhabitants thereof', but the bell's true resonance came in the 1830s, when abolitionists used it as a symbol of freedom. Although the bell has cracked several times in its centuries of use, the large and distinctive cleft dates from the 19th century, although the details remain unknown.

The Mid-Atlantic region

free), at 12th and Arch streets. The market building packs in dozens of vendors selling everything from handmade chocolates to oozing cheesesteak sandwiches. Many of the permanent stalls also sell kitchen gadgets and cookbooks, so you'll be able to source the recipe as well as the ingredients and kitchen gadgets.

Uniquely, Amish vendors frequently sell their wares at this market. Most are present on Wednesday through Saturday, and bring with them scrapple (pork mush) , and shoofly pie (made with molasses). If you don't have time to venture into Pennsylvania Dutch Country, this might be the best opportunity to look for a singular Amish or Mennonite gift.

The **National Constitution Center** (tel: 215-409-6600; www.constitution center.org; Mon–Fri 9.30am–5pm, Sat 9.30am–6pm, Sun noon–5pm; charge) focuses on the history and significance of the American Constitution, the document on which the entire US government is predicated. Lively exhibits explain how the Constitution shapes the modern government. Visitors can get in on the act by trying on judicial robes and seeing how current constitutional issues are debated in Congress.

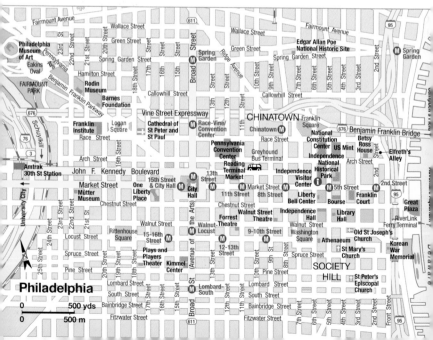

Philadelphia's imposing Benjamin Franklin Parkway, illuminated for July 4

### The old city

One of the city's oldest neighborhoods is also one of its trendiest, a lively mix of old and new. The historic zone between Front, 5th, Chestnut, and Vine streets has plenty of picturesque cobblestone lanes, like **Elfreth's Alley**, the oldest residential street in America. There are also cast-iron industrial buildings, now revamped as trendy lofts, and a smattering of cool art galleries and shops. In the warmer summer months, actors in period costume roam the streets, stopping at scheduled times to give a demonstration or lead a short tour. The 13 Storytelling Benches scattered around the city provide opportunities to listen to a story about Philadelphia. Stories are told continuously throughout the day, and last just a few minutes each. See the Historic Philadelphia website for details: http://historicphiladelphia.org/day/storytelling-benches.

### The Benjamin Franklin Parkway

Shooting northwest through Center City towards the sweeping Fairmount Park, the flower-lined Parkway has a grand, European-boulevard feel. At one end stands the grand, columned **Philadelphia Museum of Art** (tel: 215-763-8100; www.philamuseum.org; Tue–Thur and Sat–Sun 10am–5pm, Fri 10am–8.45pm; charge). Visitors can often be seen running up the front steps and huming the theme music from the movie *Rocky*; the iconic picture at the top is a must. Afterwards, dive into the galleries hung with European masterpieces by, among others, Van Eyck, Cézanne, and Picasso; work by the famed hometown painter Thomas Eakins; and many period rooms that capture a sense of times past. The museum has the second-largest collection of arms and armor in the United States, although many pieces are displayed in rotation to conserve space.

A few blocks down the Parkway stands the **Rodin Museum** (tel: 215-568-6026; www.rodinmuseum.org; Tue–Sun 10am–5pm; donation). With one of the world's largest collections of Rodin sculptures, these galleries and gardens teem with monumental yet poignant works such as *The Burghers of Calais* and the monumental *Meudon Gate*. A renovation

The Mid-Atlantic region

project for the exterior and garden landscape will rejuvenate the grounds in the spirit of the original 1929 plans; note that during the construction program, *The Thinker* was relocated to the Great Stair Hall at the Philadelphia Museum of Art, but is due to be returned to the Rodin Museum in late spring 2012.

Another famous Pennsylvania art collection is headed to the Parkway, but only after much debate. The **Barnes Foundation** (tel: 610-667-0290; www.barnesfoundation.org) is slated to move to the Museum

## Philadelphia's murals

One of Philadelphia's nicknames is the 'City of Murals' – a moniker that nods to a recent creative effort in this historic town. In 1984, city officials took a fresh approach to combating graffiti by asking the taggers to try painting murals instead. The initiative was a raging success. Now, thousands of colorful murals pop up across town and special mural classes are offered to 'at-risk' youth. Local businesses help to sponsor the work.

The **Mural Arts Program** (https://muralarts.org) spearheads these projects and organizes tours of the best images. There's a vibrant series of artworks along Mural Mile in Center City, for instance, where 17 paintings can be seen along an easy walking route southeast of City Hall.

Other standout murals include an image of baseball player Jackie Robinson sliding into a base; a tribute to Rosa Parks and mayor Frank Rizzo; and the touching 'A Love Letter For You.'

*The Thinker* by Auguste Rodin (1840–1917)

District from the suburbs of Lower Merion, to a newly built gallery on the Franklin Parkway in 2012. The Barnes collection, a breathtakingly rich trove of European and folk art, will be displayed in a re-creation of its original home, since the original trust stipulates that the paintings be kept 'in exactly the places they are.' The founder, Albert Barnes, filled his mansion with hundreds of European paintings by Renoir, Cézanne, Picasso, and others. Matisse even painted a mural in a stairwell. Alongside these artworks, Barnes hung ironwork, homely crafts, and tribal artifacts, hoping to encourage visitors to find connections in unlikely places. Viewing this collection is a truly exceptional experience. The new gallery will re-create that original experience as much as possible, with the addition of an art education center, renovation space, and a shop.

If you're interested in the wonders of science rather than those of sculpture or painting, head to the **Franklin Institute** (tel: 215-448-1200; www2.fi.edu; daily 9.30am–5pm; charge). Exhibits include the walkthrough *Giant Heart* model, which has become a Philadelphia icon; the new *Electricity* exhibit, which follows electricity from Benjamin Franklin's experiments through to modern-day uses, including a sustainable dance floor; and *Changing Earth*, which focuses on the forces of air, water, and earth. All this is overseen by a larger-than-life marble statue of the great man himself. This centerpiece of the Benjamin Franklin National Memorial sits in a rotunda. Nearby is the Frankliniana Collection, which contains Franklin artifacts, including one of his lightning rods and the odometer he used to measure the postal routes through the city of Philadelphia.

## Pennsylvania Dutch Country

Roughly an hour's drive west of Philadelphia, you're more likely to see a horse-driven buggy than a Volkswagen bug. Here in Lancaster County, life slows down under the peaceful influence of the Amish, a subset of the Mennonite church.

The Amish community here is the oldest and largest in the United States, and is directly descended from German and Swiss immigrants who settled in the area in the 17th and 18th centuries. The Amish and Mennonites follow a simple lifestyle without modern conveniences such as electricity, cars, or even zippers. Each community creates its own set of rules about what level of technology is appropriate, so you might find some youngsters speeding by on in-line skates, while others stick to the plodding speed of a pony or horse. Although there are variations, the majority of Amish do not like to be photographed, especially if their faces would be visible in the picture.

The *Electricity* exhibit at Philadelphia's Franklin Institute

**Lancaster County** is often called the 'Pennsylvania Dutch' region because of the Amish dialect, which is a variation of German (*Deutsche*). Amish crafts, such as quilts or furniture, are renowned for their high quality and workmanship, and make excellent gifts or souvenirs. Be sure to purchase from a reputable dealer, or directly from the crafts-person if at all possible.

The town of **Lancaster** ❷ is a good introduction to Amish culture and history. The **Landis Valley Museum** (tel: 717-569-0401; www.landisvalley museum.org; Mon–Sat 9am–5pm, Sun noon–5pm; charge) re-creates a 19th-century farming village, where guides in period dress demonstrate skills such as weaving and plowing. At the **Central Market** (tel: 717-735-6890; www.centralmarketlancaster.com; Tue and Fri 6am–4pm, Sat 6am–2pm;

free), locals and visitors alike stock up in what is the country's oldest farmer's market. Look for regional specialties such as Lebanon bologna or scrapple, which is a breakfast meat made of pork scraps and cornmeal.

**Adamstown**, meanwhile, tempts antiques hounds with its 'Antique Mile' along Route 272. Markets such as Renninger's and Stoudt's bring together vendors of every kind of collectible and antique, from Depression-era milk glass to rocking chairs. One unique experience is **Shupp's Grove** (www.shupps-grove.com; Apr–mid-Oct Sat–Sun 7am–5pm; free), where dealers set up tables heaped with collectibles, crafts, and vintage treasures outdoors among the trees. Although the quality can vary depending on which antique dealers are present, the possibility of finding a hidden treasure

The Amish community in Pennsylvania is the oldest and largest in the US

The neoclassical Jefferson Memorial in Washington, DC

still brings crowds out to search. You can also find home-made sandwiches and soups at Friar Tuck's Deli.

## Washington, DC

A visit to the nation's capital is nothing less than a step into history – living history, too, as you can peek into the corridors of power and watch the wheels of America's government turning day by day in **Washington, DC ❸**.

The city has a stately beauty, thanks to the first president, George Washington. He insisted that the fledging country have a European-style capital like Paris or London, and hired French architect Pierre-Charles L'Enfant to plan the city and give it the broad boulevards

### Kids' Capitol favorites

As the site of thousands of school field trips and family vacations, Washington, DC sees floods of children every day. Admission to the attractions of the city's Smithsonian Institution is free of charge and there are always plenty of kid-friendly activities and exhibits. The following are some of the other highlights for children:

- **The National Zoo** (tel: 202-633-4888; http://nationalzoo.si.edu; Apr–Oct daily 10am–6pm, Nov–Mar daily 10am–4.30pm; free). There are dozens of eye-popping critters, from gorillas to elephants, but the ultimate stars are the rare giant pandas.
- **International Spy Museum** (tel: 202-393-7798; www.spymuseum. org; May–early Sept daily 9am–7pm, mid-Sept–Apr daily 10am–6pm; charge). For older kids, this is a thrilling afternoon of espionage, with exhibits on famous agents, Cold War secrets, and a school for spies.
- **A night at a museum.** The National Museum of Natural History and the National Zoo offer sleepovers.

and impressive vistas that epitomize the Old World. The world's first planned capital was established along the Potomac River to ensure separation from the existing states, in an area that comes directly under federal control. It was designed to encompass the working levels of government, great museums, and impressive historial monuments; there are a few nice views, as well.

## Capitol Hill

As far as Washingtonians are concerned, there's only one hill in town: the area where the domed Capitol sits. Two of the three major houses of government anchor 'the Hill': the Supreme Court and the Capitol, where the Senate and the House of Representatives meet. Plenty of wheeling and dealing happens in the restaurants and pubs in the surrounding streets, and recent gentrification has made the area one of the hottest neighborhoods in town.

A neoclassical white dome gleams atop the **Capitol** (tel: 202-226-8000; www.visitthecapitol.gov; Mon–Sat 8.30am–4.30pm; free). After being burnt by the British in 1814, reconstruction continued through the 19th century. Abraham Lincoln even kept the project going through the Civil War, saying that it was a symbol of the continued union; Lincoln was assassinated before its completion. The final scaffolding was removed in January 1866. The exterior dome stands 288ft (88m) above ground, while the interior dome rises to 180ft (55m) above the rotunda floor.

Underneath the dome, the grand rotunda is adorned with frescoes and

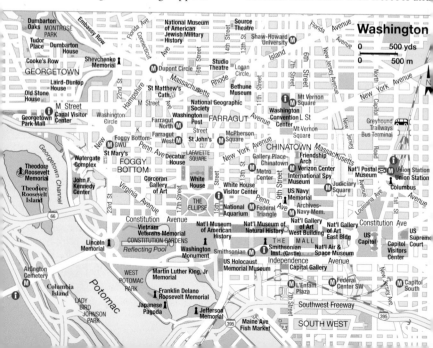

Symbols of national pride on Washington's Capitol Hill

tatuary. More statues join the ranks n the National Statuary Hall, where each state can submit two sculptures to the national collection. The statues' artistic merit may vary, but that's part of the fun. Many visitors search for the figures from their home state, although space is at such a premium that recent additions can be found in Emancipation Hall in the Capitol's visitor center.

Touring the Capitol gets more exciting when the Senate and House are in session. (Check the Capitol's website for legislative calendars.) Both chambers have galleries where visitors can watch legislation being debated. Whenever the Senate and House are in session, flags fly over their wings of the Capitol (House to the south, Senate to the north). There are also lights that twinkle near the statue of *Freedom* when either house is in a night session: a red light means that the Senate is working

late, while a white light represents the House.

The Capitol's visitor center is not immediately apparent because it's underground; look for the entrance at the intersection of First and East Capitol streets. To tour the Capitol, you must have a timed pass, ordered online before your visit. Senate and House of Representative gallery passes must be requested separately. US citizens can obtain them from the office of their representative.

Be sure to check the current security guidelines in advance; no large bags or bottles are currently allowed in the building. There can be long waits to get in through security. Once you are inside, there are shops as well as a canteen that sells the Capitol's famous bean soup.

Just behind the Capitol stands the **Supreme Court of the United States** (tel: 202-479-3000; www.supreme court.gov; daily 9am–4.30pm; free).

**Airports:** Ronald Reagan Washington National Airport (DCA); tel: 703-417-8000; **www.mwaa.com/reagan**; 4 miles (6km) south of downtown Washington, DC in Virginia. Metrorail Blue and Yellow lines: about 20 minutes to downtown, $2.55 (peak) or $2.35 (off-peak), roughly from 5.30am to 11.45pm. Taxi: 15 minutes to downtown, about $15. Washington Dulles International Airport (IAD); tel: 703-572-2700; **www.mwaa.com/dulles**; 26 miles (42km) west of downtown, in Virginia. SuperShuttle shared-ride vans: about 45 minutes to downtown, $30. Taxi: at least 40 minutes to downtown; about $50. At the time of writing, construction of a Metrorail project connecting Dulles directly to DC was under way; check **www.dullesmetro.com** for updates

**Subways:** The Metrorail is operated by Washington Metropolitan Area Transit Authority (WMATA), tel: 202-637-7000; **www.wmata.com**. Although the system is currently being upgraded and thus passengers sometimes experience delays, this is still the easiest way to navigate the city. It reaches most sightseeing neighborhoods, except Georgetown. The five color-coded lines run from about 5am on weekdays and 7am on Saturday and Sunday to midnight Sunday through Thursday, 3am on Friday and Saturday. Fares vary based on peak travel times and distance traveled, but most rides cost under $3. Buy farecards at vending machines in stations and hold on to them as they're also needed to exit stations. Other options include a $9 unlimited one-day pass and the rechargeable SmarTrip card, which is also available at station vending machines

**Buses:** Washington Metropolitan Area Transit Authority (WMATA), tel: 202-637-7000, **www.wmata.com**, runs the extensive Metrobus network. A ride costs $1.70 in exact change on the bus, or $1.50 if using a SmarTrip card (see above). Buses operate 24 hours every day, though late-night services are sporadic. Another popular sightseeing option is the DC Circulator, tel: 202-567-3040; **www.dccirculator.com**. These red-and-silver buses do loops of several key locations, including the Mall and Georgetown. They start at 7am on weekdays, 9am on weekends, running until midnight Sunday through Thursday, and about 2am on Friday and Saturday. Fares are $1, exact change, paid on board

**Taxis:** Taxis can be hailed from the street downtown. They're known for sometimes ignoring or turning down fares, however. A cab ride starts at $3, with $1.50 per mile afterward; most taxis accept payment only in cash. To call ahead for a cab, try Diamond Cab, tel: 202-387-6200, or the Yellow Cab Company, tel: 202-544-1212. Report any issues by contacting the Taxicab Commission at 202-645-6018

The highest court in America decides on the constitutionality of any Acts of any level of government, from the President to the lower courts of the states. The eight justicees hear some of the country's most crucial cases.

The Supreme Court's columned, Greco-Roman-style building is actually quite modern, built in 1935. Before then, the court was somewhat itinerant, bouncing between offices and even meeting in a tavern.

If possible, come to the Supreme Court to see a case being argued. The court sits from October through April for two weeks a month, hearing a few arguments each weekday. Call or check the website for an argument calendar, then plan to come well in advance of the scheduled times, since seats are on a first-come, first-served basis; there are about 250 seats available for the public. Note that you'll need to stow your belongings in a coin-operated locker, so bring plenty of quarters. Visitors may not tour the courtroom unaccompanied, but when court is not in session there are lectures held every hour from 9.30am to 3.30pm. There is a gift shop and cafeteria, as well as an informational film for visitors.

## The Mall

Stretching from the Capitol to the Lincoln Memorial, the **National Mall** links together several outstanding museums, evocative memorials, and a sweeping open-space park. This 2-mile (3km) expanse of greenery and water is one of the country's great vistas. It's almost always full of people strolling, playing Frisbee, or relaxing between visits to the museums. At night, the monuments shimmer under illumination.

With approximately 24 million visitors each year, the Mall is definitely at the top of the list for any trip to Washington, DC. The city's planner, Pierre-Charles L'Enfant, had designed a grand avenue for this space, but while the throughway was never constructed, the Washington Monument is located at the very spot where he had planned to place an equestrian statue of George Washington.

At the Capitol end of the Mall stands the **National Gallery of Art** (tel: 202-737-4215; www.nga. gov; Mon–Sat 10am–5pm, Sun 11am–6pm; free). This superb

Exploring Washington, DC's National Gallery of Art

collection of Western art has a split personality, between traditional and cutting-edge. The massive, neoclassical West Building (designed by John Russell Pope) was the gift of financier Andrew Mellon, who seeded the museum with his personal collection of Old Masters in 1930. The 1970s East Building is a glassy angular structure by I.M. Pei, with an Alexander Calder mobile dangling in the atrium. The two disparate buildings are connected by an underground concourse, which has been used as in installation space for *Multiverse,* a complex light sculpture by American artist Leo Villareal. The tunnel features 41,000 computer-programmed LED nodes that run through channels along the entire 200ft- (61m-) long space, making it a bright transition between the old and new.

The National Gallery's collection is extensive. The West Building showcases European art, including the only portrait by Leonardo da Vinci on public display in the Western hemisphere. In the East Building hangs 20th-century work by Jackson Pollock, Mark Rothko, and other modern masters. The National Gallery is quite big, and you'll need a plan to avoid gallery-fatigue. A good tactic is to choose just a small section of the collection, and immerse yourself in that experience.

The **Smithsonian Institution** (tel: 202-633-1000; www.si.edu) forms one of the largest presences on the National Mall. This complex of museums, research centers, and a zoo encompasses a mind-boggling array of collections. Many of the Smithsonian's prime attractions line the Mall; all of them offer free admission and share the Smithsonian's general phone number. The castle-like **Smithsonian Institution**

Aviation exhibits at the National Air and Space Museum

In April 2011, NASA announced that the space shuttle *Discovery* would be permanently retired to the Udvar-Hazy Center of the National Air and Space Museum in Chantilly, Virginia, which is not far from Washington, DC. The museum will also be receiving sections of the flight-deck training hardware from the Johnson Spaceflight Center.

In the **National Museum of Natural History** (www.mnh.si.edu; late Mar–early Sept daily 10am–7-.30pm, mid-Sept–mid-Mar daily 10am–5.30pm; free), further west along the Mall, a mounted elephant greets visitors in the entry rotunda. The NMNH is home to 185 professional scientists who study the natural world. The museum attracts 7.4 million visitors each year.

The vast Ocean Hall houses a coral-reef aquarium, and models of a 45ft- (14m-) long model of a North Atlantic right whale and a 24ft- (7.3m-) long female giant squid. Other permanent exhibits include the Hall of Geology, Gems, and Minerals, where the famous Hope diamond is displayed. The collection also includes more than 35,000 meteorites, one of the largest collections in the world. The Hall of Human Origins is one of the newest additions to the museum, and has an interactive family tree that visitors can use to trace mankind's development through six million years of evolution.

Next door is the **National Museum of American History** (www.americanhistory.si.edu; late Mar–early Sept daily 10am–7.30pm, mid-Sept to

**111**

The Mid-Atlantic region

**Building** (daily 8.30am–5.30pm), on the south side of the Mall, includes an information center for the entire organization.

One of the biggest draws, the **National Air and Space Museum** (www.nasm.si.edu; late Mar–early Sept daily 10am–7.30pm, mid-Sept–mid-Mar daily 10am–5.30pm; free), faces the National Gallery. Its galleries soar with artifacts from the entire history of flight, from the Wright brothers' first aircraft to the *Apollo 11* command module from the flight that put the first humans on the Moon. There are plenty of kid-friendly interactive exhibits, from flight simulators to wind tunnels.

The White House has been the home of every US president since John Adams in 1797

mid-Mar daily 10am–5.30pm; free), a repository of all things American, from the actual Star-Spangled Banner that inspired the national anthem to Dorothy's ruby slippers from *The Wizard of Oz*. The collections are organized thematically, from technology to the American ideal and entertainment. The basement is home to a cafeteria, as well as a fun exhibit all about American lunch boxes.

If the Statue of Liberty represents the nation to the world, the **Washington Monument** (tel: 202-426-6841; www.nps.gov/wamo; June–early Sept daily 9am–10pm, Sept–May daily 9am–5pm; free) symbolizes the nation to Americans. Construction of the 555ft (169m) white marble obelisk at the western end of the Mall began in 1848 but dragged on for decades. The slight change in color about halfway up reveals where work stopped, first because of funding shortages and then because of the

Civil War. Construction resumed in 1876, and the monument was finally completed in 1885. The pyramidal point at the top is made of aluminum, which, at the time of construction, was a rare metal, even more valuable than silver.

There's an elevator to the top of the monument, from where visitors enjoy a 360° view of the city. Picking out the White House, Capitol Dome, and other landmarks is a good way to get oriented. While entrance to the monument is free, tickets are timed. These often run out early in the day, so plan to stop by the ticket booth before 10am and then return at your alotted time. Large bags are not currently permitted.

Further west along the Mall, on the other side of 17th Street, glistens a long reflecting pool, leading to one of the country's most beloved monuments, the **Lincoln Memorial** (tel: 202-426-6841; www.nps.gov/linc;

daily 24 hours; free). A giant marble sculpture of President Abraham Lincoln, designed by Daniel Chester French, sits in a Grecian temple, its walls inscribed with Lincoln's Gettysburg Address and Second Inaugural Address. On the steps, look for the 'I have a dream' inscription, where Reverend Martin Luther King addressed 200,000 people during the famous 1963 Civil Rights demonstration.

Just north of the Lincoln Memorial is the dark gash of the **Vietnam Veterans Memorial** (tel: 202-426-6841; www.nps.gov/vive; daily 24 hours; free). Designed by Maya Lin, the memorial's shiny black-stone walls reflect back visitors' own images as they peer at the incised names of the servicemen who were killed in action or went missing during the Vietnam War. The two arms of the memorial point to the Washington Monument and the Lincoln Memorial. To find a specific name, visit one of the nearby podiums, where directories provide a comprehensive and searchable list. Visitors can make pencil-and-paper rubbings of the names of their loved ones, or talk to one of the many veterans who tend to congregate around the area. Most veterans are friendly and willing to share their stories.

To the south, around the Tidal Basin pool, stand two more important memorials, to Franklin Delano Roosevelt and Thomas Jefferson. In the spring, when the cherry trees flower, the Tidal Basin pool is a favorite spot to wander and smell the blossoms (see also p.14 and p.123).

### The White House

Just north of the Mall stands the **White House** (tel: 202-456-7041; www.whitehouse.gov), home to every American president since 1797. The White House is now only open to the public on limited tours arranged through congressional representatives or embassies, but anyone is welcome at the **Visitor Center** (daily 7.30am– 4pm) at 15th and E streets, where you can watch an informational film and explore six interpretive exhibits.

The White House is a graceful, Palladian-style building that has been altered and renovated many times over the centuries – including an unwanted 'alteration' when the British

The pretty streets of Georgetown are ideal for cycling

set it on fire in 1814. Luckily, a timely thunderstorm kept the walls from completely collapsing.

If you arrange a tour of the President's home in advance, you'll be able to visit the **East Room**, a gold-and-white reception area where presidents traditionally welcome foreign heads of state (and also sometimes lie in state). Tours also include a stop in the China Room, where porcelain used by former first families is on display, and the kitchen, where all the meals are prepared, whether for the president's family or a formal state dinner.

### Georgetown

With narrow, tree-lined streets and Georgian and Federal buildings, Georgetown feels completely different from the broad avenues of governmental Washington. Already established as a tobacco market while Washington was only in the planning stages, this neighborhood is now not only the city's oldest but also its wealthiest area. Unfortunately, the metro doesn't reach this district, which makes travel for visitors more complicated. Public parking is available, but watch the meter carefully as traffic wardens are ever-vigilant.

M Street and Washington Avenue NW are the main drags, buzzing with boutiques, pubs, and cafés. Since Georgetown University is based here, the atmosphere can become pretty raucous at night. North of M Street lie rows of old brick homes, the gracious bastion of high society.

At the southern edge of the neighborhood streaks a remnant of the **C&O Canal**, once an industrial artery

The Blue Ridge Parkway winds its way through the mountains

and now a route for cyclists, joggers, and canoers.

## Virginia

History is close to the surface in the so-called 'Old Dominion' state. Another of Virginia's nicknames is the 'Mother of Presidents', arising from the fact that no less than eight US presidents were born here. The southeastern coast is a special draw for history buffs, with its restored Colonial Williamsburg settlement and Jamestown, the first pioneer colony on the mainland. The western side of the state rumples up in the beautiful Blue Ridge Mountains, with a network of scenic drives. The oft-repeated slogan, 'Virginia is for lovers', has certainly drawn the crowds, as the state is currently the 10th-most-popular destination out of all 50 states.

## Blue Ridge Mountains

The namesake blue haze seems to hover over these glorious mountain ridges, while sparkling waterfalls trickle down alongside the roads. One of Virginia's most captivating landscapes is best explored by car on winding, slowpoke scenic routes.

One key entry point is **Shenandoah National Park** (tel: 540-999-3500; www.nps.gov/shen; daily 24 hours; charge). Its 105-mile (168km) **Skyline Drive** curves through forested slopes, giving glimpses of the Shenandoah Valley from its overlooks. The **Blue Ridge Parkway** (tel: 828-298-0398; www.blueridgeparkway. org; daily 24 hours; free) picks up where Skyline Drive leaves off, leading south toward North Carolina. The most scenic stretch of road is north of Roanoke, and the quick side trip to Roanoke Mountain has impresive views. Note that these roads can close in bad weather, as the cold climate can damage the road surface. Most closures are well marked.

## Jamestown and Williamsburg

These two communities, connected by the Colonial Parkway, epitomize colonial Virginia. **Jamestown** ❹ was at first an outpost of British settlers

Visitors to Jamestown enjoy dressing up in period garb, such as soldiers or farmers

who landed in 1607, 13 years before the *Mayflower* Pilgrims. Now the **Jamestown Settlement** (tel: 757-253-4838; www.historyisfun.org; mid-June–mid-Aug daily 9am–6pm, late Aug–early June daily 9am–5pm; charge) re-creates the first permanent English community, including replicas of the original palisade fort, the village of Powhatan Indians, and the three ships that brought the pioneers across the Atlantic.

Colonial **Williamsburg** ❺ (tel: 757-229-1000; www.history.org; daily 9am–5pm; charge), just a few miles north, is the country's biggest restoration project, with more than 500 18th-century buildings restored to their former glory. This was Virginia's capital from 1699 to 1780, and is now one of the premier tourist destinations in the region.

# ACCOMMODATIONS

With all of its lobbyist, convention, and congressional business, Washington, DC is chock-full of chain hotels, including international brands such as Sofitel, as well as luxury digs. Philadelphia, true to form, has many scrupulously preserved historic properties, along with polished modern options. Since Philly's downtown parking can be difficult, ask whether the hotel includes a parking lot or whether it can direct you to a nearby garage (which may add quite a bit extra to your costs).

## Philadelphia

**Hotel Palomar**
117 So. 17th Street
*Tel: 215-563-5006*
**www.hotelpalomar-philadelphia.com**
The Palomar matches eco-friendliness with high style. Think portraits of the Founding Fathers in Pop-Art colors, animal-print robes in the guest rooms, and great city views. **$$$**

**Lippincott House**
2023-25 Locust Street
*Tel: 215-523-9251*
**www.lippincotthouse.com**
This gracious Victorian bed and breakfast near Rittenhouse Square offers period details as well as Wi-fi and a media room. **$$–$$$**

**Penn's View Hotel**
14 N. Front Street
*Tel: 215-922-7600*

A room at the Hotel Palomar, Philadelphia

**www.pennsviewhotel.com**
This 19th-century Old Town warehouse has been transformed into a cozy, traditional hotel. **$$**

## Pennsylvania Dutch Country

**Alden House B&B**
62 E. Main Street, Lititz
*Tel: 717-627-3363*
**www.aldenhouse.com**
A restored Victorian building in downtown Lititz offering traditional rooms plus a separate carriage house. **$$**

**Eby Farm B&B**
345 Belmont Road and 459a Queen Road, Gordonville
*Tel: 717-768-3615*
**http://ebyfarm.com**
The Mennonite Eby family runs two visitor properties on their picturesque Pequea dairy farm. **$–$$**

## Washington, DC

**Hay-Adams**
16th and H streets
*Tel: 202-638-6600*
**www.hayadams.com**
If it's good enough for the Obamas, it's good enough for the rest of us. This grand, historic hotel faces the White House and has hosted many a famous face. **$$$$**

**Homewood Suites by Hilton**
1475 Massachusetts Avenue NW
*Tel: 202-265-8000*

http://homewoodsuites1.hilton.com
This chain is good for family stays, as its well-priced suites are equipped with full-sized kitchens and pull-out sofas. **$$**

### Swann House
1808 New Hampshire Avenue, NW
*Tel: 202-265-4414*
**www.swannhouse.com**
Heavy on the romance, this bed and breakfast in Dupont Circle is also a gorgeous 19th-century mansion. **$$$**

## Virginia
### Colonial Houses
Colonial Williamsburg
*Tel: 800-447-8679*
**www.colonialwilliamsburg.com/visit/hotels**
The Colonial Williamsburg Foundation runs several hotels, but these houses actually let you stay in the historic 18th-century core. The accommodations range from tavern rooms to entire homes, and have both reproduction period furnishings and modern amenities. **$$–$$$**

Williamsburg Inn in Colonial Williamsburg

### Miss Molly
Chincoteague
*Tel: 800-881-5620*
**www.missmollys-inn.com**
If you've read the well-known novel, *Misty of Chincoteague*, you'll want to stay at Miss Molly's, the 1886 Victorian inn that claims that author Marguerite Henry was inspired by her stay in this humble dwelling. **$–$$$**

# RESTAURANTS

Over the past decade, Philadelphia's restaurant scene has exploded, pollinating the city with several terrific restaurant rows. South Philly is still the place for homey Italian cooking; Walnut Street is known for glam dining rooms. Bring-your-own-bottle establishments are quite common. In Washington, DC, the finer dining rooms fill up fast when Congress is in session. While the city doesn't have many restaurant districts, or pockets of ethnic eateries, you can find nearly any cuisine with a bit of sleuthing.

| Restaurants price categories |
| --- |
| Prices are for a main course meal for one, excluding alcoholic drinks: <br> **$** = less than $15 <br> **$$** = $15–$25 <br> **$$$** = $25–$50 <br> **$$$$** = more than $50 |

## Philadelphia
### Paradiso
1627 E. Passyunk Avenue
*Tel: 215-271-2066*
**www.paradisophilly.com**
South Philly-raised chef Lynne Marie Rinaldi pushes her neighborhood's Italian cooking in a more modern direction. **$$$**

### Pat's King of Steaks
1237 E. Passyunk Avenue
*Tel: 215-468-1546*
**http://patskingofsteaks.com**
Several cheesesteak vendors elbow each other for top billing, but Pat's, founded in 1930, claims to have invented the sandwich and still hand-chops its meat. **$**

### Geno's Steaks
1219 S. Ninth Street
*Tel: 215-389-0659*
**www.genosteaks.com**
If you prefer your cheesesteak meat sliced rather than chopped, then the neon-glow of Geno's will become familiar. The great rivalry between Pat's and Geno's dates back to 1966, when Geno's first opened. **$**

### 10 Arts by Eric Ripert
10 S. Broad Street
*Tel: 215-523-8273*
**www.10arts.com**
The namesake celebrity chef describes this bistro as 'Ripert in jeans'. His masterful technique gets turned to homier dishes, such as brook trout with hazelnut brown butter, and buttermilk fried chicken. **$$$$**

## Pennsylvania Dutch Country
### Miller's Smorgasbord
2811 Route 30
*Tel: 1-800-669-3568*
**www.millerssmorgasbord.com**
A heaping smorgasbord is the quintessential Lancaster County experience. Rich, gut-busting home cooking, with dishes such as chicken-pot pie and cheesecake, makes a return trip to the buffet a guarantee. **$$**

## Washington, DC
### 2 Amys Pizza
3715 Macomb Street NW
*Tel: 202-885-5700*
**www.2amyspizza.com**
Blistered, simple, and decadent Neapolitan-style pizza. The thin crusts are famous throughout the capital city, and guests can wait up to an hour for a table. **$–$$**

### Ben's Chili Bowl
1213 U Street, NW
*Tel: 202-667-0909*
**www.benschilibowl.com**
Loved by celebrities, locals, and presidents, this 1950s joint built its reputation on the chili half-smoke, a pork-and-beef sausage on a bun, topped with mustard, onions, and spicy chili sauce. **$**

The bright lights of Geno's Steaks, on the corner of Philadelphia's South Ninth Street

### Oyamel
401 7th Street NW
*Tel: 202-628-1005*
**www.oyamel.com**
DC has fallen hard for the sophisticated Mexican cooking of José Andrés. This branch of his restaurant family serves small plates, ceviche, and tacos. **$$**

### Palena
3529 Connecticut Avenue NW
*Tel: 202-537-9250*
**www.palenarestaurant.com**
Modern, seasonal American cuisine draws Washingtonians here for special occasions, burger cravings, and everything in between. The formal dining room offers a fixed-price menu, but the adjoining Palena Café ($$–$$$) has more casual fare. At the time of writing, a market was due to open. **$$$$**

## Virginia
### Old Chickahominy House
1211 Jamestown Road, Williamsburg
*Tel: 757-229-4689*
**www.oldchickahominy.com**
'Welcome, wayfarer' proclaims this reconstructed 18th-century house. The Old Chickahominy dishes up traditional cooking, from biscuits layered with Virginia ham to tender chicken and dumplings. Save room for the home-made pie for dessert. **$$**

# NIGHTLIFE AND ENTERTAINMENT

After-dark options in Philadelphia and Washington, DC are getting better by the year. Philadelphia's Avenue of the Arts (www.avenueofthearts.org), along South Broad Street, is anchored by the Kimmel Center. Bars and other nightspots, meanwhile, crowd into the Old City neighborhood. Washington's performing-arts scene is even stronger, concentrated in the Kennedy Center. The city may be full of suited politicos, but even the conservative types like to cut loose. Georgetown, Adams-Morgan, and Dupont Circle have the busiest nightlife.

## Bars and pubs

**Black Squirrel**
2427 18th Street NW, Washington, DC
*Tel: 202-232-1011*
www.blacksquirreldc.com
A welcoming gastropub in a busy nightlife neighborhood, with over a dozen hard-to-find beers on tap.

**Dock Street Brewing Company**
701 S. 50th Street, Philadelphia
*Tel: 215-726-2337*
www.dockstreetbeer.com
Philly's first microbrewery, founded in 1985, consistently wins raves for its beers. Classic ambers, IPAs, and cream ales sometimes make room for experimental brews such as 'prisoner of hell,' spiked with chilis.

**Southwark**
701 W. 4th Street, Philadelphia
*Tel: 215-238-1888*
www.southwarkrestaurant.com

This bar-restaurant became a serious drinker's destination for its classic cocktails, such as Sazeracs (rye whiskey and bitters).

**Wisdom**
1432 Pennsylvania Avenue SE,
Washington, DC
*Tel: 202-543-2323*
www.dcwisdom.com
Get wise to expertly mixed cocktails, following the menu's detailed codes, and an impressive line-up of absinthes.

**World Cafe Live**
3025 Walnut Street, University City,
Philadelphia
*Tel: 215-222-1400*
www.worldcafelive.com.
Not just a bar, not just a concert venue, World Cafe Live mixes the best of both worlds, with two theaters and two restaurants. Everything is engineered to make the live-music experience the

Philly's Old Town at night is bustling with activity

best, including the acoustics and sight-lines. You can eat, drink, and enjoy the performances.

## Classical music and opera

### The Kennedy Center
2700 F Street, NW, Washington, DC
*Tel: 202-467-4600*
**www.kennedy-center.org**
The Kennedy Center hosts the National Symphony Orchestra, the KC Jazz Club, the Washington National Opera, ballet companies, educational programs, and much more.

### Kimmel Center for the Performing Arts
260 S. Broad Street, Philadelphia
*Tel: 215-893-1999*
**www.kimmelcenter.org**
Philadelphia's orchestra, chamber orchestra, opera, and ballet company all perform at this prestigious venue.

## Live music

### 9:30 Club
815 V Street NW, Washington, DC
*Tel: 202-265-0930*
**www.930.com**
A famed venue for rock acts old (The Cars) and brand-spanking new (Raphael Saadiq).

### Black Cat
1811 14th Street NW, Washington, DC
*Tel: 202-667-7960*
**www.blackcatdc.com**
All-ages shows for up-and-coming musicians, dance music, pool tables, vegetarian grub – it's all here.

### Painted Bride Art Center
230 Vine Street, Philadelphia
*Tel: 215-925-9914*
**www.paintedbride.org**
A vibrant catch-all of music, dance, and other artistic endeavors, the Bride is a good place for world music and jazz.

### Trocadero Theatre
1003 Arch Street, Philadelphia
*Tel: 215-922-6888*

Philadelphia's Merriam Theater

**www.thetroc.com**
Once a vaudeville house, the Troc is now an indie-rock-band showcase.

## Theater

### Merriam Theater
250 S. Broad Street, Philadelphia
*Tel: 215-893-1999*
**www.merriam-theater.com**
Broadway musicals and blockbuster plays rotate through this historic venue, which is affiliated with the Kimmel Center.

### Shakespeare Theatre Company
Lansburgh Theatre, 450 7th Street NW; Sidney Harman Hall, 610 F Street NW, Washington, DC
*Tel: 202-547-1122*
**www.shakespearetheatre.org**
One of the world's best Shakespeare companies inhabits two spaces, and mounts innovative productions in both.

### Woolly Mammoth
641 D Street NW, Downtown NW, Washington, DC
*Tel: 202-393-3939*
**www.woollymammoth.net**
For something a little different, the Wooly Mammoth frequently presents avant-garde productions that you won't find on Broadway. With an intimate, 256-seat theater, it is often compared to Chicago's Steppenwolf Theater, as a place where future stars are born.

# SPORTS AND ACTIVITIES

As relatively flat, riverside cities, Philadelphia and Washington, DC have good waterfront zones for cycling and jogging. Philly also benefits from Fairmount, the world's largest landscaped urban park.

## Baseball

**Philadelphia Phillies**
1 Citizens Bank Way, Philadelphia
*Tel: 215-463-1000*
http://philadelphia.phillies.mlb.com
Whenever the Phillies hit a home run in their Citizens Bank Park, a giant Liberty Bell rings.

**Washington Nationals**
1500 S Capitol Street, SE, Washington, DC
*Tel: 202-675-6287*
http://washington.nationals.mlb.com
Relatively new team with a stadium, Nationals Park, opened in 2008.

## Boating

**Boathouse at Fletcher's Cove**
4940 Canal Road, NW, Washington, DC
*Tel: 202-244-0461*
www.fletcherscove.com
Right on the C&O Canal, Fletcher's rents kayaks, canoes, and rowboats; they also have tackle for Potomac River fishing.

## Bicycling

**Fairmount Park**
1 Boathouse Row, Philadelphia
*Tel: 215-568-6002*
www.fairmountpark.org
This vast urban park along the Schuykill River has its own bike-rental stand and a network of cycling-friendly roads. Popular for jogging, too.

**C&O Canal Towpath**
Georgetown
*Tel: 301-739-4200*
www.nps.gov/choh
The 13-mile (21km) section of the Chesapeake and Ohio Canal runs from Georgetown to Great Falls and is the most popular section with bikers, although you can definitely cycle the complete 200-mile (322km) trail all the way to Cumberland, Maryland if you feel adventurous. Watch out for the mules that still pull passenger barges along the canal.

## Football

**Philadelphia Eagles**
1020 Pattison Avenue, Philadelphia
*Tel: 215-463-5500*
www.philadelphiaeagles.com
Philly is a diehard football town, complete with tail-gating at Lincoln Financial Field before fans root for the Birds.

## Soccer

**Washington United**
2400 E. Capitol Street, SE, Washington, DC
*Tel: 202-547-3134*
www.dcunited.com
Robert F Kennedy stadium is home to some of the best soccer in the United States. The DC United are followed passionately by local fans, and excitement peaks when international matches are scheduled.

Boating on the Potomac River in Washington, DC

# TOURS

With centuries of history embedded in their streets, Philadelphia and Washington, DC are especially good cities for narrated tours. Occasionally, tour guides veer from accuracy into anecdote, but hey, it's a good story.

## Boat tour

**Capitol River Cruises**
31st Street and K Street, NW, Washington, DC
*Tel: 301-460-7447*
**www.capitolrivercruises.com**
Board a historic riverboat for a narrated ride on the Potomac River, with views of the major memorials, the Kennedy Center, and famous landmarks.

## Bus tours

**Philadelphia Trolley Works and 76 Carriage Company**
*Tel: 215-389-8687*
**www.phillytour.com**
This company offers narrated rides through the historic downtown in trolley-style or double-decker buses. For a more picturesque option, book a horse-drawn carriage.

**Tourmobile Sightseeing**
Washington, DC
*Tel: 202-554-5100*
**www.tourmobile.com**
A hop-on/hop-off open-air tram makes the rounds of major Washington sights, including Arlington National Cemetery.

## Food tours

**Lancaster County Tours**
*Tel: 1-888-999-4479*
**www.lancastercountytours.com**
Nibble and sip your way through Pennsylvania Dutch Country. Special theme trips rotate through most months, with beer-and-pretzel tours in June and August.

**Taste of Philly Food Tour**
*Tel: 215-545-8007*
**www.tasteofphillyfoodtour.com**

Horse-drawn carriage in Philadelphia

Get an insider's look, and many tasty samples, at the Reading Terminal Market.

## Walking tours

**Spies of Washington Tour**
*Tel: 703-569-1875*
**www.spiesofwashingtontour.com**
Four routes touch on espionage in various DC neighbourhoods, from Georgetown to Capitol Hill. Several other theme walks cover local history, the African-American community, and more.

**Tour de Force**
Washington, DC
*Tel: 703-525-2948*
**www.atourdeforce.com**
Individually tailored, one-on-one tours run by a native historian. Itineraries focus on monuments, diplomatic Washington, or whatever your special interest might be. Driving tours are also available.

**Constitutional Walking Tour**
Philadelphia
*Tel: 215-525-1776*
**www.theconstitutional.com**
This 75-minute walking tour hits the highlights of Philly's historic center, including the facts and folklore of the city. The walks visit more than 20 sites, and there are multiple options, including self-guided routes and the popular Spirit of '76 ghost tours.

# FESTIVALS AND EVENTS

Independence Day is an especially big deal in this region; the historic cities of Philadelphia and Washington, DC both stage huge celebrations. Washington also hosts some of the country's biggest parades on federal holidays such as Veteran's Day and Memorial Day.

## January
**Philadelphia Mummers Parade**
January 1
*Tel: 215-336-3050 (Mummers Museum)*
http://phillymummers.com
An ancient tradition, local clubs of musicians and clowns parade in elaborate costumes to welcome in the new year.

## March
**Lancaster County Mud Sales**
*Tel: 717-299-8901*
http://www.padutchcountry.com/members/mud_sales.asp
Throughout the year, but mainly in early spring thaws, local fire companies hold sales and auctions to raise funds. This tradition is a great source for Amish arts and crafts.

## Late March–early April
**National Cherry Blossom Festival**
Washington, DC
*Tel: 877-442-5666*
www.nationalcherryblossomfestival.org
The Tidal Basin is planted with Japanese cherry trees, a gift from Tokyo. When these bloom in early spring, the city turns out to stroll under the frothy pink blossoms. In 2012, the festival celebrates its centennial.

The National Cherry Blossom Festival is held at Washington, DC's Tidal Basin every spring

## June–early July
**Smithsonian Folklife Festival**
Washington, DC
*Tel: 202-633-6440*
www.festival.si.edu
The Smithsonian puts on the capital's premier cultural event in late spring/early summer. The city hums with concerts, storytelling, crafts and cooking demonstrations, and ecology exhibits.

## July
**National Independence Day**
Washington, DC
www.july4thparade.com
The 4th of July is especially important in the nation's capital. Parades and spectacular concerts run throughout the day; at night, cannons boom and fireworks burst over the Capitol building.

**Welcome America!**
Philadelphia
*Tel: 215-683-2200*
www.welcomeamerica.com
Philly celebrates the 4th of July with a week-long party – live music, a hoagie sandwich day, outdoor movies, a food fair, all capped with a parade, concerts, and fireworks on the 4th itself.

## September
**Philadelphia Live Arts Festival & Philly Fringe**
*Tel: 215-413-9006*
www.livearts-fringe.org
For two weeks each year, performers converge on Philadelphia from all over the world for a theatre, dance, music, and spoken word blowout.

# The South

The South conjures up images of antebellum plantation homes, alligators, Mardi Gras, and sun-drenched beaches. While Charleston, the Everglades, New Orleans, and Miami certainly fulfill these expectations, there's also plenty more on offer. Visitors can experience fantasy at the Walt Disney World Resort, technology at the Kennedy Space Center, and history in St Augustine.

## Atlanta, Miami, and New Orleans

**Population:** Atlanta 541,000; Miami 433,000; New Orleans 355,000

**Local dialing code:** Atlanta 404; Miami 305; New Orleans 504

**Local tourist offices:** Atlanta: 65 Upper Alabama Street; tel: 404-577-2148; www.atlantacitytourist.com. Miami: 701 Brickell Avenue; tel: 305-539-3000; www.miamiandbeaches.com. New Orleans: 2020 St Charles Avenue; tel: 504-566-5011; www.neworleanscvb.com

**Main police stations:** Atlanta: 226 Peachtree Street; tel: 404-853-3434. Miami: 400 NW 2nd Avenue; tel: 305-603-6640. New Orleans: 715 South Broad Street; tel: 504-821-2222

**Main post offices:** Atlanta: 400 Pryor Street. Miami: 3191 Grand Avenue. New Orleans: 701 Loyola Avenue

**Hospitals:** Atlanta: Emory University Hospital, 1364 Clifton Road; tel: 404-712-2000. Miami: Jackson Memorial Hospital, 1611 Northwest 12th Avenue; tel: 305-585-1111. New Orleans: Ochsner Hospital, 1315 Jefferson Highway; tel: 504-842-3900

**Local newspapers/listings magazines:** Major papers include the *Atlanta-Journal Constitution,* the *Miami Herald,* and the *Times-Picayune* of New Orleans

**Time zones:** EST for North Carolina, South Carolina, Georgia, and Florida; CDT for Louisiana

Think of the South and a swarm of contrasting images comes to mind. Bible Belt churches and rowdy spring-break beaches. Tennessee country music and Atlanta hip-hop. Memorials to the Civil War and the civil-rights marches. Bayous, bluegrass, and the Great Smoky Mountains. The southern states have a complex history and culture, and a distinct sense of pride.

Florida, the southernmost state in the continental US, brings with it another state of mind. In 1962, John Steinbeck declared that 'the very name Florida carried the message of warmth and ease and comfort. It was irresistible.' The Sunshine State still tempts vacationers and annual snowbirds with that promise of warmth and relaxation. The quirky towns in he tropical Keys, the trendy clubs of Miami, and the vast theme parks of Orlando are just three of the perennial draws. It's easy to get around Florida – and anywhere in the South – so long as you're willing to spend time behind the wheel.

# North Carolina

North Carolina's eyes are fixed firmly on the prizes of the future. Textiles, tobacco, and tourism have been the state's main industries until recently. Now banking and high-tech companies have come to the fore. But tourism is a mainstay as visitors seek out the wild coast or cruise the scenic byways, especially the famed Blue Ridge Parkway in the Great Smoky Mountains.

## The Piedmont area

Sweeping through the middle of North Carolina, the Piedmont area encompasses the original Tobacco Road, where tobacco has rolled from the red-clay fields to dealers ever since colonial times. Piedmont is the most

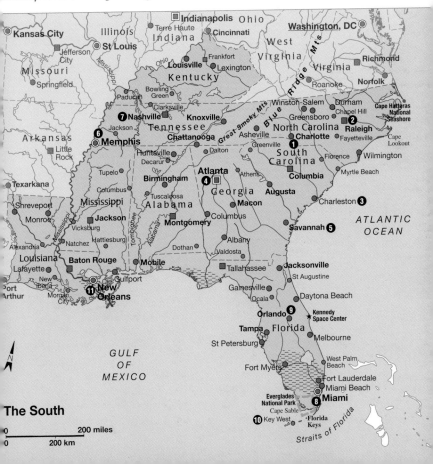

The South

The skyline of Charlotte, one of the world's busiest banking centers

urban and industrial zone, although small-town pleasures can nevertheless be found.

**Charlotte ❶** bloomed from a regional sales center to one of the world's busiest banking centers in just a few decades. The city's skyscrapers add a visual crown to the 'Queen City.' **The Square**, where Trade and Tyron streets cross, marks the heart of Center City, with plenty of hotels, restaurants, arts centers, and nightspots radiating from this crossroads.

The developing arts scene helps to offset the city's business-centric character. The latest major addition is the **Bechtler Museum of Modern Art** (tel: 704-353-9200; www.bechtler.org; Mon and Wed–Sat 10am–5pm, Sun noon–5pm; charge), which opened in 2010. The Mario Botta-designed building glows in terracotta tile, with a dramatically cantilevered upper floor. The collections focus on mid-century European works.

Further north is the **Triangle Area**, pegged between three major cities: the state capital, Raleigh, to the east; Durham to the north; and Chapel Hill to the west. Each has a university and sprawling research center.

**Raleigh ❷** is a mix of 19th-century government buildings, museums, and lush parks. Highlights include the **North Carolina Museum of Art** (tel: 919-839-6262; www.ncartmuseum.org; Tue–Thur and Sat–Sun 10am–5pm, Fri 10am–9pm; free). Its new wing, opened in 2010, houses a permanent collection that ranges from Rodin sculptures to African masks.

**Chapel Hill** remains the quintessential college town. It grew up around the University of North Carolina, founded in 1795, with a colonial campus and Franklin Street as its main drag. UNC locks horns with nearby Duke University in one of college basketball's fiercest rivalries.

Duke is based in **Durham**, otherwise known as Bull City. The nickname comes from the post-Civil War Bull Durham Tobacco Company. Union soldiers occupying the town tasted the local bright-leaf tobacco and couldn't get enough. This sudden, huge demand established tobacco as North Carolina's main crop.

The city you see today has tobacco warehouses and factories that are either still in use or have been 'repurposed' for new urban plans. **Duke University** (tel: 919-684-8111; www.duke.edu; general campus daily 24 hours; free), with its neo-Gothic stone buildings and famed medical research center, was built with tobacco fortunes. There's a fine chapel on campus, as well as the **Nasher Museum of Art** (tel: 919-684-5135; www.nasher.duke.edu; Tue–Wed and Fri–Sat 10am–5pm, Thur 10am–9pm, Sun noon–5pm;

charge). Rotating exhibits range from Greco-Roman sculpture to paintings by Picasso.

### The Outer Banks

North Carolina's coast is fringed with barrier islands and peninsulas. These Outer Banks are shifting sands, shaped by currents and hurricanes. During the area's seafaring heyday, hundreds of ships were wrecked here, and the area was known as the Graveyard of the Atlantic. That era's lighthouses still flash to guide navigators.

Many miles of the golden dunes are protected as the **Cape Hatteras National Seashore** (tel: 252-473-2111; www.nps.gov/caha; daily 24 hours; free). You can climb up the barber-pole-striped **Cape Hatteras Lighthouse** (tel: 252-473-2111; www.nps.gov/caha; mid-Apr–Memorial Day and Labor Day–mid-Oct daily 9am–4.30pm, Memorial Day–Labor Day daily 9am–5.30pm; charge), if you can manage the hundreds of stairs.

The distinctive Cape Hatteras Lighthouse

### Great Smoky Mountains

The far west side of North Carolina rumples up into the Appalachian Mountains, including the **Blue Ridge and Great Smoky ranges**, so called for the blue-gray haze that often veils the mountains beneath.

The famed **Blue Ridge Parkway** (tel: 828-298-0398; www.blueridge parkway.org; daily 24 hours except for weather closures; free) weaves through these mountains, tempting millions of drivers a year on to its scenic curves. It's a route that feels timeless – no billboards, no gas stations alongside, just milepost markers, overlooks, and every so often, a glimpse of a waterfall.

## South Carolina

The Palmetto State is making a characteristically leisurely transition from Old to New South. South Carolina was the first state to secede from the Union in December 1860, heralding the slide into Civil War. Despite the devastating conflict that ensued, relics of the antebellum age are everywhere.

### Charleston

Pirate attacks, wars, and tornadoes have struck **Charleston ❸** for centuries, but Charlestonians have always picked up the pieces. The town evokes the courtly atmosphere that people associate with the Old South. The downtown **Historic District** is packed with antebellum buildings. A stroll down **Meeting Street** takes you past the Citadel military college, neoclassical homes, and the **City Market** (tel: 843-853-8000; http://the charlestoncitymarket.com; Mar–Oct daily 8.30am–5.30pm, Nov–Feb daily 8.30am–5pm; free), still bustling with food and craft vendors.

From **the Battery**, a lovely palmetto-shaded park at the end of

The Blue Ridge Parkway offers a scenic route through the mountains

Atlanta's Georgia Aquarium claims to be the largest of its type in the world

of many of them. One of the finest is the **Aiken-Rhett House** (Mon–Sat 10am–5pm, Sun 2pm–5pm; charge) at 48 Elizabeth Street. It has been preserved just as it was in the 1850s. You can mooch around the kitchens, slave quarters, library, and parlors.

## Georgia

The classic song *Georgia on My Mind*, sung by native son Ray Charles, is as poignant and elegant as the state itself. From the moss-draped streets of 'Slow-vannah' to the atmospheric towns along the Antebellum Trail, there's a leisurely pace to life.

### Atlanta

The symbol of **Atlanta** ❹, the phenix, salutes the city's ability to rise from the ashes. After being destroyed in the Civil War, it became the federal head-quarters for Reconstruction. Millions of gallons of Coca-Cola, one CNN media juggernaut, and one Olympics later, Atlanta is a dynamic urban center for the region.

Downtown Atlanta is becoming more fun to visit, as restaurants, bars, and shops join the skyscrapers and government buildings. The symbolic heart is **Five Points**, the intersection of Marietta, Peachtree, and Decatur streets. Moving northwest, Marietta Street borders Centennial Olympic Park. On the far side of this green space fizzes the **New World of Coca-Cola** (tel: 404-676-5151; www.worldofcoca-cola.com; Sun–Thur 10am–5.30pm, Fri–Sat 9am–6.30pm;

the peninsula, you can look across the harbor to **Fort Sumter** (tel: 843-883-3123; www.nps.gov/fosu; mid-Mar–Labor Day daily 10am–5.30pm, Labor Day–Nov daily 10am–4pm, Dec–Feb daily 11.30am–4pm; fee for the ferry). Visitors take one of the boats run by Spirit Tours (tel: 843-722-2628; www.spiritlinecruises.com) to visit the flashpoint of the Civil War, where the South Carolina's militia captured a Union military base.

There are several historic or rep-lica homes and plantations in these parts. The **Historic Charleston Foundation** (tel: 843-723-1623; www.historiccharleston.org) over-sees the maintenance and running

charge). Invented by an Atlanta pharmacist in 1886, the secret recipe became the world's most popular soda. The museum brims with memorabilia; at the café you can try a wide variety of concoctions.

Just next door is another liquid attraction: the **Georgia Aquarium** (tel: 404-581-4000; www.georgiaaquarium.org; Memorial Day–Labor Day Sun–Thur 9am–6pm, Fri 9am–10pm, Sat 9am–9pm, Labor Day–Memorial Day Sun–Fri 10am–5pm, Sat 9am–6pm; charge). Claiming to be the world's largest, the aquarium features creatures from all the oceans of the globe, from local species such as horseshoe crabs and right whales to exotic creatures such as beluga whales, African electric fish, and the giant octopus. Visitors can even sign up to swim with whale sharks.

The towering **Millennium Gate**, raised in 2008, now welcomes people to the Midtown neighborhood, the cultural core. The biggest draw is the **High Museum of Art** (tel: 404-733-4444; www.high.org; Tue–Wed and Fri–Sat 10am–5pm, Thur 10am–8pm, Sun noon–5pm; charge). Swooping white ramps curl around a central atrium.

East of Downtown stretches Auburn Avenue and one of the most moving places in the South: the **Martin Luther King National Historic Site** (tel: 404-331-5190; www.nps.gov/malu; Memorial Day–Labor Day daily 9am–6pm, Labor Day–Memorial Day daily 9am–5pm; free). At 407 Auburn Street stands Ebenezer Baptist Church, where Dr King was baptized, where he preached nonviolence, and where he was eulogized. In 2011, a restoration was unveiled that brought the sanctuary in line with how it looked in the 1960s. At 501 Auburn Avenue is the home where King was born. Nearby, the crypt of King and his wife, Coretta Scott King, anchors the **King Center** (tel: 404-526-8900; www.thekingcenter.org; Memorial Day–Labor Day daily 9am–6pm, Labor Day–Memorial Day daily 9am–5pm; free).

A few miles north of Downtown beckons **Buckhead**, the city's poshest neighborhood. At the **Atlanta History Center** (tel: 404-814-4000; www.atlantahistorycenter.

---

### Regional barbecue

While the true origins of the barbecue are lost in the smoke of time, several Southern states consider it their regional specialty. Locals swear allegiance to their regional barbecue styles and hotly debate which is best.

- **Eastern North Carolina:** a whole hog seasoned with a peppery vinegar sauce, cooked over hot coals, served finely chopped or shredded into 'pulled pork.'
- **Western North Carolina:** wood-smoked pork shoulder sliced or cut into chunks, with a vinegar 'dip' sauce sweetened by a drop of ketchup.
- **South Carolina:** wood-smoked whole hog, sometimes with a mustard-based sauce.
- **Tennessee:** pork ribs dry-rubbed with spices, then smoked. Wet ribs are served with a tomato-based sauce.

The Mercer-Williams House Museum in Savannah

com; Mon–Sat 10am–5.30pm, Sun noon–5.30pm; charge), get a crash course in local history and culture. The main campus includes historic homes, displays of photos and artifacts, even a farm.

## Savannah

To go with the flow in **Savannah** ❺, you'll need to switch gears to a low speed. When you're strolling through the city's grassy squares, hearing the clip-clop sound of the horse-drawn carriages, and enjoying the evening air, you simply can't hurry.

There aren't many must-see individual attractions here. Instead, visitors relish the beauty of the city streets, lined with moss-covered oaks and timbered houses with intricate ironwork details. The **Historic District** is one of the country's biggest, covering a 2½-mile (4km) radius. **Bull Street** runs the length

of the district, north to south, connecting the squares like beads on a chain. Beside the Savannah River, down flights of steps, old warehouses and shipping offices have turned into restaurants and boutiques, flanking the cobblestoned **Riverwalk**.

**Telfair Museums** (tel: 912-790-8800; http://telfair.org), the oldest public-museum organization in the South, links together several old and new cultural landmarks. The **Jepson Center for the Arts** (Sun–Mon noon–5pm, Tue–Wed and Fri–Sat 10am–5pm, Thur 10am–8pm; charge) showcases modern art and photography, with particular attention given to major American figures such as Chuck Close and Richard Avedon. Meanwhile, the **Owens-Thomas House** (Tue–Sat 10am–5pm, Mon noon–5pm, Tue 1pm–5pm; charge) is a pristine example of Georgian Regency

# ★ RHYTHM AND MELODY

From blues to country, jazz to rock, many of the rhythms that have swept the world originated in the United States. No matter which town you visit, you're likely to hear about a legend who was born there, played there, or got into a colorful scrape while passing through.

Many different musical styles can be found in the United States, but those in the South typically reflect the immigrant histories of the region's people. European folk music – from polkas to Irish jigs – introduced certain beats, while religious spirituals and the cadences of slaves' working music formed the base for much modern popular music. Even today, you should come to the South to hear the best of what's new in the studio, whether it's the latest in jazz, country, blues, or pop.

## Jazz

This musical genre may be America's greatest contribution to the music world, and it all started in New Orleans around the turn of the 20th century. Marching-band and African rhythms, Creole and parlor-piano sounds combined into a new kind of syncopation. Pianist Jelly Roll Morton and trumpeter Louis Armstrong were the sound of the times.

## Blues

New Orleans also had a major role in blues history. In 1903, W.C. Handy

The blues is characterized by a set of specific chord progressions

adopted a slide-guitar style and set down the early notations for the blues. Robert Johnson came along a decade later, and in his short life established himself as the king of the Mississippi Delta bluesmen; his spare songs continue to influence guitarists today. In the 1930s, local bluesmen started migrating north, seeding Tennessee and Chicago with their style.

## Rock

'The blues had a baby and they named it rock'n'roll,' sang bluesman Muddy Waters. While it's impossible to pin down the very first rock song, many of the most influential early rockers went through Sam Phillips's Sun Studio in Memphis. In the young Elvis Presley, Phillips found the key: a white kid who could sing rhythm and blues with an injection of country-style energy. Phillips also started the career of Johnny Cash, who brought a new intensity to country music.

## Country

Tennessee cottoned on to country music right from the start. In the late 1920s, Tennessee singers popularized traditional songs by combingin them with melodic rhythm guitar and vocal harmonies. An example of this can be found in the famous Carter Family. The Grand Ole Opry radio show, based in Nashville, sent those unique sound over the airwaves. It also made a star of Hank Williams, who used his tough upbringing and stormy love life as fodder for heart-wrenching lyrics.

The banjo and fiddle are popular instruments in country and folk music

Instrumentation can vary, but most jazz music involves a horn secton

architecture, with even its slaves' quarters remaining intact.

## Tennessee

If you've ever sipped a Jack Daniel's whiskey or hummed along to Elvis, Johnny Cash, or Dolly Parton, you've already gotten a little taste of Tennessee. Bordered by the Mississippi in the west, and dominated by the Appalachians in the east, it has two main cities, Memphis and Nashville. Memphis dubs itself the home of rock'n'roll, while Nashville is the king of country music.

### Memphis

Starting on the east bank of the Mississippi River, **Memphis** ❻ sprawls eastward. Downtown, the oldest section by the river, thrums to the beat of **Beale Street** (www.beale street.com). This thoroughfare has been a major music scene for many generations. WC Handy put down the first recorded blues song here. BB King, John Lee Hooker, Muddy Waters, Memphis Minnie – they've all played Beale. Bars, clubs, and restaurants still line the road.

Near the eastern end of Beale Street stands **Sun Studio** (tel: 1-800-441-6249; www.sunstudio.com; daily 10am–6pm; charge), a veritable shrine for music fans. Here, producer Sam Phillips recorded Johnny Cash, Roy Orbison, and many more legends. As the story goes, the young Elvis first came here to record a song for his mother's birthday present. It's not just a museum, though; top acts, including U2, still come here to record their latest albums.

A free hourly shuttle from Sun Studio runs over to the second-mostvisited home in America (after the White House): **Graceland** (tel: 901-332-3322 ; www.elvis.com; June–Aug Mon–Sat 9am–5pm, Sun 9am–4pm, Sept–Oct and Mar–May

Memphis' Beale Street is the birthplace of the Blues

Nashville's Country Music Hall of Fame

Mon–Sat 9am–5pm, Sun 10am–4pm, Nov–Feb daily 10am–4pm; charge). Elvis bought the 23-room home for himself and his parents in 1957; they're all now buried in the garden out back. The home is an over-the-top 1970s time capsule. Don't miss the car collection, which includes the King's classic pink Cadillac.

Music fans shouldn't miss the **Stax Museum of American Soul Music** (tel: 901-946-2535; www.stax museum.com; Apr–Oct Mon–Sat 10am–5pm, Sun 1–5pm, Nov–Mar Tue–Sat 10am–5pm, Sun 1–5pm; charge). The exhibits evoke the glory days of 'Soulsville USA' in the 1960s and 70s, when Isaac Hayes, Otis Redding, Aretha Franklin, and many other great singers laid down their now-famous tracks.

Another must-see is the somber but enlightening **National Civil Rights Museum** (tel: 901-521-9699; www.civilrightsmuseum. org; June–Aug Mon and Wed–Sat 9am–6pm, Sun 1pm–6pm, Sept–May Mon and Wed–Sat 9am–5pm, Sun

1–5pm; charge), built around the courtyard of the Lorraine Motel, where Dr Martin Luther King, Jr. was shot. Exhibits span the entire history of America's civil rights struggles, from the early slave rebellions to the political sit-ins and great rallies and marches of the 1960s.

### Nashville

Tennessee's capital is often referred to as the 'Athens of the South' for its concentration of top schools, and 'Music City, USA' for its rich musical culture. Walking down **Broadway**, the main drag of downtown **Nashville** ❼, you'll likely see a hopeful musician carrying a guitar.

If you're on Broadway in broad daylight, stop by **Hatch Show Print** (tel: 615-256-2805), the oldest letterpress printer in the US. They were the brilliant minds behind those boldly graphic music posters; you can buy reproductions here. Down the block is **Gruhn Guitars** (tel: 615-256-2033; www.gruhn.com), renowned for vintage and handmade instruments. Overseeing it all is **Ryman Auditorium**, the 'mother church for country music' (see Nightlife listings, p. 153).

Plunge into the big-hearted and big-haired world of country music at the **Country Music Hall of Fame** (tel: 615-416-2001; http://country-musichalloffame.org; Mar–Dec daily 9am–5pm, Jan–Feb Mon and Wed–Sun daily 9am–5pm; charge). With films, photos, guitars, and sparkling and spangled costumes, it evokes

An aerial view of Miami Beach shows the sand and Intracoastal Waterway

the outsize personalities and talents of famous country, blues, folk, and rockabilly artists.

## Florida

The Sunshine State is the most popular destination for travelers from both within the US and beyond. Discover the breadth of variety available in its dazzling cities and stunning beaches.

## Miami

**Miami ❽** is the big dot on the Florida map. Brash and beautiful, it's the state's most complex city, a crossroads of Latin American, Caribbean, and Yankee cultures. It is large in size as well as personality; Greater Miami, made up of over 30 municipalities, reaches over 500 sq miles (1,300 sq km). Full of energy yet also casual, it quickly latches on to new hotels and nightclubs, even in the face of grittier urban concerns.

### Central Miami

Downtown Miami is a busy area of shops, restaurants, and nightspots, based around Flagler Street and Biscayne Boulevard. Right by the water twinkles **Bayside Marketplace** (tel: 305-577-3344; www.baysidemarketplace.com; Mon–Thur 10am–10pm, Fri–Sat 10am–11pm, Sun 11am–9pm; free), an outdoor mall with cafés, boutiques, and music at night.

Modern-art fans seek out the **Miami Art Museum** (tel: 305-375-3000; www.miamiartmuseum.org; Tue–Fri 10am–5pm, Sat–Sun noon–5pm; charge), which focuses on modern and contemporary works. At the time of writing, the MAM planned to move to a new bayfront building designed by Herzog & de Meuron in 2013.

It's livelier south of downtown, in the Cuban neighborhood of **Little Havana**, centered on a 30-block section around 'Calle Ocho' (Southwest

**Airport:** Miami International Airport (MIA); tel: 305-876-7000; www.miami-airport.com; 6 miles (10 km) west of downtown. Airport Flyer express bus: at least 20 minutes to downtown; the fare is $2.35. SuperShuttle shared-ride vans: about 30 minutes to downtown, about $16. Taxi: at least 20 minutes to downtown; about $22

**Trains:** Miami's two commuter-train lines are operated by the Metro-Dade Transit Agency, tel: 305-891-3131; **www.miamidade.gov/transit**. Metrorail, Miami-Dade County's 22-mile elevated rapid-transit system, operates daily services from about 5am to midnight. A single ride is $2; a 1-day pass costs $5.00; and a 7-day

pass costs $26. To ride Metrorail, you must purchase a rechargeable EASY Card or EASY Ticket, available at vending machines in rail stations. The free and frequent Metromover trains run on a 4½-mile (7km) elevated line, with stops at many of the city's major attractions. The Metromover system operates daily from 5am to midnight

**Taxis:** Taxis in Miami can be expensive. Meters start at about $2.50 for the first quarter-mile and cost around $2.40 for each additional mile. Taxis aren't readily available on the street, so it's best to call ahead. Major cab companies include Yellow Cab (tel: 305-444-4444) and Miami Dade Taxi (tel: 305-551-1111)

The South

8th Street) running east from 37th Avenue. Cubans make up a significant proportion of Greater Miami's population and here is where they sip strong Cuban coffee and hang out in **Domino Park** to play chess.

Further south still are two of Miami's cheeriest neighborhoods, **Coral Gables** and **Coconut Grove**. Coral Gables has a Mediterranean look, and is renowned for its 1920s landmark, the Biltmore Hotel. Coconut Grove was once an artist's hang-out, but is now gentrifying into a shopping and nightlife destination.

Nearby is Miami's grandest home, hidden behind rock walls: the **Vizcaya Museum and Gardens** (tel: 305-250-9133; www.vizcayamuseum.com; Mon and Wed–Sun 9.30am–4.30pm;

The blue lights of the Colony Hotel in the Art Deco District on Miami's Ocean Drive

charge). In the early 1900s, industrialist James Deering turned this into a kaleidoscope of European design, from the Renaissance-style exterior to the rococo music room.

## Miami Beach

Connected to mainland Miami by causeways across Biscayne Bay, this barrier island is where Miami gets its reputation as a leisure destination. The miles of beaches, fronted by hotels and condos, have gone through a succession of ups and downs – from elite playground in the 1940s and-50s to urban decay in the 1970s to the New Riviera of the 1990s.

Miami Beach's latest rebirth began at the bottom of the island, in the **South Beach** neighborhood. In the 1970s, preservationists started beating the drums for the Art Deco buildings that crowded this area, remnants of an earlier heyday. In 1979, an official historic district was founded and things started to turn around.

Now, the **Art Deco District** is almost as much of an attraction as

The ultimate fairy-tale castle at Walt Disney World Resort's Magic Kingdom

If you can tear yourself away from the turquoise-and-flamingo paint jobs and tropical drinks, drop into the **Bass Museum of Art** (tel: 305-673-7530; www.bassmuseum.org; Wed–Sun noon–5pm; charge). Its collection of European art, which includes Flemish altarpieces and Renaissance paintings, contrasts with visiting shows of modern art.

## Orlando

It's hard to believe that this area of central Florida was once quiet farmland. Starting with Walt Disney's visionary theme park, **Orlando ❾** is now dominated by fantasy resorts, thrill rides, water parks, and every other mind-bending amusement you can imagine.

the beaches. More than 500 stylish buildings are sheltered between Ocean Drive, Alton Road, and 6th to 23rd streets. Get your bearings at the **Art Deco Welcome Center** (tel: 305-672-2014; www.mdpl.org; Mon–Sat 10am–4pm; free), which has maps, pamphlets, and tours on offer. Many of the most whimsical buildings are on Collins and Washington avenues, and on Ocean Drive.

**Ocean Drive** is the most see-and-be-seen strip, with its grand Art Deco hotels, people-watching cafés, and bronzed bodies on display. Across the street is **Lummus Park**, a busy promenade. The **public beaches** get less crowded as you head north.

### Walt Disney World Resort

If you dream of **Walt Disney World Resort** (tel: 407-939-6244; http://disneyworld.disney.go.com; charge) as a giant amusement park, think again. Disney World is a city in its own right, with four elaborate theme parks, two water parks, two nighttime entertainment districts, golf courses, hotels, over 100 restaurants, its own police force, and an average daily population of well over 100,000 people. This all-encompassing approach provides an all-in-one holiday, luring travelers back year after year. The 'happiest place on earth' is also the most visited vacation destination on the planet. And it's no wonder why.

The **Magic Kingdom** (Mon–Wed 9am–1pm, Thur 9am–midnight, Fri 8am–midnight, Sat–Sun 9am–11pm, with exceptions) is Disney World's oldest park and the one closest to Walt Disney's original vision of a 'timeless land of enchantment'. It's perfectly calibrated to younger children, as it captivates with elaborate design and whimsical 'imagineering' rather than fast-paced special effects.

Disney World's second park, **Epcot** (Mon–Thur and Sat–Sun 9am–9pm, Fri 8am–9pm, with exceptions) is modeled on a Worlds' Fair. A huge silver golf-ball structure anchors **Future World**, the first of its two main areas. The second zone is the **World Showcase**, a whistle-stop tour through 11 pavilions themed for different countries, from Mexico to China.

The third park, **Disney's Hollywood Studios** (Mon 9am–7pm, Tue–Thur 9am–10pm, Fri–Sun 9am–midnight, with exceptions), combines some of Disney's best rides with a behind-the-scenes look at movie-making. A 12-story sorcerer's hat towers above the park, ushering visitors into attractions based on popular live-action movies and TV shows.

Even after all the animated creatures and imaginary critters, you can still be wowed by real wildlife at **Disney's Animal Kingdom** (daily 9am–8pm, with exceptions). With over 500 acres and more than 1,700 animals, this vast park highlights the wonders of the natural world. You're welcomed to the park by the **Tree of Life**, an enormous, intricately carved faux-banyan tree.

Staying at one of the Disney Resort hotels that pop up between these various parks and attractions accords visitors some special privileges in addition to the convenient location. Best of all is that hotel guests are eligible for the Extra Magic Hours – an extra hour, before or after the standard public entry times, or access to the parks.

'Toy Story Mania!' at Disney's Hollywood Studios

series. Many feel that Universal has exceeded the high expectations of Potter fans.

The Wizarding World is technically part of the **Islands of Adventure** park (daily 9am–9pm, with exceptions), which clusters several theme zones around a central lagoon. These experiences are shaped around cartoon and children's book characters, and include the Marvel Super Hero Island and Seuss Landing.

The **Universal Studios** park (daily 9am–9pm, with exceptions) turns back to its roots in film and TV production. Attractions include the Shrek 4-D show, and more thrills-and-chills options, such as the Revenge

**141**

## Universal Studios

A few miles away from the House of Mouse is its great rival, **Universal Studios** (tel: 407-363-8000; www.universalorlando.com; charge). These three theme parks and water park were inspired by the art and production of Hollywood movies. Like Disney, Universal is laid out in a pattern of 'neighborhoods', each with special rides, facilities, and shows. It caters more to teens and 20-somethings, with more adrenaline than adorableness.

**The Wizarding World of Harry Potter** (Sun–Thur 9am–8pm, Fri–Sat 9am–9pm, with exceptions) made its debut in 2010, casting its spell over fans of the magical book

### Theme-park sanity strategies

Theme parks can be overwhelming. Avoiding a family meltdown involves some careful planning and adopting realistic expectations.

- Consider your kids' tolerances of dark rides, thrills, delayed mealtimes, and waiting in lines.
- Take breaks. There's always another ride around the next corner, but if you're exhausted you won't enjoy it so much. Swim in your hotel's pool, hang out in a park, or otherwise hit the pause button.
- Investigate special passes to help reduce waits for rides. Disney has its free FASTPASS service, for instance, which holds your place. Universal charges for an Express Plus pass, which lets you jump a line.

The South

of the Mummy coaster, which zooms through fireballs.

**Universal CityWalk** comes into its own at night, when restaurants, bars, and live music venues get into gear. A big movie theater means that even locals flock here for entertainment.

### SeaWorld and Discovery Cove

Dubbed an 'adventure park,' **SeaWorld** (tel: 1-888-800-5477; www. seaworld.com/orlando; mid-June– mid-Aug daily 9am–10pm, late Aug–early June, daily 9am–7pm, with exceptions; charge) is smaller in scale but makes a big impact. The marine park is full of surprises and educational – sliding enlightening info about marine biology and conservation into the splashy shows.

If all these tanks of fish are making you want to dive in yourself, head next door to the sister park, **Discovery Cove** (tel: 1-877-557-7404; www.discoverycove.com; daily 9am–5.30pm; charge). This all-inclusive resort revolves around animal encounters, so that you can take a dip with tropical fish and other creatures.

## Elsewhere in South Florida

Outside Miami, southern Florida offers two radically different experiences. West and south of Miami stretches the 'river of grass,' the Everglades National Park. This vast, endangered region of inundated prairie and mangrove swamps is an extraordinarily important wildlife sanctuary. Down at the state's southern tip is a sprinkling of islands known as the Florida Keys. At the very end is the 'Conch

An air-boat ride through the Everglades

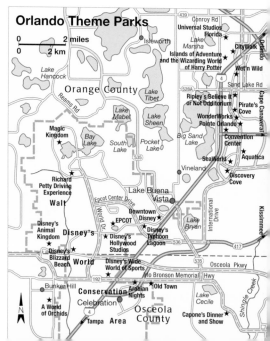

The idyllic Smathers Beach on the south side of Key West

Republic' of Key West, a good-time community of off-kilter characters.

### The Everglades

**Everglades National Park** (tel: 305-242-7700; www.nps.gov/ever; daily 24 hours; charge) is a breathtaking water world. This subtropical wilderness is the only one of its kind in the US, an 'edge place' where northern and southern flora and fauna meet. The two main entry points are at the north and south ends. To the north, closer to Miami, you'll find the **Shark Valley entrance** (daily 8.30am–6pm), located off Highway 41 (which is otherwise known as the Tamiami Trail). From here, a 15-mile (24km) paved road loops around an observation tower, making an outstanding cycling route.

The southern entrance has the main information area, the **Ernest Coe Visitor Center** (mid-Dec–mid-Apr daily 8am–5pm, mid-Apr–mid-Dec daily 9am–5pm). A few miles further in you'll find two of the most popular hiking trails. The short, paved Gumbo Limbo Trail runs through a jungly hardwood hammock forest. Along the Anhinga Trail, you'll get up close to herons, turtles, and egrets in a sawgrass marsh.

### Key West

A ragged skein of islands drifts out from Florida's southern shore, connected tenuously by the **Overseas Highway**, a 43-bridge exercise in forced linear travel. At the very end of the line, you tumble into Key West ❿. The inimitable character of this spot comes from its history as a haven for wanderers and free-thinkers. The easiest way to explore is on a bike.

**Old Town**, the 19th-century core of the city, faces into the Gulf of Mexico. As sunset approaches, tourists flock to **Mallory Square** to watch the sky turn pink and orange, applauding as the sun dips below the horizon. A block off the square, you can ogle glinting treasure at the **Mel Fisher Maritime Heritage Museum** (tel: 305-294-2633; www.melfisher.org; Mon–Fri 8.30am–5pm, Sat–Sun 9.30–5pm; charge).

**Duval Street** is Margaritaville headquarters – a strip of bars, souvenir shops, and squalling karaoke. Hard-

# 🚗 A DRIVE ALONG THE SPACE COAST

Summer 2011 saw the end of an era: the final space-shuttle launched from Kennedy Space Center. Hop in a car to explore the area around Cape Canaveral and you can still experience the starry thrill of space travel.

The swath of coastline between Titusville, Cocoa Beach, and Melbourne has been linked to America's space program since the early 1960s. Many visitors make a day trip to the Kennedy Space Center, which is under-an-hour's drive from Orlando, but the beaches make the area worth an overnight stay.

The space shuttle *Endeavour's* final launch was on May 16, 2011

Drive from Orlando on State Road 528 to the exit for State Road 407. This leads to State Road 405, which has signs directing you to Merritt Island and the **Kennedy Space Center** (tel: 321-867-5000; www.nasa.gov/centers/kennedy/home; daily 9am–6pm; charge). Although at first glance it appears small compared with the theme parks, even with a full day you'll be hard pressed to fit everything in. In addition to the visitor complex, there's the Space Center bus tour that takes you to three outlying sites over roughly three hours.

Even though the shuttle program has ended and the five space shuttles have retired, there is still going to be a lot of action from Cape Canaveral. NASA will continue to launch satellites, probes, and drones into space from these launch pads, so don't fear that you've missed your opportunity for the countdown. Future space travel will probably take the form of private enterprise, but you can be sure that Florida's Space

### Tips

- Total distance:  180 miles (290km)
- Time:  One to two days
- While on the Kennedy Space Center's bus tour, keep an eye out for alligators. It's a self-guided tour, but most visitors take about three hours to see all the sights.
- If you'd like to have dinner in the area, drive south on US 1 to Cocoa Beach, a classic beach town.

Coast will be front and center of whatever tomorrow holds.

At the visitor complex, you will have a couple of opportunities to meet NASA astronauts. At **Astronaut Encounter**, astronauts give presentations on space travel and answer questions. With an advance reservation, you could also have **Lunch with an Astronaut** at the complex's restaurant. The **Astronaut Hall of Fame**, meanwhile, collects memorabilia from all sorts of space explorers. There is also a G-force Trainer, a dizzying centrifuge.

Just outside stand several rockets that took astronauts to outer space. You can even get into an Apollo or Mercury capsule to get an idea of what the tight quarters felt like. For a more realistic experience, but without the G-force, head over to the **Shuttle Launch Experience** for a simulated but relatively tame ride. Two IMAX theaters show 3D films narrated by Hollywood stars and featuring real footage from space flights.

The bus tour takes you to an observation platform and to the **Apollo/Saturn V Center**, which is dedicated to the first flight that took man to the Moon. Visitors can gawk at the enormous *Saturn V* rocket.

Coming back down to earth, save some time to enjoy the **Merritt Island National Wildlife Refuge** (tel: 321-861-0669; www.fws.gov/merrittisland; daily sunrise–sunset; free). There is no public access directly from the space center, so drive back across State Road 405, then north on US 1 through Titusville. The island is a habitat for

An anhinga on Merritt Island

hundreds of wildlife species, many of which are threatened or endangered. You might see alligators, ospreys, and river otters, especially on the **Black Point Wildlife Drive**. A highlight is the **Manatee Observation Deck**, beside the Haulover Canal on State Road 3. The rare, placid manatees are most frequently spotted in spring and fall.

drinking author Ernest Hemingway used to stroll over here when he was living in the town in the 1940s and 50s. His house has been preserved as the **Hemingway Home and Museum** (tel: 305-294-1136; www. hemingwayhome.com; daily 9am–5pm; charge). You can see his study and be inspected by the many six-toed cats who now live here.

## New Orleans

Most of the world's musicians wish they were from, or could live in, **New Orleans ⓫**. Stroll along almost any street and you'll hear a seductive beat or saxophone wail. This is the birth-place of jazz. Today, festivals spring up nearly every week, with Mardi Gras lording it as the most spectacular of all.

The city has shown incred-ible resilience since the Hurricane Katrina disaster in 2005. Businesses have steadily reopened and the major festivals continue every year. Thankfully, the city's oldest and most tourist-centric neighborhoods, including the French Quarter, weren't flooded. Most importantly, the catastrophe didn't quash the city's spirit, nor its enthusiasm for food, drink, and a good time.

### *The French Quarter*

Known locally as the Vieux Carré (Old Square), this historic quarter lies between Canal and North Rampart streets, Esplanade Avenue, and the Mississippi River. The city took root here in the 18th century, but many of the buildings date to the 19th century. Their intricate wrought-iron galleries are a 'N'awlins' signature – some of the finest examples line Royal Street.

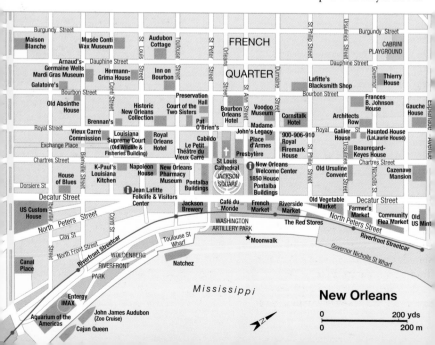

New Orleans' historic French Quarter, or Vieux Carré (Old Square), by night

visitors a taste of Mardi Gras all year round. Exhibits on the city's most famous parade explain the development and meaning behind many of the 'Fat Tuesday' traditions, from the elaborate costumes to bead-tossing.

Behind Jackson Square, right on the river, lies the **French Market** (tel: 504-522-2621; www.frenchmarket.org; roughly 9am–6pm; free), a mother lode of boutiques, produce stands, and restaurants, including the legendary Café du Monde.

At night, **Bourbon Street** becomes the hub of the Vieux Carré, with its bars, music clubs, and restaurants. It's rowdy, but some of the city's renowned restaurants can be found here. The bars and clubs on the section of the street northeast of the intersection with St Ann Street is also the center of New Orleans' thriving gay community.

Start exploring at **Jackson Square**, which is anchored by St Louis Cathedral and bounded by Chartres, Decatur, St Peter and St Ann streets. Street musicians, artists, and vendors keep this car-free area lively.

On the square you will find two important sites of the Louisiana State Museum, which oversees several historic structures in this neighborhood. The **Cabildo** (tel: 504-568-6968; http://lsm.crt.state.la.us/cabildo/cabildo.htm; Tue–Sun 10am–4.30pm; charge) houses exhibits on Louisiana's past, from the period of its early settlement through Reconstruction. Fittingly, the building itself is historically significant, as the Louisiana Purchase Transfer was signed here in 1803.

The other major landmark on the square is the **Presbytère**, which gives

### Mardi Gras in New Orleans

Mardi Gras celebrations in New Orleans date back to 1856, when a secret society launched a night-time parade, dubbing itself the Mystick Krewe of Comus.

Mardi Gras has official colors: purple symbolizing justice, gold for power, and green for faith. Krewes parade in dazzling costumes, with marching bands and huge floats. Krewe members toss 'throws' or trinkets to the thousands of fans. Doubloon throws are favorite souvenirs – aluminum coins emblazoned with the year and the krewe's coat of arms.

# ACCOMMODATIONS

When booking a room in the South, pay careful attention to the calendar. Florida, for instance, has a specific high season from November to March, but hurricanes threaten for the rest of the year. In New Orleans, demand for rooms during major festivals such as Mardi Gras means that you

need to book at least six months ahead. As a convention city, Atlanta has lots of hotel chains but can still fill up early. Note that there is nowhere to stay in the Everglades, since the severe hurricanes of 2005 wiped out the only lodge.

## Accommodations price categories

Prices are for two people in a double room, including goods and sales tax:

**$** = less than $75
**$$** = $75–$150
**$$$** = $150–$225
**$$$$** = $225–$350
**$$$$$** = more than $350

**Arrowhead Inn**
106 Mason Road, Durham
*Tel: 919-477-8430*
**www.arrowheadinn.com**
An 18th-century home turned bed and breakfast, complete with rockers on the front porch and acres of garden. **$$–$$$**

**Sanderling Inn**
1461 Duck Road, Outer Banks
*Tel: 1-800-701-4111*
**www.sanderlinginn.com**
One of the state's most celebrated resorts. Guests hardly need to leave the property, owing to the tennis club, spa, and a restaurant in a historic lifesaving station. **$$–$$$$**

## South Carolina

**Planters Inn**
112 N. Market Street, Charleston
*Tel: 843-722-2345*
**www.plantersinn.com**
Next to the City Market in the Historic District, this gracious 1844 bed and breakfast has reproduction period decor, including romantic four-poster beds. **$$$**

## Georgia

**Ballastone Inn**
14 E. Oglethorpe Avenue, Savannah
*Tel: 912-236-1484*
**www.ballastone.com**
This Historic District home has gone through good times (Girl Scouts offices) and bad (a bordello in the 1920s). Now it's acclaimed

as a particularly romantic getaway, with 19th-century period details. **$$–$$$**

**Mansion on Peachtree**
3376 Peachtree Road NE, Atlanta
*Tel: 404-995-7500*
**www.rwmansiononpeachtree.com**
The Mansion goes for streamlined luxury, with taupe-and-dove-gray rooms, deep soaking tubs, and a luxurious spa. **$$$**

## Tennessee

**Elvis Presley's Heartbreak Hotel**
3677 Elvis Presley Boulevard, Memphis
*Tel: 901-332-1000*
**www.elvis.com/graceland/heartbreak_hotel**
If you're making an Elvis pilgrimage, this is as close as you'll get to sleeping in Graceland. Guest rooms have pictures of the King; a few more-expensive themed suites have Elvis-worthy extravagant decor. **$$**

**Hutton Hotel**
1808 West End Avenue, Nashville
*Tel: 615-340-9333*
**www.huttonhotel.com**
An eco-friendly, chic spot that's halfway between downtown and the Vanderbilt University campus. **$$–$$$**

## Miami

**Gansevoort South**
2377 Collins Avenue, Miami Beach
*Tel: 1-866-932-6694*
**www.gansevoortmiamibeach.com**

North Carolina's Sanderling Inn is located on the beach next to a bird sanctuary

A large, flashy new kid, trying hard to be cool. There's a rooftop pool and bar with great views, plus a ground-floor infinity pool. Grey-and-white rooms get pops of strong color from chairs, headboards, etc. **$$$–$$$$**

### Pelican
326 Ocean Drive, Miami Beach
*Tel: 305-673-3373*
**www.pelicanhotel.com**
Here you will find wackily decorated themed rooms such as 'Me Tarzan, You Vain' and 'Executive Zebra'. **$$–$$$**

### The Tides
1220 Ocean Drive, Miami Beach
*Tel: 305-604-5070*
**www.tidessouthbeach.com**
The Art Deco 'diva of Ocean Drive' is steeped in luxury; every guest gets a personal assistant. Suites have beachy color schemes with snazzy accessories, such as zebra rugs. All have ocean views. **$$$$**

## Orlando

### Disney's Fort Wilderness Lodge & Campground
Near the Magic Kingdom
*Tel: 707-939-7429*
**http://disneyworld.disney.go.com**
Inspired by western national-park lodges, this pine lodge has a pioneer theme and

a spouting Old Faithful-style geyser near the swimming pool. Close by are hundreds of campsite pitches (the cheapest lodging options in the House of Mouse), as well as some cabins. **$–$$$$**

### Disney's Grand Floridian Resort & Spa
Near the Magic Kingdom
*Tel: 707-939-7429*
**http://disneyworld.disney.go.com**
Situated right beside the monorail line for easy park access, this hotel channels Old Florida's graciousness. It feels a little more grown-up than some of the other resort lodgings. **$$$$**

### Loews Pacific Royal Resort
Universal Studios
*Tel: 1-888-273-1311*
**www.universalorlando.com**
With a huge lagoon-style pool, a small sand beach, and Saturday 'luaus' (Hawaiian feasts), this Pacific Rim-themed hotel is particularly relaxing. **$$$**

### Nickelodeon Suites Hotel
14500 Continental Gateway
*Tel: 407-387-5437*
**www.nickhotel.com**
This is an extremely kid-centric kind of place, with characters including SpongeBob and Dora the Explorer waving everywhere.

Suites have separate, brightly decorated bunk-bed rooms for children. **$$–$$$**

## Elsewhere in Southern Florida
**Ivey House**
107 Camellia Street, Everglades City
*Tel: 239-695-3299*
**www.iveyhouse.com**
The owners of this eco-friendly lodge offer several excursions into the Everglades. Besides comfortable rooms in the main inn, there are inexpensive accommodations in a lodge with shared bathrooms. **$–$$**

**The Marquesa Hotel**
600 Fleming Street, Key West
*Tel: 305-292-1919*
**www.marquesa.com**
This complex feels as intimate as a bed and breakfast, but offers the amenities of a larger property. Two buildings are restored Victorian, while two are modern (and have larger bathrooms in their guest rooms). There are also two pools, and a notably good restaurant. **$$–$$$**

**Simonton Court**
320 Simonton Street, Key West
*Tel: 1-800-944-2687*
**www.simontoncourt.com**

There's a little of everything at Simonton Court, from inn rooms in what was once a cigar factory, to cottages and town houses. Several of the breezy-chic rooms have private decks. **$$$–$$$$**

## New Orleans
**Magnolia Mansion**
2127 Prytania Street
*Tel: 504-412-9500*
**www.magnoliamansion.com**
This bed and breakfast is steeped in both atmosphere and attitude. A verandah-wrapped mansion with elaborately decorated rooms, such as the blood-red Vampire Lover's Lair or the purple, gold, and green Mardi Gras Getaway. Guests must be 21 or older. **$$**

**Windsor Court**
300 Gravier Street
*Tel: 504-523-6000*
**www.windsorcourthotel.com**
Situated just a couple of blocks from the French Quarter, this genteel inn is known for its warm yet polished service, large guest rooms, and impressive art collection. At the time of writing, the Windsor Court had embarked on a renovation to improve on perfection. **$$$**

# RESTAURANTS

Rich cultural influences as well as the down-home linchpins of barbecue and seafood are responsible for continually converting new fans to Southern cooking. New Orleans is the most food-obsessed city, where debating the merits of restaurants is practically a sport. Miami's Cuban community offers a chance to taste some of the most authentic Cuban food in the US.

### Restaurant price categories
Prices are for a main course meal for one, excluding alcoholic drinks:

**$** = less than $15
**$$** = $15–$25
**$$$** = $25–$50
**$$$$** = more than $50

## North Carolina
**Lantern**
423 West Franklin Street, Chapel Hill
*Tel: 919-969-8846*
**www.lanternrestaurant.com**

This place doesn't just offer your standard Southern fare. Local provisions make their way into Asian-influenced dishes, such as five-spice pork belly or a seafood hotpot with wild shrimp. **$$$**

## South Carolina

**Anson**
12 Anson Street, Charleston
*Tel: 843-577-0551*
www.ansonrestaurant.com
A long-standing favorite for precisely executed Low Country food: shrimp and grits,
she-crab soup, and fried oysters. **$$$**

## Georgia

**Atlanta Fish Market**
265 Pharr Road NE, Atlanta
*Tel: 404-262-3165*
www.buckheadrestaurants.com/
atlanta-fish-market
A towering copper fish sculpture guards the
door here. Match a fish (salmon, catfish, etc)
with its preparation (blackened, sautéed, with
hush puppies on the side). **$$–$$$**

**Elizabeth on 37th**
105 E. 37th Street, Savannah
*Tel: 912-236-5547*
www.elizabethon37th.net
A more formal take on modern Southern
cooking in a former mansion. The seafood
stands out, as do local desserts such as
sherry-doused cream cake. **$$$$**

**The Varsity**
61 North Avenue, Atlanta
*Tel: 404-881-1706*
www.thevarsity.com
'What'll ya have?' chirp the staffers at this
classic drive-in. Chili dogs, onion rings, and
sweet tea are the way to go. **$**

## Tennessee

**The Capitol Grille**
231 6th Avenue N., Nashville
*Tel: 1-888-888-9414*
www.capitolgrillenashville.com/food.aspx
The dining room of the historic Hermitage
Hotel packs in Nashville's finest. Southern
classics are prepared with produce from a
dedicated farm. **$$$–$$$$**

**Prince's Hot Chicken Shack**
123 Ewing Dr., Nashville
*Tel: 615-226-9442*

Sloppy Joe's bar in Key West

Hot chicken is a Music City specialty: juicy
fried chicken with an eye-wateringly spicy
crust. Prince's invented the style and takes
no prisoners. **$**

**The Rendezvous**
Rendezvous Alley, behind 52 S. 2nd Street,
Memphis
*Tel: 901-523-2746*
www.hogsfly.com
The scent of smoke will lead you to this
cellar institution, where it's all about the
spice-rubbed ribs. **$$**

## Miami

**Michael's Genuine Food & Drink**
130 NE 40th Street
*Tel: 305-573-5550*
www.michaelsgenuine.com/miami
Rigorously fresh and locally sourced
American meals. Simple but never boring
dishes such as wood-oven roasted local
snapper dusted with fennel pollen. **$$–$$$**

**Sugarcane Raw Bar and Grill**
3250 NE 1st Avenue
*Tel: 786-369-0353*
www.sugarcanerawbargrill.com
Angle for a seat at this popular mash-up,
where tapas, sushi, and Japanese-style
grilled snacks happily co-exist. There's an
interesting blend of high- and low-brow in
dishes such as duck confit and waffles.
**$$–$$$**

### Versailles
3555 SW 8th Street
*Tel: 305-444-0240*
Everyone comes by for *ropa vieja* (shredded beef) or Cuban sandwiches. **$–$$**

## Orlando
### California Grill
Disney's Contemporary Resort
*Tel: 407-939-3463*
http://disneyworld.disney.go.com/dining
This restaurant serves decent California-inflected cooking, though the real attraction is the view from the windows. **$$$–$$$$**

### Emeril's Tchoup Chop
Loews Pacific Royal Resort
*Tel: 407-503-2467*
www.universalorlando.com
A fun, loose interpretation of South Seas cuisine. Dishes include seared yellowfin tuna with Thai rice and wasabi butter. **$$$**

### Whispering Canyon Café
Disney's Wilderness Lodge
*Tel: 407-939-3463*
http://disneyworld.disney.go.com/dining
Family-style servings of rib-sticking classics, from pancakes to burgers, in an Old West setting. **$$**

## Elsewhere in Southern Florida
### Blue Heaven
729 Thomas Street, Key West
*Tel: 305-296-8666*
www.blueheavenkw.com
A fun, scruffy, hippie shack where cats roam around diners lining up for jerk chicken and vegetarian gumbo. **$$–$$$**

### Pit Bar-B-Q
16400 SW 8th Street
*Tel. 305-226-2272*
www.thepitbarbq.com
This roadside stop dishes up tender, oak-smoked ribs, or fried yucca, and 'gator nuggets if you dare. **$$**

All the trimmings at Disney's Old West-style Whispering Canyon Café

### Seven Fish
632 Olivia Street, Key West
*Tel: 305-296-2777*
www.7fish.com
Polished simplicity makes this a local favorite. One of the best dishes is the most basic – point to 'fresh fish.' Don't miss the Key lime cheesecake, either. **$$$**

## New Orleans
### Café du Monde
800 Decatur Street
*Tel: 504-525-4544*
www.cafedumonde.com
For sugar-dusted beignets, chicory coffee, people-watching, and pure NOLA atmosphere, this historic 1875 café cannot be beaten. **$**

### Commander's Palace
1403 Washington Avenue
*Tel: 504-899-8221*
www.commanderspalace.com
Renovated after Katrina, the Palace is a local institution, revered for its refined Creole cuisine. The menu looks both back and forwards with dishes including turtle soup, a daily gumbo, and oysters poached with bacon and absinthe. **$$$–$$$$**

**Elizabeth's**
601 Galler Street
*Tel: 504-944-9272*
**www.elizabeths-restaurant.com**

Diners flock to this cozy neighborhood spot for its down-home cooking: oyster po'boys, fried green tomatoes with local shrimp, and 'pork candy' bacon. **$$**

# NIGHTLIFE AND ENTERTAINMENT

No trip to the South is complete without a night spent listening to live music at a local dive. This region is the home of blues, jazz, country, and rock – not to mention their many variations. Wander into almost any bar in Nashville, Memphis, or New Orleans, and the house band will be outstanding. Miami is one of the few major Southern cities that is more partial to DJs and velvet ropes than live bands.

## Bars

**Club One**
1 Jefferson Street, Savannah
*Tel: 912-232-0200*
**www.clubone-online.com**
Drag legend Lady Chablis rules the roost at this bar, cabaret, and club.

**Manuel's Tavern**
602 N. Highland Avenue, Atlanta
*Tel: 404-525-3447*
**www.manuelstavern.com**
The very model of a neighborhood bar, where politics and sports are hashed out with gusto.

**Mova Lounge**
1625 Michigan Avenue, Miami Beach
*Tel: 305-534-8181*
**www.movalounge.com**
Playful gay and lesbian bar with a roster of theme evenings.

**Pat O'Brien's**
718 St Peter Street, New Orleans
*Tel: 504-525-4823*
**www.patobriens.com**
Where the Hurricane cocktail was invented and is still poured nightly.

**Satisfaction**
905 W. Main Street, Brightleaf Square, Durham
*Tel: 919-682-7397*
**www.satisfactionrestaurant.com**

Fueled by its heated sporting rivalries, Bull City has a busy sports-bar scene. Satisfaction rakes in fans with its better-than-average pub grub and dozens of TVs.

**Sloppy Joe's**
201 Duval Street, Key West
*Tel: 305-294-5717*
**www.sloppyjoes.com**
This Conch Republic institution was one of Hemingway's haunts. Everyone sloshes through at least once.

## Dance clubs

**Bongo's Cuban Café**
601 Biscayne Boulevard
*Tel: 786-777-2100*
**www.bongoscubancafe.com**
Backed by singer Gloria Estefan, at night this venue transforms from a restaurant into a big salsa club.

**Mynt**
1921 Collins Avenue, Miami Beach
*Tel: 305-532-0727*
**www.myntlounge.com**
A vast space for posing, preening, and occasionally dancing, with a tight door policy.

## Live music

**B.B. King's Blues Club**
143 Beale Street, Memphis
*Tel: 901-524-5464*
**www.bbkingclubs.com**

The club's 'King of the Blues' plays here occasionally, but even without his royal presence, the house band and touring musicians are outstanding. Upstairs is a cozy bar named for King's hometown, Itta Bena.

### Grand Ole Opry
2804 Opryland Drive, Nashville
*Tel: 615-871-6779*
**www.opry.com**
America's longest-running radio show still broadcasts from Music City. After leaving Ryman *(see below)*, it moved to a purpose-built Grand Ole Opry House and churns out several shows a week. Audiences might catch modern stars such as Carrie Underwood or the unstoppable old-time hillbilly Little Jimmy Dickens.

### Maple Leaf Bar
8316 Oak Street, New Orleans
*Tel: 504-866-9359*
**http://mapleleafbar.com**
Jammed with regulars and burning up with hot jazz and sweaty dancers. Don't miss the ReBirth Brass Band.

### Preservation Hall
726 St Peter Street, New Orleans
*Tel: 504-522-2841*
Absolutely no frills (including no seats, no air-conditioning) but filled with soul-stirring traditional jazz.

### Ryman Auditorium
116 5th Avenue N., Nashville
*Tel: 615-889-3060*
**www.ryman.com**
Originally built for religious purposes, Ryman has been the ultimate house of country-music worship for nearly a century. From 1943 to 1974, the Grand Ole Opry show was broadcast from here, cementing its reputation. It still rocks, with performers from Alison Krauss to Taylor Swift.

### The Station Inn
402 12th Avenue S., Nashville
Tel: 615-255-3307
**www.stationinn.com**

B.B. King's Blues Club

Don't let the unprepossessing looks deceive you: this is a legendary bluegrass venue. Favorite regulars include the Time Jumpers and the hilarious Doyle & Debbie Show, a send-up of country music.

### Wild Bill's
1580 Vollintine Avenue, Memphis
*Tel: 901-726-5473*
A true urban juke joint, with beer by the quart and blistering music, especially when the Soul Survivors take the stage.

## Performing arts
### Adrienne Arsht Center for the Performing Arts
1300 Biscayne Boulevard, Miami
*Tel: 305-949-6722*
**www.arshtcenter.org**
The dramatic spaceship-style architecture of this arts campus is enough of a draw on its own. It is, however, home to the excellent Miami City Ballet, the Florida Grand Opera, the New World Symphony, and also plays host to touring Broadway shows.

### Fox Theatre
660 Peachtree Street NE, Atlanta
*Tel: 404-881-2100*
**www.foxtheatre.org**
Once a 1920s Egyptian-themed movie palace, the Fox now hosts the Atlanta Opera, the Atlanta Ballet, musical and theater performances that roll through town, and even a rock show or two.

# SPORTS AND ACTIVITIES

Although extreme heat and humidity in summer mean that you have to pace yourself, there are still plenty of activities on offer.

## Baseball

**Atlanta Braves**
755 Hank Aaron Drive, Atlanta
*Tel: 404-522-7630*
http://atlanta.braves.mlb.com
Originally built for the Olympics, Turner Field is now the home stadium of the Braves.

## Basketball

**Miami Heat**
American Airlines Arena, 601 Biscayne Boulevard
*Tel: 786-777-1000*
www.nba.com/heat
Star player Lebron James brought new attention to this team.

## Boating

**Everglades Adventures**
Everglades City
*Tel: 239-695-3299*
www.evergladesadventures.com
Paddling a kayak or canoe among the mangroves gives visitors a whole new perspective on the Everglades. Naturalist guides point out rare birds and draw your attention to alligators along the way.

## Car racing

**Atlanta Motor Speedway**
1500 Tara Place, off Highway 19, Hampton
*Tel: 770-946-4211*
www.atlantamotorspeedway.com
Besides annual NASCAR races, the track burns with Friday-night drag racing and 'Thursday Thunder' face-offs in summer.

**Charlotte Motor Speedway**
5555 Concord Parkway. South, Concord
*Tel: 704-455-3200*
www.charlottemotorspeedway.com
What's the South without NASCAR? Races here are some of the best in North Carolina; there's a dirt track, too. Don't forget a fried-bologna sandwich.

## Fishing

Fishing off Key West is famously diverse; you can go after tuna, tarpon, grouper, or wahoo. 'Charter Boat Row', on North Roosevelt Avenue, lines up dozens of charter boats for serious and less-than-serious excursions.

**New Horizons**
Key West
*Tel: 305-294-4929*
www.fishbruce.com
An open boat, light tackle, and some of the most knowledgeable folks in town.

## Golf

**Doral Golf Resort and Spa**
4400 NW 87th Avenue, Miami
*Tel: 305-592-2000*
www.doralresort.com
Colorfully named championship courses: the Blue Monster and the Great White Shark.

Kayaking the Everglades

# TOURS

In addition to the organizations described below, check the tour offerings of the Orlando theme parks. Each has behind-the-scenes or special-access tours.

## Boat tours

**Savannah Riverboat Cruises**
*Tel: 1-800-786-6404*
www.savannahriverboat.com
Paddle around the harbor on an hour-long sightseeing cruise. Special offerings include a cruise about Gullah culture (African-Americans culture the Lowcountry) and a night-time ghost-story tour.

## Driving tours

**American Dream Safari**
Memphis
*Tel: 901-527-8870*
www.americandreamsafari.com
Get an expertly chauffeured ride in a vintage Cadillac, seeking out Elvis sites, gospel music, and more.

**Backbeat Tours**
Memphis
*Tel: 901-272-2328*
www.backbeattours.com
Guides strum the guitar with classic songs while showing off their city from aboard the 'Miss Claudy' bus.

**Nash-Trash Tours**
Nashville
*Tel: 615-226-7300*
http://nashtrash.com
Climb aboard a big pink bus and see the sights of Nashville, while listening to the commentary of the Jugg Sisters, who fill you in on the gossip about local country stars. Nash-Trash also run a Murder Mystery Dinner Tour.

## Walking tours

**Charleston Pirate Tours**
Tel: 843-442-7299
http://charlestonpiratetour.com
Explore Charleston's Historic District with a 'pirate' guide, complete with macaw. There's also an evening cemetery tour covering the town's ghost legends.

**Historic New Orleans Tours**
Tel: 504-947-2120
www.tourneworleans.com
A top-notch and reliable company with nearly a dozen walking and chauffeured-van itineraries: a post-Katrina rebirth tour; walks dedicated to jazz, voodoo, or the French Quarter; even a scandalous cocktail-hour gathering.

**Little Havana Walking Tours**
Miami
*Tel: 305-375-1492*
www.historymiami.org
Get the behind-the-scenes story of this vibrant neighborhood.The tour includes a stop at a cigar factory.

**Savannah Walks**
*Tel: 912-238-9255*
http://savannahwalks.com
Most of the itineraries on these strolls cover local history, including the colorful tales from the popular book, *Midnight in the Garden of Good and Evil*. There's a pub crawl, too.

Savannah's waterfront

# FESTIVALS AND EVENTS

Music and food fuel many of the South's festivals – after all, there's a lot to celebrate. As well as the special events below, check the parade and firework schedules of the Orlando theme parks. They go all out for holidays, too, with special parties such as Mickey's Not-So-Scary Halloween.

## February
**South Beach Wine & Food Festival**
Miami
Tel: 305-627-1646
www.sobefest.com
Celebrity chefs and food personalities throw a giant fund-raising fair with tastings galore.

## February or March
**Mardi Gras**
New Orleans
www.mardigrasneworleans.com
On the Tuesday before Ash Wednesday is one of the country's most epic parties, with eye-popping costumes, hypnotic music, and plenty of decadence.

## March
**Calle Ocho**
Little Havana, Miami
Tel: 305-644-8888
www.carnavalmiami.com/calle8
A street fair devoted to Miami's Cuban population, with music, art, and lots of food.

## April
**Dogwood Festival**
Piedmont Park, Atlanta
Tel: 404-817-6642
www.dogwood.org
When the dogwood trees bloom, Atlanta celebrates with music, crafts booths, and the 'disc dog' tournament for pooches.

## April–May
**New Orleans Jazz & Heritage Festival**
Tel: 504-410-4100
www.nojazzfest.com
A celebration of New Orleans music, food, and culture, with traditional jazz just the beginning. Big names, local bluesmen, Cajun, zydeco, swamp pop – whatever you want, it's all here.

## May
**Memphis in May**
Tel: 901-525-4611
www.memphisinmay.org
This month-long giant party includes the Beale Street Music Festival and the World Championship Barbecue Cooking Contest.

## June
**CMA Music Festival**
Nashville
Tel: 1-800-262-3378
www.cmaworld.com/cma-music-festival
The biggest country-music festival, with a line-up of live gigs, meet-and-greets, and late-night shows at downtown clubs.

## July
**Annual Hemingway Days Festival**
Key West
Tel: 305-294-5717
http://sloppyjoes.com/lookalikes.htm
To toast Key West's most famous former resident, Sloppy Joe's bar hosts a lookalike contest. There are also fishing and arm-wrestling contests, and plenty of drinking.

## August
**Elvis Week**
Memphis
Tel: 901-332-3322
www.elvis.com/elvisweek
Around the week of Elvis's death (August 16), Graceland goes off the deep end with tribute events, including a candlelight vigil and a charitable race.

## December
**Art Basel Miami Beach**
Tel: 305-674-1292
www.artbaselmiamibeach.com
The biggest and trendiest art show in the US is the sister event to the Swiss art fair.

Listings

# The Heartland

The heart of the Midwest could be described as a place of unpretentious achievement. Chicago and Minneapolis-St Paul may often be compared with New York City – as 'Second City' and 'Mini-Apple', respectively – but each holds its own with great restaurants and cultural offerings. South Dakota's Badlands, meanwhile, epitomize the rough and tough beauty of the wilderness.

## Chicago and Minneapolis-St Paul

 **Population:** Chicago: 2,695,600; Minneapolis–St Paul 666,800

 **Local dialing codes:** Chicago: 312 and 773; Minneapolis–St Paul: 612 and 651; Badlands 605

 **Local tourist offices:** Chicago: 2301 South Lake Shore Drive; tel: 312-567-8500; **www.choosechicago. com**. Minneapolis–St Paul: 250 Marquette Avenue South; tel: 612-767-8000; **www.minneapolis.org**

 **Main police stations:** Chicago: 3510 South Michigan Avenue; tel: 312-744-4000. Minneapolis–St Paul: 350 South 5th Street, tel: 612-673-3000

 **Main post offices:** Chicago: 540 N. Dearborn Street; Minneapolis–St Paul: 2746 Blaisdell Avenue

 **Hospitals:** Chicago: tel: 312-926-2000; Minneapolis–St Paul: Northwestern Memorial Hospital, 251 East Huron

 **Local newspapers/listings magazines:** The *Chicago Tribune* and the *Chicago Sun-Times* compete to be the top daily in the Windy City. The *Star Tribune* is the newspaper for Minneapolis-St Paul

 **Time zone:** CDT

The Heartland is the industrial and agricultural core of the US. From the Great Lakes, across the prairies, to the Great Plains, the Midwest is based on dairy and pig farming, corn and wheat, along with large manufacturing plants.

Punctuating the vast swaths of farmland, the region's cities are continually becoming more prominent in the public consciousness. In some cases, the headlines are grim (Detroit). But Chicago and the 'Twin Cities' of Minneapolis and St Paul continue to impress with their museums, restaurants, and theaters. Minneapolis has more theater seats per capita than any other American city outside New York. Chicago draws architecture buffs, since it nurtured the 20th-century Prairie School of architecture led by Frank Lloyd Wright, and has several landmark buildings in the style.

In contrast to these urbane attractions, western South Dakota beckons with a wilder appeal. The Badlands and Wind Cave national parks have an otherworldly beauty, with their canyons and famous echoing caverns.

## Chicago

Braced against the shores of Lake Michigan, **Chicago ❶** is a brash place with strong civic pride. This is the birthplace of the Mob legends, the electric blues, Chicago School skyscrapers, and deep-dish pizza. It's also known for outstanding theater, comedy, and the theatrics of tempestuous politics. Local politicians' penchant for filibustering is one of

Chicago gave the world the first skyscraper, which was designed after a fire swept through the city in 1871

## Chicago transportation

 **Airport:** O'Hare International Airport (ORD); tel: 773-686-3700; http://flychicago.com; 18 miles (29km) northwest of downtown. The blue line of the Chicago Transit Authority's 'L' train system: about 40 minutes to downtown, $2.25 fare, runs 24 hours daily. This is one of the world's busiest airports, so be sure to leave extra time for navigating the huge terminals. Taxi: at least 35 minutes to downtown (but traffic often adds significant time), roughly $40

 **'L' Trains:** The Chicago Transit Authority (CTA), tel: 312-836-7000; www.transitchicago.com, runs the city's extensive rail system, locally known as the 'L', short for 'elevated' – since the trains were originally on elevated tracks. Now the 'L' operates both above and below ground. Of the eight color-coded routes, the red and blue lines run 24 hours a day. The other trains pause for a few hours, usually between 1am or 2am and 4am or 5am. Buy a stored-fare Transit Card at vending machines at any rail station; rides cost $2.25. Or get a Fun Pass, with unlimited rides on the CTA, for one day ($5.75), three days ($14), or a week ($23). To use any card, swipe at station turnstiles

 **Taxis:** Taxis, which can be any color but have a medallion on the hood, are generally easy to hail from the street in the Loop and around the Magnificent Mile. To call a dispatcher, try Yellow Cab Chicago, tel: 312-829-4222. Fares start at $2.25, then $1.80 per mile and $0.33 per minute for time in traffic, plus a $1 fuel surcharge. Cab drivers accept both cash and credit cards. To report any issues, contact the Business Affairs & Consumer Protection department, www.cityofchicago.org

The Chicago Theater is on State Street

The Loop is named for the elevated train tracks that wind their way the downtown area

the sources of Chicago's nickname, the Windy City. A delightful surprise for most visitors is the 15-mile (24km) stretch of parkland and beaches along the lakefront. This provides plenty of opportunities to sunbathe or stroll just blocks from the skyscrapers.

The city that showed the world how to build high-rises learnt the technique from necessity. In 1871, a disastrous fire swept through and Chicago had to rebuild in a hurry, with fireproof buildings making the most of available space. The architects who worked out how to use a metal skeleton to make towering yet graceful structures became known as the Chicago School.

### The Loop and South Michigan Ave

With the 'L' tracks rattling around, **the Loop** neighborhood means business. LaSalle Street is the core of the financial district. The major downtown department stores, wonders of the early 20th century, stand on State Street and Wabash Avenue. Look out for Louis Sullivan's Carson Pirie Scott building on State Street, with its lavish carvings. Several vibrant, modern public sculptures pop up on these blocks, including Pablo Picasso's steel *Untitled* on Daley Plaza.

Looming above is the **Willis Tower** (formerly known as the Sears Tower), one of the world's tallest buildings, at 110 stories. Its **Skydeck** (tel: 312-875-9696; www.theskydeck.com; Apr–Sept daily 9am–10pm, Oct–Mar daily 10am–8pm; charge) on the 103rd floor boasts views of up to 50 miles.

A block further east runs South Michigan Avenue, bordering the lakefront **Grant Park**. At the park's northwest corner, near East Washington Street in the **Millennium Park** area, curves the silvery sculpture *Cloud Gate*. Known affectionately as **the Bean**, this massive steel swoop reflects the nearby towers like a funhouse mirror, making it a favorite photo op.

Further south along the avenue, guarded by two bronze lions, is the **Art Institute of Chicago** (tel: 312-443-3600; www.artic.edu/aic;

# ⭐ FRANK LLOYD WRIGHT IN CHICAGO

A college dropout, Frank Lloyd Wright was also one of the most influential architects of the 20th century. His early life and work are intertwined with the Chicago area, where he galvanized the Prairie School of Design and developed its aesthetic of streamlined, modern functionality.

Franky Lloyd Wright got his first break when he joined the Chicago architecture firm of Adler & Sullivan as a draftsman in 1887. Louis Sullivan, now considered the father of skyscrapers, had been among the first to embrace the steel-framed architecture that allows buildings to be constructed to ever-taller heights. Sullivans' 'form follows function' dictum had a deep impact on his protégé.

After a few years, Wright borrowed money from Sullivan to build his first independent project: a home in the suburb of Oak Park. By 1893, Wright ventured out on his own and added studio space to this house, which has now become an icon of Wright's design ethos.

Now open to the public, the **Frank Lloyd Wright Home and Studio** (tel: 312-994-4000; www.gowright.org; daily 10am–5pm; tour charge) reveals some of Wright's signature design elements. The landscapes flat, sweeping prairies inspired long, horizontal lines and natural materials in his buildings. An open floor plan centers around fireplaces, with built-in furniture ensuring maximum efficiency. Wright and his family lived here until 1909, when he bolted to Europe with his mistress, Mamah Cheney, who was married to one of his clients.

The Frederick C. Robie House

Wright's buildings frequently use horizontal lines that draw the eye outward

Before he left Illinois, Wright dreamed up more than 20 buildings, giving Oak Park the world's largest concentration of his work. In 1905 he was commissioned to rebuild Oak Park's **Unitarian church.** Making a bold break from standard religious architecture, Wright devised a blocky concrete structure without a spire or a dramatic front entrance. The interior is illuminated with high-placed windows, keeping the focus on the congregation. Here, Wright said, he became an architect of space rather than structure.

In 1908 Wright started designing and building another home that would become a Modernist landmark: the **Frederick C. Robie House** (tel: 312-994-4000; www.gowright.org/visit/robie-house.html; Thur–Mon 9am–4pm; charge) on Chicago's South Side. With narrow bands of window and glass, wide eaves, and a gently pitched roof, Robie House epitomizes Prairie style.

In 1911, Wright returned to America with Cheney and settled on family land in Wisconsin, building his home, Taliesin. Tragedy struck three years later when Julian Carlton, a male servant from Barbados, set fire to Taliesin and brutally murdered seven people with an axe, including Cheney. Wright rebuilt Taliesin, although it burnt down again in 1925 after wiring from the telephone system caught fire. This fire destroyed a set of Japanese prints that served as inspiration for much of Wright's work. Despite much personal turmoil, Wright lived and worked all over the United States, making his mark on 20th-century architecture and design.

Wright designed many interiors for his buildings, including light fixtures and furniture

Gustave Caillebotte's *Paris Street; Rainy Day* (1877) at the Art Institute of Chicago

daily 10.30am–5pm, Thur until 8pm; charge). One of the country's greatest museums, the Institute possesses stellar 20th-century American paintings (by Edward Hopper and Jackson Pollock, among others) and a vast trove of French Impressionist art, including dozens of paintings by Claude Monet. In 2009, the Art Institute opened a modern-art wing designed by Renzo Piano, making it the second-largest museum in the US. The glass-and-steel structure gracefully echoes the classic lines of the original building. Inside, it accommodates the 20th- and 21st-century collections.

Grant Park's south end tapers to Museum Point, which is anchored by the **Field Museum** (tel: 312-922-9410, http://fieldmuseum.org; daily 9am–5pm; charge). This natural-history and archeology collection includes an

## Chicago's gangster era

After nearly a century, the name Chicago still conjures up images of mobsters with machine-guns and fedoras. The most notorious period of organized crime was the 1920s, when Prohibition gave rise to speakeasies, illegal distilleries, and bootlegging. Legendary mobster Al Capone controlled the Chicago Outfit.

New York-raised 'Scarface' Capone landed in Chicago in 1919. Within a few years, he was raking in millions of dollars; unlike most crime bosses, he courted publicity and met with politicians and reporters. He also ordered numerous hits, including the infamous Saint Valentine's Day Massacre in 1929, when Capone's henchmen executed seven members of a rival gang.

Eventually, paperwork got the better of Capone. In 1931, he was sentenced to 11 years for income-tax evasion, and after bouncing around the prison system, ended up on Alcatraz Island, the toughest penitentiary in the US.

Ancient Egypt display with mummies, and paleological specimens such as 'Sue', the largest complete *T. rex* skeleton yet found. Sue is estimated to have been 29 years old at the time of her death, and while she's referred to as female, her gender is unknown.

Nearby, thousands of sea creatures swim in the **Shedd Aquarium** (tel: 312-939-2438; www.sheddaquarium. org; Memorial–Labor Day daily 8.30am–6pm, Labor Day–Memorial Day daily 9am–5pm; charge). Stingrays circle in a coral-reef tank; beluga whales peer at visitors from the Oceanarium; and fish and turtles swarm in the Caribbean-reef exhibit.

The third draw at Museum Point is the **Adler Planetarium and Astronomy Museum** (tel: 312-922-7827; www.adlerplanetarium.org; Mon–Fri 10am–4pm, Sat–Sun 10am–4.30pm; charge). Projected images of the Milky Way flicker across the dome of the main theater, while interactive displays touch on space exploration and the solar system.

### Near North

North of the Loop, on the other side of the Chicago River, the city streets get even grander. Here, North Michigan Avenue is called the **Magnificent Mile** on its march up to Oak Street. This is the swanky main drag of the Near North neighborhood, and is lined with indoor malls, department stores, and flagships of mega-brands such as Ralph Lauren and Chanel. Once at Oak Street, the shopping circuit continues with boutiques and art galleries. Two landmark buildings dominate the avenue: the Gothic-style **Tribune Tower**, close to the river, and the 100-story **John Hancock Center**, with its dramatic dark diagonal struts, at the intersection with East Chestnut Street. Take a close look at the facade of the Tribune Tower, which is studded with unique stone fragments from landmarks all over the world.

The **Museum of Contemporary Art** (tel: 312-280-2660; www.mca chicago.org; Tues 10am–8pm, Wed–Sun 10am–5pm; charge) champions new artists. Displays of young Chicago artists and other up-and-comers share space with more established names such as Olafur Eliasson.

The John Hancock Center rises over the Old Chicago Water Tower

A burst of carnival cheer comes from **Navy Pier** (tel: 312-595-7437; www.navypier.com; Memorial Day–Labor Day Sun–Thurs 10am–10pm, Fri–Sat 10am–midnight, Sept–Oct Sun–Thurs 10am–8pm, Fri–Sat 10am–10pm, Nov–Mar Mon–Thurs 10am–8pm, Fri–Sat 10am–10pm, Sun 10am–7pm; free but charge for some attractions). This former military training ground extends from East Grand Avenue into Lake Michigan, and comprises a children's fun zone, a mall, and a cultural center. The Pier Park section is best for children, with its carousel, mini golf, and Ferris wheel (which is modeled on the very first Ferris wheel, built for the Chicago 1893 World's Columbia Exposition). The **Chicago Children's Museum** (tel: 312-527-1000; www.chicagochildrensmuseum.org; Mon–Wed and Fri–Sun 10am–5pm, Thurs 10am–8pm; charge) keeps kids busy with arts rooms, an invention lab, a recreated archeological dig, and more. At the far end of the complex you'll find the Chicago Shakespeare Theater.

### Lincoln Park

Starting at North Avenue, Lincoln Park reaches for miles up the shoreline of Lake Michigan. This narrow strip of land accommodates all sorts of diversions, from beaches to tennis courts to botanical gardens. The main attraction is the **Lincoln Park Zoo** (tel: 312-742-2000; www.lpzoo.org; Memorial Day–Labor Day Mon–Fri

The Gold Coast of Chicago stretches from Oak Street Beach to Lincoln Park

Chicago's Navy Pier is a former military pilot-training ground-turned-entertainment area

10am–5pm, Sat–Sun 10am–6.30pm, Sept–Oct and April–May daily 10am–5pm, Nov–Mar 10am–4.30pm; free). The African Journey section features rhinos, giraffes, ostriches and hippos, while a 'children's zoo' has North American species, including beavers, bears, owls and wolves.

## Minneapolis–St Paul

Because of their relative proximity, **Minneapolis ❷** and St Paul, on opposite sides of the Mississippi River, get lumped together as the 'Twin Cities.' They're fraternal rather than identical twins, though. St Paul tends to be more conservative, with a small-town (some would say stodgy) vibe when compared to Minneapolis, with its high-rises and the cutting-edge Walker Art Center. Locals are also proud of their ability to tolerate long cold winters, and of their homespun humor – best exemplified by radio personality and author Garrison Keillor.

### Minneapolis

Over the past decade, several dazzling new buildings have risen up in this half of the Twin Cities, giving it a reputation as an architect's darling.

One of the most impressive is the **Walker Art Center** (tel: 612-375-7600; www.walkerart.org; Tue–Wed and Fri–Sun 11am–5pm, Thur 11am–9pm; charge). Famed architecture firm Herzog & de Meuron designed the museum's expansion in 2005, likening the shimmering new structure to a lantern. Inside is a collection of modern and contemporary art. The adjacent **Minneapolis Sculpture Garden** (daily 6am–midnight; free), partially managed by the Walker, takes art outdoors with sculptures exhibited in a park setting. Just across the river, the **Frederick R. Weisman Art Museum** (tel: 612-625-9494; www.weisman.umn.edu) is due to reopen in fall 2011 with a dramatic extension by star architect Frank Gehry.

> ### The *über*-mall
>
> The sheer numbers boggle the mind. The **Mall of America** (tel: 952-883-8800; www.mallofamerica.com), in the suburb of Bloomington, is one of the most-visited tourist attractions in the country, with over 500 stores, a Nickelodeon theme park, an aquarium, a wedding chapel, and hundreds of daily mall walkers. As if all this were not enough, an ongoing expansion will add hotels, a water park and, of course, more stores. The 'Sprawl of America' is located roughly 15 minutes south of downtown Minneapolis by car.

### St Paul

Just to the east is St Paul, Minnesota's state capital. Visitors should make for **Summit Avenue,** which runs between the Mississippi and the Cathedral of St Paul, and is lined with over four miles of Victorian homes.

## South Dakota

Southwestern South Dakota is where the landscape gets interesting. The Badlands rise out of the prairie; its stark landscape was once referred to as 'Hell with the fires burned out.' The Black Hills, further west, have two riveting sights: the complex underground caverns of Wind Caves National Park and the inspiring sculpture of four great American presidents on Mount Rushmore.

### Badlands National Park

Several chunks of dramatic terrain strung together make up **Badlands National Park ❸** (tel: 605-433-5361; www.nps.gov/badl; daily 24 hours; charge). The spires, buttes, canyons, and jagged ridges are a fossil-hunter's paradise. Shaped by erosion, these striking formations continue to evolve. The terrain is often compared to a moonscape for its severe and ethereal beauty.

The main route through the park is the Badlands Loop Road, which has several overlook pullouts. The road passes the **Ben Reifel Visitor Center** (tel: 605-433-5361; www.nps.gov/badl; mid-May–Aug daily 7am–7pm, early Sept–Oct and mid-Apr–mid-May daily 8am–5pm, Nov–mid-Apr daily 8am–4pm; free), with its natural-history exhibits and ranger programs. Near the center is the Fossil Exhibit Trail, which offers a glimpse of the rich fossil beds.

Badlands National Park in South Dakota

The carved presidential heads at Mount Rushmore National Monument

## The Black Hills

Underneath the Black Hills snake over 130 miles (210 km) of underground passages and caves – the subterranean lure of **Wind Cave National Park** (tel: 605-745-4600; www.nps.gov/wica; daily 24 hours; free). Cave tours, for which there is a fee, leave from the **Wind Cave Visitor Center** (tel: 605-745-4600; www.nps.gov/wica; mid-June–mid-Aug daily 8am–7pm, mid-Apr–mid-June and mid-Aug–Sept daily 8am–6pm, Oct–mid-Apr daily 8am–4.30pm; free). The tours reveal the signature boxwork formations, where thin calcite blades form a honeycomb pattern on the ceiling. Of the five itineraries, one of the most popular is the candlelight tour. So far, Wind Cave is believed to be the fourth-largest cave system in the world, but exploration continues. Wear sturdy shoes with non-slip soles and bring a sweater.

North of Wind Cave rises one of the nation's most iconic and unconventional artworks: **Mount Rushmore National Monument** (tel: 605-574-2523; www.nps.gov/moru; daily 24 hours; parking charge). Here, giant portraits of American presidents George Washington, Thomas Jefferson, Abraham Lincoln, and Theodore Roosevelt gaze sternly from a rock face in the Black Hills.

This massive sculptural project was the vision of sculptor Gutzon Borglum, who began work on the project in 1925 and continued until his death in 1941. He and his crew did much of the work with dynamite. The **Lincoln Borglum Visitor Center and Museum** (tel: 605-574-2523; www.nps.gov/moru; May–mid-Aug daily 8am–10pm, mid-Aug–Sept daily 8am–9pm, Oct–Apr daily 8am–5pm; free) includes an interactive exhibit on the blasting technique. At night, the sculptures are illuminated.

# ACCOMMODATIONS

Although both Chicago and Minneapolis are known for great modern architecture, their best-known hotels are often historic piles rather than cutting-edge. Bear in mind also that Chicago is a convention hub, so when major events are being hosted, rooms sell out well in advance. To avoid peak times, check the convention calendar on the visitor bureau's website.

## Chicago

**The Drake**
140 East Walton Place
*Tel: 312-787-2200*
**www.thedrakehotel.com**
Opened in 1920, the Drake keeps pace with the polished neighborhood, right off the Magnificent Mile. The lobby still has a whiff of history; its hundreds of guest rooms are more modern and neutral. It's worth paying a bit extra for a lake view. **$$$**

**Majestic Hotel**
528 W. Brompton Place
*Tel: 773-404-3499*
**www.majestic-chicago.com**
Tucked into a residential neighborhood between Lincoln Park and Wrigley Field, this option is modest, rather than majestic, but quite comfortable. **$$–$$$**

**theWit**
201 N. State Street
*Tel: 312-467-0200*

The historic Drake, Chicago

**www.thewithotel.com**
The first hotel in a budding chainlet by Doubletree, theWit balances the efficiency of a business hotel with a warm, vacation-style mindset. Terrific views of its north-Loop neighboring buildings, especially from its rooftop bar. **$$$**

## Minneapolis–St Paul

**Aloft Minneapolis**
900 Washington Avenue S., Minneapolis
*Tel: 612-455-8400*
**www.starwoodhotels.com/alofthotels**
A hop away from the Guthrie Theater, Aloft fits right in with the glassy modern buildings here. The decor can feel a bit prefab but the amenities are top-notch. **$$**

**St Paul Hotel**
350 Market Street, St Paul
*Tel: 651-292-9292*
**www.saintpaulhotel.com**
Fittingly for this half of the Twin Cities, the St Paul is elegantly historic. Having celebrated its centennial in 2010, it carefully maintains its classic rooms and local-favorite grill restaurant. **$$$**

## South Dakota

**Cedar Pass Lodge**
Badlands Loop Road, Badlands National Park
*Tel: 605-433-5460*
http://cedarpasslodge.com
A line of rustic cabins lets visitors see the Badlands at dusk and dawn. The lodge is only open in high season, but there's an adjacent campground that's open year-round. **$–$$**

# RESTAURANTS

Even New York City chefs sometimes point to Chicago as one of the best culinary destinations in the country. From avant-garde gastronomy to homey comfort food, the city consistently impresses. (As with hotels, though, top restaurants fill quickly when there's a convention in town.) Minneapolis and St Paul have their fair share of steakhouses, but they are also nurturing refined seasonal and regional cooking, and earning good reputations.

Chicago's Pizzeria Uno

## Chicago

### Alinea
1723 North Halsted Street
*Tel: 312-867-0110*
**www.alinea-restaurant.com**
Topping many a best-of-list, Alinea is a constantly changing, experimental marvel. The prix-fixe menus transform familiar flavors with cutting-edge technique. In spring 2011, chef Grant Achatz followed up this success with a seasonal restaurant, Next, and an adjoining cocktail bar, Aviary, both equally avant-garde (953–955 W. Fulton Market). **$$$$**

### Frontera Grill
445 North Clark Street
*Tel: 312-661-1434*
**www.fronterakitchens.com**
Rick Bayless, one of the country's most influential champions of Mexican cuisine, got his start here, showcasing well-executed dishes. Twinned restaurant Topolobampo is quieter and fancier ($$$$). **$$$**

### Pizzeria Uno
29 E. Ohio Street
*Tel: 312-321-1000*
**www.unos.com**
This is the birthplace of deep-dish pizza. While Uno is now a nationwide chain, the original location packs in crowds for its oozing, meaty pizza pies. **$$**

## Minneapolis–St Paul

### Cafe Latté
850 Grand Avenue, St Paul
*Tel: 651-224-5687*
**www.cafelatte.com**
Although technically a cafeteria, this favorite lunch spot dishes out elaborate salads, sandwiches, and pizzas, plus rich layer cakes and cheesecakes. **$$**

### Heartland
289 E. 5th Street, St Paul
*Tel: 651-699-3536*
**www.heartlandrestaurant.com**
The neighboring farmers' market shapes the daily menu at this sleek regional restaurant. To get a taste without the formality and high prices, try the attached market deli for soup and sandwiches. **$$$$**

### Manny's Steakhouse
825 Marquette Avenue, Minneapolis
*Tel: 612-339-9900*
**http://mannyssteakhouse.com**
Everyone comes through this steakhouse at some point, craving its porterhouse, sirloin, and lively barroom scene. This is a quintessentially American experience. **$$$–$$$$**

# NIGHTLIFE

Chords from electric guitars resonate through Chicago, from Chicago-style blues clubs to indie-rock joints. Several outstanding live-music venues cluster in the Lincoln Park and Wicker Park neighborhoods, along with easy-going pubs. In Minneapolis, the Warehouse District is the place to go after dark.

## Bars and pubs

**Billy Goat Tavern**
430 N. Michigan Avenue, Chicago
*Tel: 312-222-1525*
**www.billygoattavern.com**
Immortalized in a 'Saturday Night Live' comedy skit, the historic Billy Goat is a scruffy, heart-of-gold dive bar in what's now the posh Miracle Mile.

**Nye's Polonaise Room**
112 E. Hennepin Avenue, Minneapolis
*Tel: 612-379-2021*
**www.nyespolonaise.com**
Opened in 1950, Nye's is in something of a time warp, complete with the 'world's most dangerous polka band', which usually plays on weekends.

**The Violet Hour**
1520 N. Damen Avenue, Chicago
*Tel: 773-252-1500*
**www.theviolethour.com**
This sexy, speakeasy-style bar shakes up a range of impeccable cocktails, both classic and innovative.

## Live music clubs

**Buddy Guy's Legends**
700 S. Wabash Avenue, Chicago
*Tel: 312-427-1190*
**www.buddyguys.com**
A blues club stocked with musical memorabilia, this atmospheric venue books top-tier acts including, the namesake owner.

**First Avenue & 7th Street Entry**
701 1st Avenue N., Minneapolis
*Tel: 612-332-1775*
**www.first-avenue.com**
This is where Prince took off; the club rumbles with up-and-coming rock acts, DJ dance nights, and the occasional burlesque show.

**Metro**
3730 N. Clark Street, Chicago
*Tel: 773-549-0203*
**www.metrochicago.com**
This old auditorium has a star-studded musical history; seemingly every major rock and alternative band passes through, from R.E.M. to the Decemberists. Downstairs is a dance club.

A blues club in Chicago provides late-night entertainment

# ENTERTAINMENT

Between Chicago and Minneapolis–St Paul, you'll be spoilt for choice in the performing arts, particularly when it comes to theater.

## Theater and comedy

**Goodman Theatre**
170 N. Dearborn Street, Chicago
*Tel: 312-443-3800*
**www.goodmantheatre.org**
For both new plays and revivals, the Theater District's Goodman is the reliable front-runner. Some of the city's best actors headline works such as 'Red' or 'The Seagull'.

**Fitzgerald Theater**
10 E. Exchange Street, St Paul
*Tel: 651-290-1200*
**http://fitzgeraldtheater.publicradio.org**
As the seat of Garrison Keillor's 'Prairie Home Companion' live radio show, the Fitzgerald's walls regularly ring with laughter.

**Guthrie Theater**
818 S. 2nd Street, Minneapolis
*Tel: 612-377-2224*
**www.guthrietheater.org**
This renowned theater got even more buzz when it debuted its new home in 2006. French architect Jean Nouvel delivered an imaginative riff on Midwestern grain silos covered in blue glass and steel. The three stages offer productions of everything from Shakespeare to 'God of Carnage.'

Architect Jean Nouvel's Guthrie Theater

**The Second City**
1616 N. Wells Street, Chicago
*Tel: 312-337-3992*
**www.secondcity.com**
The country's most famous and consistently hilarious comedy club, known for long-form improv and famous graduates (Tina Fey, Stephen Colbert, John Belushi).

**Steppenwolf Theatre Company**
1650 N. Halsted Street, Chicago
*Tel: 312-335-1650*
**www.steppenwolf.org**
An ensemble company with a taste for putting on challenging plays, Steppenwolf has graduated from fringe to venerable over the past few decades.

# SPORTS AND ACTIVITIES

Anyone hearing debates about 'da Bears' or the Cubs Curse knows that Chicago takes its spectator sports very seriously. With several legendary teams (sometimes legendary for *not* winning), the Windy City is renowned for its devoted fans.

## Baseball

**Chicago Cubs**
1060 W. Addison Street, Chicago
*Tel: 773-404-2827*
**http://chicago.cubs.mlb.com**

Though they may not win championships, the Cubs have a passionately loyal fan base, and their 1914 ballpark, the ivy-covered Wrigley Field, stands as virtually a monument to the sport.

### Chicago White Sox
333 W. 35th Street, Chicago
*Tel: 312-674-1000*
http://chicago.whitesox.mlb.com
The South Side stadium, US Cellular Field, may lack the atmosphere of Wrigley, but Sox fans are also a loyal bunch.

### Minnesota Twins
1 Twins Way, Minneapolis
*Tel: 1-800-338-9467*
http://minnesota.twins.mlb.com
With a new stadium, Target Field, opened in 2010, the Twins will hopefully climb back to their championship records.

## Basketball
### Chicago Bulls
1901 W. Madison Street, Chicago
*Tel: 312-455-4000*
www.nba.com/bulls
While the years of constant championships with legendary player Michael Jordan are now over, the Bulls are still an exciting team with a lively fan base.

## Football
### Chicago Bears
Lake Shore Drive at 16th Street, Chicago
*Tel. 847-295-6600*
www.chicagobears.com
One of the top teams in the history of the National Football League, 'da Bears' get most fired up when facing their rivals, the Green Bay Packers, at the Soldier Field stadium.

## Ice-skating
### McCormick Tribune Ice Rink
Millennium Park, S. Michigan Avenue at E. Randolph Street, Chicago
http://explorechicago.org/city/en/millennium.html
From November to March, this rink gets out the Zamboni (the machine that resurfaces the ice) for the public, with free entry

# TOURS

While bad weather conditions mean that many outdoor itineraries can't run year-round, Chicago offers several notable architecture tours.

## Boat tour
### Chicago Architecture Foundation
224 S. Michigan Avenue, Chicago
*Tel: 312-922-3432*
http://caf.architecture.org
The CAF takes to the Chicago River for its best-selling Architecture River Cruise. This gives visitors a fresh perspective on the city's landmark buildings.

## Walking tours
### Chicago Architecture Foundation
224 S. Michigan Avenue, Chicago
*Tel: 312-922-3432*
http://caf.architecture.org
The CAF taps the city's most popular walking tours. Some walks follow a specific theme, such as skyscrapers or Art Deco, while others explore neighborhoods in depth.

A boat tour along the Chicago River offers a relaxing way to see the sights

# FESTIVALS AND EVENTS

The celebratory season really kicks in during summer, when parks fill with special events – though even in the dead of winter, there are festivals that forge on.

Lollapalooza is held in Chicago's Grant Park

## January
### St Paul Winter Carnival
Throughout St Paul
www.winter-carnival.com
Launched in 1886 to prove that St Paul wasn't the equivalent of Siberia in winter, this annual carnival cheers for nearly two weeks with parades, ice carving, and a treasure hunt.

## March
### Great Northern Bluegrass Music Festival
Schaumburg, IL
www.bluegrassmidwest.com
If you like your fiddles staccato rather than legato, stop by the Bluegrass Festival in Schaumburg, which has a Friday-night jam session, an open stage on Saturday, and a heart-warming Gospel session on Sunday morning.

## June
### Chicago Blues Festival
Grant Park, Chicago
www.chicagofestivals.net
The world's largest free blues festival booms through a mid-June weekend, with big-name musicians such as B.B. King and Bonnie Raitt often featuring on the roster.

## July
### Taste of Chicago
Grant Park, Chicago
www.explorechicago.org
For more than a week, usually from late June through early July, Grant Park turns into a mammoth food-and-music fair.

### Sommerfest
Minneapolis–St Paul
www.minnesotaorchestra.org
The summer season of the Minnesota Orchestra hits all the highlights, including symphonic, chamber, jazz, and rock.

## August
### Lollapalooza
Grant Park, Chicago
www.lollapalooza.com
Once a touring festival, Lolapalooza now only rocks out in Chicago, with major head-liners such as Coldplay and Eminem.

### Iowa State Fair
Des Moines
www.iowastatefair.org
The largest event in the state of Iowa, the State Fair attracts visitors from all over the country's heartland. The Fair inspired author Phil Strong to write State Fair, and musicians Rodgers and Hammerstein to write a Broadway musical. Don't miss the famous butter cow, which has been present every year since 1911.

## Late August–Labor Day
### Minnesota State Fair
Minneapolis–St Paul
www.mnstatefair.org
Held in permanent fairgrounds in the Twin Cities, this is one of the country's biggest state fairs. Among other attractions, it offers agricultural shows, concerts, midway rides, and every fried food you can imagine (and some you can't).

# Texas and the Southwest

Characterized by wide-open spaces, the Southwest stretches across most of the Sun Belt, with the ranchlands and oilfields of Texas, the highlands of New Mexico, and Arizona's deserts. The most breathtaking sight within all these sun-baked vistas? The Grand Canyon, which is a truly awesome sight.

## Houston, Austin, Santa Fe, and Phoenix

 **Population:** Houston 2.25 million; Austin 710,000; Santa Fe 72,000; Phoenix 1.5 million

 **Local dialing codes:** Houston 713; Austin 512; Santa Fe 505; Phoenix 602

 **Local tourist offices:** Houston: 901 Bagby Street; tel: 713-437-5200; www.visithoustontexas.com. Austin: 301 Congress Avenue; 1-800-926-2282; www.austintexas.org. Santa Fe: 201 W. Marcy Street; 1-800-777-2489; www.santafe.org. Phoenix: 125 N. Second Street; 1-877-225-5749; www.visitphoenix.com

 **Main police stations:** Houston: 1200 Travis Street; tel: 713-884-3131. Austin: 715 E. 8th Street; tel: 512-974-5000. Santa Fe: 2515 Camino Entrada; tel: 505-428-3710. Phoenix: 620 W. Washington Street; tel: 602-262-7626

 **Main post offices:** Houston: 401 Franklin Street; Austin: 10109 Lake Creek Parkway; Santa Fe: 120 S. Federal Place; Phoenix: 4949 E. Van Buren Street

 **Hospitals:** Houston: Methodist, 6565 Fannin Street; tel: 713-790-3311. Austin: Seton Medical Center Austin, 1201 W. 38th Street; tel: 512-324-1000. Santa Fe: Christus St Vincent, 455 St Michaels Drive; tel: 505-983-3361. Phoenix: Banner Good Samaritan Medical Center, 1111 E. McDowell Road; tel: 602-839-2000

 **Local newspapers/listings magazines:** The main newspapers include the *Houston Chronicle*, *Austin American Statesman*, and the *Arizona Republic*

 **Time zones:** CST for the far-west corner of Texas; MST for Arizona, New Mexico, and most of Texas

Texas, the Lone Star State, is a world unto itself. Everything is on a grand scale, from the state's sheer size to the big hair favored by Houston matrons and the belt buckles on the cowboys and cowgirls. Cattle and oil originally fueled its economy and still shape life here. While Texas summons up images of longhorns and oil wells, its identity is in fact increasingly urban.

It has some of the largest cities in the US, with the inevitable sprawling suburbs, high-rises, and freeway snarls.

Arizona and New Mexico, on the other hand, are best known for their surreal landscapes and Native American heritage. Everything, from the flat-topped mesas to the adobe buildings in large towns such as Santa Fe, seems to be toasted by sunlight and history. These are favorite states for road trips, especially as New Mexico retains a good section of the legendary Route 66.

Don't even consider traveling in this region without a car. While you can fly into the major cities, the distances between sights, neighborhoods, and towns are more than shoe leather or local buses can cover. Be careful with your timing, since summer's intense heat and (in the case of much of Texas) high humidity can make even hardy

Wheels are essential for exploring this vast region – a favorite for road trips (see p.22)

travelers wilt. Come prepared with some of the determined spirit of the pioneers who settled here.

## Texas

Texas is a state renowned for its stark contrasts: gleaming cities and sleepy 'cowtowns'; rodeos and high-powered

**Texas and the Southwest**

0    200 miles
0    200 km

## Houston transportation

 **Airport:** George Bush Intercontinental Airport (IAH); tel: 281-233-3000; **www.fly2houston. com/iahhome**; 22 miles (35km) north of downtown. Super Shuttle: 713-523-8888; **www.supershuttle. com**, starting at $25 for a shared ride to downtown hotels. Taxi: at least 40 minutes to downtown (traffic can add significant time), roughly $50

 **Light Rail:** An alternative to driving in Houston is the light-rail network of the Metropolitan Transit Authority (Metro), tel: 713-635-4000; **www. ridemetro.org**. Routes connect downtown with the museum district and other key areas. Rides cost

$1.25 each. Fares can be paid in cash with exact change, or by using a Metro Q fare card, which can be purchased and loaded with a monetary amount at rail stations

 **Taxis:** It's usually best to call ahead for a taxi; they're hard to find on the street, although downtown does have some cab stands marked by a taxi icon. Two reliable dispatchers are Yellow Cab, tel: 713-236-1111, and United Cab, tel: 713-699-0000. There's a flat $6 fare in the central business district. Otherwise, taxis cost $4 for the first mile and $1.87 for every following mile, with $0.33 per standing minute

industry, the Gulf of Mexico's beaches and arid deserts. It's a place where economic, social, and geographic boundaries intersect. It's also the second-largest state in the US (after Alaska), and each part has a distinct character. East Texas has much in common with the South, for instance, while Latino culture comes to the fore along the Rio Grande River.

### Houston

**Houston ❶** is an eccentric boom-town, definitely the weirdest and most dynamic metropolis in Texas. It's steeped in oil, cowboy culture,

Houston skyscrapers by night

The Minute Maid Park baseball stadium in downtown Houston

**Downtown Houston** is demarcated by Interstate 45 and US 59. It's spiky with high-rises such as Pennzoil Place, designed by Philip Johnson as an optical illusion, with its two towers seeming to join and separate depending on your angle. This neighborhood also has the city's major theaters and the famous Minute Maid Park baseball stadium.

Southwest of downtown, on either side of the Southwest Freeway, cluster the attractions of the **Museum District** (www.houstonmuseumdistrict.org), comprising 18 sites ranging from a zoo to several dazzling art collections. **The Menil Collection** (tel: 713-525-9400; www.menil.org; Wed–Sun 11am–7pm; free) stands out as an art museum, not only in Texas but in the world. This is an extraordinary private collection, a perfect

space history, rapid-fire growth, sludgy traffic, and even sludgier humidity. Because of the oil-price fluctuations in the 1970s, Houston grew faster than other Texas cities. Without overall planning, it became a sprawling city with a network of freeways. The inner city is surrounded by Interstate 610, otherwise known as the Loop. Most visitor attractions can be found inside the Loop.

Texas and the Southwest

## Texas musical traditions

What do Beyoncé, Buddy Holly, Willie Nelson, the Dixie Chicks, and Janis Joplin have in common? They're all Texan – but they represent just a fraction of the state's musical mother lode. After centuries as a cultural crossroads, Texas has produced stars in folk, hip-hop, and every musical style in between.

The accordion-based *conjunto* has especially deep roots, since German immigrants introduced the instrument to Mexicans in the 1840s. You'll hear a bit of polka in these folk tunes, too.

Country and cowboy music is closely tied to Texas, of course. Bob Wills and the Texas Playboys sprang Western swing on the world in the 1930s, firing up dancehalls with distinctive fiddling and a yodeling yelp. In the 1970s, Austin-based Willie Nelson and Waylon Jennings shaped a new kind of country music influenced by rock and blues.

African-American workers brought the blues to east Texas, providing the setting for legendary bluesmen such as Sam 'Lightnin'' Hopkins. After World War II, Houston and Dallas became blues hotbeds, with artists such as 'Big Mama' Thornton. Now Houston is known as the hometown of superstar Beyoncé.

example of what oil millions and taste can buy. The Menils had an especially good eye for modern art ranging from the European Surrealists to American Pop Art. Jumping back through the centuries, they also amassed impressive collections of Byzantine relics and indigenous art from Africa, Pacific Islands, and the Pacific Northwest. The main building, designed by Renzo Piano, encourages an up-close-and-personal viewing experience. The Menil campus also includes the **Rothko Chapel** (tel: 713-524-9839; www.rothkochapel.org; daily 10am–6pm; free). This non-denominational space is hung with 14 huge, abstract canvases by Mark Rothko, which feature great slabs of intense, dark color.

For another immersion in art history, head to the **Museum of Fine Arts** (MFAH, tel: 713-639-7300; www.mfah.org; Tue–Wed 10am–5pm, Thur 10am–9pm, Fri–Sat 10am–7pm, Sun 12.15–7pm; charge). It's an immense organization, with two main gallery buildings facing each other across South Main Street, plus a sculpture garden and house museums. The two main buildings display important collections of Impressionist art, 19th- and 20th-century American work, and African tribal art. The galleries themselves are eye-catching, with contributions by Mies van der Rohe and Rafael Moneo.

'Houston, we've had a problem.' As home base for NASA's Apollo lunar missions, the Johnson Space Center in Houston is a key location for America's space program. Tourists can get a glimpse of these extraterrestrial efforts at the official visitor center, **Space Center Houston** (tel: 281-244-2100; www.spacecenter. org; Mon–Fri 10am–5pm, Sat–Sun 10am–6pm, extended summer hours; charge), about 25 miles (40km) southeast of downtown. The Space Center has teamed up with the Disney Imagineers to dream up fun, interactive exhibits. A 'living in

The Johnson Space Center in Houston

The attractive River Walk winds through downtown San Antonio

space' module, for instance, recreates the living quarters in a space station, where daily activities such as eating and sleeping are transformed by microgravity. A NASA tour takes guests to the Mission Control Centers and the massive *Saturn V* rocket.

### San Antonio

A cultural crossroads, **San Antonio** ❷ is where the US and Mexico merge – and with an added splash of German tradition thrown in. For visitors, it's one of the most accessible Texas cities, with its lovely River Walk winding through Downtown.

For Texans, San Antonio is celebrated as the cradle of independence. In 1836, when the territory belonged to Mexico, a symbolic battle was fought here as a group of 187 rebels tried to hold off 5,000 Mexican troops under General Santa Anna. They died in the trying, and their fortress is now a museum-cum-shrine called **the Alamo** (tel: 866-769-8419; http://thealamo.org; June–Aug Mon–Thur 9am–5.30pm, Fri–Sat 9am–7pm, Sun 10am–5.30pm, Sept–May Mon–Sat 9am–5.30pm, Sun 10am–5.30pm; donation). Exhibits explain the significance of the siege and how it galvanized the fight for independence with the battle cry 'Remember the Alamo!' Displays also highlight the famous Americans who fell, including the adventurer Davy Crockett.

Nowadays, town life revolves around the San Antonio River and its bordering, tree-fringed **River Walk**, or **Paseo del Río** (www.thesan antonioriverwalk.com; free), which follows a horseshoe bend for nearly 3 miles (5km). The River Walk is lined with cafés, boutiques, hotels, and bars, making it a perfect place to stroll.

### Austin

**Austin** ❸ is two capitals in one: it's the state capital but also boasts of being the live-music capital of the US. Within a few blocks, a visitor can bounce from the whopping State Capitol Building to the famous Sixth Street music clubs.

Downtown Austin is easy to explore on foot. Government buildings surround the Capitol but **South Congress Avenue**, or **SoCo,** is a magnet for boho stores, vintage boutiques, cafés, and galleries. On the first Thursday of every month, the avenue between Barton Springs Road and Elizabeth Street takes part in a block party as stores stay open late.

One of Austin's more unusual tourist attractions is **Bat Bridge** (www.austinbatsbridge.com; free). Technically called Governor Ann Richards Bridge, this has became a huge urban bat colony, with well over a million Mexican free-tail bats roosting under the bridge. From March through October, at dawn and dusk, the bats swarm out to feed while sightseers gather to watch their flight.

### Corpus Christi and the Barrier Islands

The arcing Gulf Coast shoreline embraces pristine beaches, scruffy beach towns, and new developments. In summer, the Gulf is often as warm as bathwater.

**Corpus Christi** ❹ is a popular destination, with a pleasant but low-key downtown. Like many Gulf communities, it has a sea wall as protection against hurricanes. In its bay sits the World War II-era aircraft carrier **USS Lexington** (tel: 361-888-4473; www. usslexington.com; Memorial Day–Labor Day daily 9am–6pm, Labor Day–Memorial Day daily 9am–5pm; charge), now a naval museum. Visitors clamber around on board the 'Blue Ghost,' which has vintage aircraft stationed on its flight deck.

Thin barrier islands form another protective layer against storms. From Corpus Christi, it's easy to get to

The streets of Austin are filled with bars, restaurants, and cafes

Selling arts, crafts and jewelry at Santa Fe's Palace of the Governors

Some of the state's pueblos have been continuously inhabited for more than 1,000 years. The vistas and the heritage of ancient cultures have helped draw tribes of artists and other creative people over the last century.

### Santa Fe

Founded by the Spanish in 1610, **Santa Fe** ❺ is the oldest capital city in the US. In the historic town center, rosy adobe buildings and shady arcades evoke the frontier past, as keen-eyed shoppers browse the galleries and boutiques.

Old Santa Fe centers on **the Plaza,** where San Francisco Street and Lincoln Avenue intersect. It's always busy, but especially so in the summer when concerts pop up in the bandstand. On its north side sits the Palace of the Governors; in the palace's arcade, Pueblo artisans sell jewelry and crafts.

**Canyon Road,** running along the south bank of the Santa Fe River, is the artists' main drag, lined with studios and galleries. Keep an eye out for Gypsy Alley, an offshoot with yet more galleries.

The 20th-century artist Georgia O'Keeffe painted many of her signature works in New Mexico, and the local landscape is often referred to as 'O'Keeffe Country.' The **Georgia O'Keeffe Museum** (tel: 505-946-1000; www.okeeffemuseum.org; Sun–Wed 10am–5pm, Thur–Sat 10am–7pm; charge) has the world's largest collection of her work.

**Mustang Island State Park** (tel: 361-749-5246; www.tpwd.state.tx.us; charge), with its 5 miles (8km) of rolling beach dunes.

Another good bet is **South Padre Island National Seashore** (tel: 1-800-767-2373; www.sopadre.com/island), really a long, skinny sandbar. With its windswept dunes and mellow weather, it has become the most popular beach getaway in Texas.

## New Mexico

Dubbed the Land of Enchantment, New Mexico seduces with its otherworldly scenery and its deep historic roots. Part of the Rocky Mountain range, Sangre de Cristos, pushes jaggedly through the middle of the state.

## Ranch hand for a weekend

If you're dreaming of riding the range, saddle up at a dude or guest ranch. The rough-and-tumble dude ranches of the early 1900s have morphed into comfortable (sometimes even luxurious) places to stay.

For the most authentic experience, look for a working ranch with family-style meals. Many offer cookouts or chuckwagon dinners, plus roping lessons, fishing, and other activities. Most require a two-night minimum stay.

A popular region is the Hill Country in central Texas, around Bandera, dubbed 'the cowboy capital of the world'. Two good options are **Dixie Dude Ranch** (tel: 830-796-7771; www.dixieduderanch.com) and the cushy **Silver Spur** (tel: 830-796-3037; www.ssranch.com).

Arizona has guest ranches spread all over; some are easy to reach from major cities. There are several in the desert around Tucson, for instance, such as the posh **Tanque Verde Ranch** (tel: 520-296-6275; www.tanqueverderanch.com).

If, after a taster, you're still hungry for more, enroll at **Arizona Cowboy College** (tel: 480-471-3151; www.cowboycollege.com), which offers week-long courses in riding, roping, and working cattle.

Another cultural standout is the **Museum of International Folk Art** (tel: 505-476-1200; www.internationalfolkart.org; daily 10am–5pm, Labor Day–Memorial Day closed Monday; charge). This is one of the world's pre-eminent folk-art centers, displaying everything from tribal masks to toys.

## Arizona

When you see Arizona's Grand Canyon, you won't believe your eyes. It's a frequent experience in this state, where stunning landscapes await you around almost every bend. The canyon is an emblem of the American West, but is only one of Arizona's

You can try your hand at ranching in the cowboy capital of the West

Contemplating one of the seven natural wonders of the world: the Grand Canyon

wonders. From the stark buttes of Monument Valley to the cultural treasures of Phoenix and Tucson, Arizona keeps visitors constantly amazed.

## Grand Canyon

Thrilling, humbling, beautiful beyond words – the Grand Canyon lives up to its reputation as one of the seven natural wonders of the world. It grows only more fascinating when you venture below its rim.

About five million people a year come to gaze down into this vast gash in the earth at **Grand Canyon National Park ❻** (tel: 928-638-7888; www.nps.gov/grca; South Rim daily 24 hours, North Rim daily mid-May–mid-Oct; charge). Here, the Colorado River has eroded the rock, leaving a mile-deep (1.6km) chasm, with the water rushing far below. The river bisects the park. Most visitor facilities and campgrounds cluster on the **South Rim**. The **North Rim**, which

gets snowy in winter, has limited visitor services. *(See also pp. 180–1.)*

**Grand Canyon Village** has most of the park's lodgings, trailheads, restaurants, and museums. The **Grand Canyon Visitor Center** (tel: 928-638-7888; www.nps.gov/grca; daily 8am–5pm; free), freshly revamped in 2011, is the place to get maps, brochures, and schedules for ranger-led programs. Free shuttle buses leave from the center to nearby scenic outlooks such as **Mather Point**.

Another popular stop is the **Yavapai Point Observation Station** (daily 8am–7pm; charge), along Hermit's Road. Three-dimensional models and other exhibits provide insight into the canyon's geology, and there's a breathtaking view into the canyon.

To hike into the canyon, you should be in good physical shape and well prepared. Getting all the way to the river is an overnight hike; don't attempt to go down and back

Monument Valley is called Tsé Bii' Ndzisgaii by the Navajo tribe

in one day. **Bright Angel Trail** is a popular day hike into the canyon as it has some shade and may have water access. There are also much easier hiking trails along the rim.

Another thrilling way to explore the canyon is on a white-water rafting trip on the Colorado *(see p.196)*. And if you prefer dry land, those

### Grand Canyon safety tips

- In summer, temperatures soar well over 100°F (37°C), and it gets even hotter below the rim. Avoid hiking between 10am and 4pm.
- Wear a hat, loose layers of clothing, and plenty of sunblock.
- Always bring extra water, both with you and in your car. For every hour spent hiking, drink at least a half-quart (1 pint) of water and eat a snack.
- Do not swim in the Colorado River, no matter how tempting it looks.
- Keep your gas tank full since service stations are few and far between.

classic mule rides are still offered, too; contact the park's concessionaire, **Xanterra** (tel: 303-297-2757; www.grandcanyonlodges.com) for details.

### Monument Valley

Over by the Utah/Arizona border, this iconic landscape of red sandstone is the crown jewel of the Navajo tribal park system. You've surely seen it in old Western movies or *Thelma and Louise*, its craggy buttes rising suddenly from the valley floor.

**Monument Valley Park** (tel: 435-727-5874; www.navajonationparks.org/htm/monumentvalley; scenic drive May–Sept daily 6am–8.30pm, Oct–Apr daily 8am–4.30pm; charge) is best explored from the scenic driving route, 17 miles (27km) long and unpaved. Be sure to prepare with plenty of gas, water, and snacks. At sunrise, rock formations such as the Owl, Mittens, and Totem Pole glow. John Ford Point, named for the film director, is the most famous view.

## Phoenix

Effective irrigation and ice-cold air-conditioning have birthed the sprawling city of **Phoenix** ❼. The intense heat in the Valley of the Sun meant that only after World War II did the town start to boom, with golf courses and high-rises quickly supplanting the old dude ranches. With more than 320 days of sun each year and a setting ringed by mountains, Phoenix now attracts visitors year-round.

Downtown has blossomed into a cultural district, with museums and performance venues. One must-see attraction is the **Heard Museum** (tel: 602-252-8840; www.heard.org; Mon–Sat 9.30am–5pm, Sun 11am–5pm; charge), an outstanding collection of Native American and other indigenous art. It's a great introduction to the various tribes in the Southwest. Among the items on display is a trove of hundreds of sacred Hopi *kachina* dolls, which are items meant to be treasured rather than played with.

Architecture buffs flock east of downtown, to Frank Lloyd Wright's home and architecture school, called **Taliesen West** (tel: 480-860-2700; www.franklloydwright.org; tours daily 9am–4pm; charge). The low-slung buildings, using local stones and other natural materials, seem to blend with the landscape. Hands-on classes for children and architecture students still take place here, giving it an artistic buzz.

Of the desert drives outside Phoenix, the most spectacular is the winding **Apache Trail**. The 45-mile (72km) route snakes its way past the Superstition Mountains, sheer cliffs, and reservoir lakes. There are plenty of hairpin turns and some graded dirt sections, but also scenic pullouts.

The Heard Museum in Phoenix showcases Native American art

# HOOVER DAM AND THE GRAND CANYON WEST

A few hours' drive from Las Vegas, you'll find two spectacular man-made wonders: the monumental Hoover Dam and the airy Skywalk over the Grand Canyon's west rim. Both require a good head for heights.

After an early breakfast, leave Las Vegas via Interstate 215, joining US Highway 93 just east of Boulder City. Then begins a 3-mile (5km) switchback descent into Black Canyon to bring you to the **Hoover Dam.**

The towering dam is one of the wonders of the modern industrial world. Built between 1931 and 1936, it was the most ambitious public-works project of the Great Depression. Spanning Black Canyon below the confluence of the Colorado and Virgin rivers, it created the largest man-made lake in the US. This reservoir, **Lake Mead,** covers about 247 miles (398km) and is a popular spot for boating and fishing.

Rising over 720ft (220m), the curved concrete wall of the dam is 660ft (198m) thick at the base, tapering to 45ft (13.5m) at the top. For free, you can walk on the sidewalk along the top of the dam, gaze down at the dizzying dam face, and admire the Art Deco statues and mosaics. At the **Hoover Dam Visitors' Center,** you can sign up for one of two tours. One takes you into the power plant to see huge generators; the other tour goes further, into

The Hoover Dam was constructed in hard times, between 1931 and 1936

## Tips

- Distance: 246 miles (396km)
- Time: A full day
- Make sure you start with a full gas tank and bring snacks and water.
- As you drive across Hoover Dam, you might change time zones; check the clocks at each end of the dam. In winter, it is one hour later in Arizona (which is on Mountain Time) than in Nevada (which is on Pacific Time). Since Arizona does not observe Daylight Saving Time, in summer the time is the same on both sides.

Unbeatable views from the cantilevered glass-and-steel Skywalk

tunnels inside the enormous structure. The generators provide electricity for the city of Los Angeles; Lake Mead supplies water for other cities in California.

As you drive across Hoover Dam, you cross into Arizona. Continue south for 42 miles (68km) on US Highway 93 to the turn-off marked with a large bill-board for **Grand Canyon West.** Follow Pearce Ferry Road for 30 miles (48km) to a well-marked Y-junction, where the right fork – the scenic but unpaved Diamond Bar Road – goes another 15 miles (24km) to Grand Canyon West.

Owned by the Hualapai tribe, whose reservation spans more than 100 miles (160km) of the Grand Canyon rim, this recreation area is outside the bounds of Grand Canyon National Park. It's thus one of the only places where you can take a helicopter ride into the canyon.

The main attraction is the gasp-inducing **Skywalk** – the first in a number of developments planned for the reservation. Opened in 2007, this cantilevered glass-and-steel walkway curves out from the canyon's rim. The horse-shoe-shaped deck gives a bird's-eye view of the nearby Colorado River, 4,000ft (1,200m) below. Note that cameras and other possessions aren't allowed on the Skywalk; these must be stashed in lockers while you 'walk on air'.

To get back to Las Vegas, retrace your route, drive over the Hoover Dam, and head back to Highway 93.

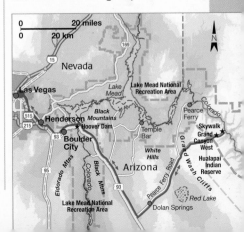

The area around Sedona, Arizona, is nicknamed 'Red Rock Country'

### Sedona

Dramatic red-rock formations surround this New Age community, a major stop on the Southwest's spiritual-seeker circuit. Whether or not you believe in power vortexes or healing crystals, the natural beauty of **Sedona** ⓽ is undeniable. At sunset, the sandstone begins to glow.

It's quite easy to get out into the desert from town. Highway 89A swoops through the Verde Valley to Sedona, passing fantastical rock formations. Just north of town is a turn-off to **Slide Rock State Park** (tel: 928-282-3034; www.pr.state.az.us/parks/SLRO; daily 8am–4pm; charge), where you'll find a great swimming hole with a natural rock chute. Several hiking trails kick off here, too.

Hundreds of pueblo ruins lie hidden in the red rocks. Some of the easiest to visit are southwest of town, in the Coconino National Forest, at the **Honanki Heritage Site** (tel: 928-527-3600; www.redrockcountry.

org; daily 10am–6pm; charge). The indigenous Sinagua tribe lived here from roughly AD1100 to 1300; the remains of their dwellings are tucked into cliff faces. You can also glimpse some ancient petroglyphs on the rock

## Tucson

Known locally as the Old Pueblo, Tucson was founded by the Spanish in 1775. Like Phoenix, **Tucson** ⓽ is ringed by dramatic mountain scenery, but unlike its northern neighbor, it has retained more of its Mexican character.

You can get a feel for the city's past in the **Presidio Historic District** downtown, around the intersection of Broadway Boulevard and Stone Avenue. Preserved 19th-century homes, colorful adobe, and portions of the original Presidio wall betray a complex history.

One of the best ways to learn about the surrounding desert is to visit the **Arizona-Sonora Desert Museum**

Picture the tumbleweed and old shutters creaking in the wind on rusty hinges: Arizona has dozens of ghost towns, the remnants of abandoned mining camps. Most are concentrated in the northwest and southeast corners of the state. While many are just a bit of rubble, several atmospheric locations still exist.

**Tombstone** (www.cityoftombstone.com) is one of the best-known – a hokey tourist magnet but one with serious history. 'The Town too Tough to Die' was the scene of the infamous OK Corral gunfight in 1881.

**Goldfield Ghost Town** (www.goldfield ghosttown.com) is relatively easy to reach as it's not far from Phoenix. With gold-panning and staged weekend gunfights, it plays up to its Old West history.

Once a gold-mining boomtown, **Oatman** (www.oatmangoldroad.org) still has a handful of residents, as well as wild burros roaming the streets. It's a popular stop for road-trippers on Route 66 through western Arizona. Many call in at the Oatman Hotel, where you can get a snack and an earful of ghost stories.

---

(tel: 520-883-2702; www.desert museum.org; June–Aug Sun–Fri 7am–4.30pm, Sat 7am–10pm, Sept and Mar–May daily 7.30am–5pm, Oct–Feb daily 8.30am–5pm; charge). The museum is only a small part of this organization; there's also a large

zoo, garden, hummingbird aviary, and nature trail, with all sorts of local flora and fauna.

### Saguaro National Park

Once the Arizona-Sonora Desert Museum has filled you in on the background information, venture out to **Saguaro National Park** (tel: 520-733-5158; www.nps.gov/sagu; daily 7am–sunset; charge), which bookends Tucson. This offers a rare chance to see the giant saguaros, those tall, branching cacti that symbolize the Old West. The saguaros are indigenous to the Sonora Desert, and this park preserves large stands of these increasingly rare plants. Of the two halves of the park, the western half, called the **Tucson Mountain District,** has the best views of the saguaro forests. From the **Bajada Loop Drive,** a 6-mile (10km) unpaved road, visitors get postcard-perfect views of the prickly giants.

The Roman Catholic cathedral of St Augustine, on South Stone Avenue in Tucson

Texas and the Southwest

# ACCOMMODATIONS

In the Sun Belt, hotels in the cities and the countryside often have opposing high seasons. Lodgings for the Grand Canyon and Monument Valley, for example, book up many months in advance of the summer tourism surge, while business centers such as Houston often have lower rates and more available rooms in the summer. In some beautiful spots, like Sedona, rooms can be pretty basic for the price; guests are paying for the views instead. For high-end resorts, visitors should look to Tucson and Phoenix.

## Houston

**Hotel Icon**
220 Main Street
*Tel: 713-224-4266*
**www.hotelicon.com**
A downtown hotel, it is spacious and colorful; bathrooms have claw-foot or whirlpool tubs with 'bath butlers' ready to draw a bubble bath. **$$–$$$**

**Hotel Zaza**
5701 Main Street
*Tel: 713-526-1991*
**www.hotelzazahouston.com**
Located within Houston's Museum District, Zaza channels artistic flair with dramatically designed guest rooms and excellent views. The specialty suites (**$$$$**) are done up like stage sets in various international themes, from Morocco to the West Indies. **$$$**

## San Antonio

**Menger Hotel**
204 Alamo Plaza
*Tel: 210-223-4361*
**http://mengerhotel.com**
Built in 1859, The Menger retains its Victorian-era lobby and other period features. Some rooms are filled with antiques while others are modern additions. **$$**

## Austin

**The Driskill**
604 Brazos Street
*Tel: 512-474-5911*
**www.driskillhotel.com**
Austin's original grand hotel was built in 1886. Now it's polished and clubby, and situated within walking distance of Sixth Street's music spots. **$$–$$$**

## Santa Fe

**Inn of the Anasazi**
113 Washington Avenue
*Tel: 505-988-3030*
**www.innoftheanasazi.com**
Drawing on the aesthetics of Navajo culture, this hotel near the Plaza stands out for its Native American accents, from the woven rugs to the artwork. Each room has a beamed ceiling, *kiva* fireplace, and four-poster bed. **$$$–$$$$**

## Grand Canyon National Park

**Desert View Campground**
Off Highway 64, 26 miles (42km) east of Grand Canyon Village
*Tel: 1-877-444-6777*
**www.recreation.gov**
Open May through mid-October, this campground has spectacular canyon views from a watchtower. **$**

**El Tovar Hotel**
South Rim
*Tel: 928-638-2631*
**www.grandcanyonlodges.com**
Run by Xanterra, the park's concessionaire, this 1905 log-and-stone landmark is by far the park's nicest hotel option. It has a good restaurant and eye-popping canyon views from the lounge. **$$–$$$**

## Monument Valley

**View Hotel & Restaurant**
4 miles (6.5km) east of Highway 163
*Tel: 435-727-3470*
**www.monumentvalleyview.com**
As the only hotel in Monument Valley, this is the best seat in the house. Every room has a stunning view. **$$$**

## Phoenix

**Royal Palms Resort and Spa**
5200 East Camelback Road
*Tel: 602-840-3610*
**www.royalpalmshotel.com**
The Royal Palms is especially atmospheric, with towering palms, Spanish mission-style rooms, and an open-air spa. **$$$**

## Sedona

El Portal Sedona
95 Portal Lane
*Tel: 928-203-9405*
**www.elportalsedona.com**
Built to look ancient, with thick adobe walls, this exquisite boutique inn is more of an

Royal Palms Resort and Spa

Arts-and-Crafts-style hacienda inside, with modern conveniences such as Wi-fi. **$$$**

## Tucson

**Canyon Ranch Health Resort**
8600 E. Rockcliff Road
*Tel: 1-800-742-9000*
**www.canyonranch.com**
Canyon Ranch is practically a verb, shorthand for 'to lose weight and rejuvenate at a luxurious retreat in a stunning location'. **$$$$**

# RESTAURANTS

Tex-Mex and Southwestern cooking both draw from Mexican cuisines but add their own twists. When it comes to Texas barbecue, the best spots are often the humblest, with little more than paper plates and picnic tables. In a beef-heavy region, Austin is a rare vegetarian-friendly town.

### Restaurant price categories

Prices are for a main course meal for one, excluding alcoholic drinks:

**$** = less than $15
**$$** = $15–$25
**$$$** = $25–$50
**$$$$** = more than $50

## Houston

**Brennan's of Houston**
3300 Smith Street
*Tel: 713-522-9711*
**www.brennanshouston.com**
This place has taken many knocks (most recently, burning down in 2008's hurricane), but has been resurrected for a loyal public. It's a gracious, New Orleans-style space with a Texas-Creole menu, including turtle soup and crawfish in season. **$$$–$$$$**

**Ninfa's on Navigation**
2704 Navigation Boulevard
*Tel: 713-228-1175*
**http://mamaninfas.com**
Said to be the original home of the fajita, this casual spot is mobbed by both visitors and locals. The kitchen turns out plenty of Tex-Mex favorites, including enchiladas, tacos, and quesadillas, while there's a constant shake of margaritas at the bar.
**$–$$**

Food and music at Mi Tierra, San Antonio

### San Antonio
**Mi Tierra**
218 Produce Row
*Tel: 210-225-1262*
**www.mitierracafe.com**
This local favorite serves everything from breakfast huevos rancheros to late-night enchiladas. **$–$$**

### Austin
**Threadgill's**
301 W. Riverside Drive
*Tel: 512-472-9304*
**www.threadgills.com**
Serving up musical memorabilia along with Southern cooking. The great jukebox makes the chicken-fried steak even tastier. **$–$$**

### Santa Fe
**Aqua Santa**
451 W. Alameda Street

*Tel: 505-982-6297*
**(No website)**
In a cozy adobe dining room, guests tuck in to seasonal, sophisticated dishes such as Caesar salad with fried oysters and delicate panna cotta. **$$$**

### Phoenix
**Chelsea's Kitchen**
5040 N. 40th Street
*Tel: 602-957-2555*
**www.chelseaskitchenaz.com**
In its minimalist ranch-house dining room, Chelsea's serves American crowd-pleasers, such as short ribs and wedge salads. **$–$$**

### Sedona
**Elote Café**
771 Route 179
*Tel: 928-203-0105*
**www.elotecafe.com**
With locally sourced ingredients, this food stands out, especially the namesake dish, *elote* (corn) roasted and topped with cheese, spicy sauce, and lime juice. **$$**

### Tucson
**Janos and J Bar**
3770 E. Sunrise Drive
*Tel: 520-615-6100*
**www.janos.com**
Janos, the more formal restaurant, splashes out on dishes such as diver's scallops and Mexican lime tart. Next door, the more casual bar offers seasonal tasting menus. **$$–$$$$**

## NIGHTLIFE AND ENTERTAINMENT

The region's honky-tonk bars, independent breweries, and old-fashioned dancehalls keep the nightlife scene firmly grounded. Austin is known for its music scene, with more live music venues than you can hit in a month. But there are highbrow pleasures, too, including the renowned opera companies of Houston and Santa Fe.

### Bars
**La Carafe**
813 Congress Street, Houston
*Tel: 713-229-9399*

Set aside the longneck beers and head for this historic building for a wine tasting instead. Candlelight and an eclectic jukebox create an atmosphere of romance and fun.

### The Lost Leaf
914 N. 5th Street, Phoenix
*Tel: 602-258-0014*
**www.thelostleaf.org**
Hung with local art and often humming with live music, the Leaf is known for its huge roster of beers on tap.

## Live music and dancing
### Broken Spoke
3201 S. Lamar, Austin
*Tel: 512-442-6189*
**www.brokenspokeaustintx.com**
A timeless Texas dancehall, with boot-scootin' and great honky-tonk music.

### The Landing
123 Losoya Street, San Antonio
*Tel: 210-223-7266*
**www.landing.com**
This River Walk institution is one of the country's oldest jazz clubs, and it's still among the best.

### Stubb's Bar-B-Q
801 Red River, Austin
*Tel: 512-480-8341*
**http://stubbsaustin.com**
How could you beat barbecue and outstanding music? Greats such as Lucinda Williams hit the outdoor stage with the scent of pork in the air.

## Performing arts
### Alley Theatre
615 Texas Avenue, Houston
*Tel: 713-220-5700*
**www.alleytheatre.org**
A much-lauded company that presents both classic and modern works, ranging from *Amadeus* to the hilarious *Santaland Diaries*.

### Houston Grand Opera
550 Prairie Street
*Tel: 713-228-6737*
**www.houstongrandopera.org**
Sharing the downtown Wortham Theater Center with the Houston Ballet, this opera company is known for staging experimental new work alongside classics.

### Santa Fe Opera
301 Opera Drive, off US 84
*Tel: 505-986-5900*
**www.santafeopera.org**
This is an opera house with a difference, as it is partially open-air. As such, it frequently pairs stellar performances with literally stellar night-sky views.

# SPORTS AND ACTIVITIES

There are dozens of ways to have an adventure in the Southwest's stunning landscapes. Despite the heat (which should be taken seriously), you can join millions of visitors in exploring trails, rafting on rivers, and cycling in the cities. Arizona also has a special allure for golfers.

## Baseball
### Houston Astros
501 Crawford Street
*Tel: 713-259-8000*
**http://houston.astros.mlb.com**
With its name quickly changed from Enron Field to Minute Maid Park in 2002, Houston's downtown stadium is a comfortable spot with a retracting roof. The home team is a member of the National League.

## Bicycling
### Fair Wheel Bikes
1110 E. 6th Street, Tucson
*Tel: 520-623-3761*
**http://fairwheelbikes.com**
Tucson's a bike-friendly city; the pros at this rental and retail store are a fount of information. They can direct you to paved in-town paths or, for the more intrepid, to nearby mountain-biking trails.

Hualapai River Runners in Peach Springs, Arizona

**West End Bicycles**
5427 Blossom, Houston
*Tel: 713-861-2271*
**www.westendbikes.com**
Rent bikes here to hit the hike-and-bike trail in Houston's Buffalo Bayou, a loop with one end in downtown, near the Theater District. The trail is dotted with sculptures.

## Fishing
**Bryan Ray's South Padre Island Fishing Adventures**
One Padre Blvd, SeaRanch Marina
*Tel: 956-433-6469*
**www.fishingadventuresspi.com**
Expert Ray takes clients to either the bay or offshore waters for game fish such as tarpon and king mackerel.

## Golf
**Boulders Golf Club**
Carefree, 33 miles (53km) north of Phoenix, AZ
*Tel: 480-488-9028*
**www.bouldersclub.com**
Two award-winning courses studded with massive boulders.

## White-water rafting
**Hualapai River Runners**
Peach Springs, AZ
*Tel: 1-888-868-9378*
http://grandcanyonwest.com/rafting.php
These one-day rafting trips are organized in the western end of the Grand Canyon. All equipment is provided and full instruction and supervision is given.

# TOURS

There's lots to explore, and there are plenty of ways to do it, from 'flightseeing' by helicopter or biplane, to taking a jeep tour through the desert, to good, old-fashioned walking and hiking.

## Flightseeing
**Sedona Air Tours**
Sedona, AZ
*Tel: 1-888-866-7433*
**www.sedonaairtours.com**
Though they're not cheap, these tours are worth it as the red rocks look even more surreal from above. Both helicopter and open-cockpit biplane are available.

## Jeep tours
**Pink Jeep Tours**
Sedona, AZ
*Tel: 1-800-873-3662*
**www.pinkjeep.com**
A four-wheel drive is the best way to see the red rocks and ruins around Sedona. But do the jeeps really need to be painted this screaming pink?

**Southwest Desert Adventures**
Phoenix, AZ
*Tel: 480-962-6620*
**www.yellowjeeps.com**
Guides drive groups through the Sonoran desert, sharing info on local ecology and history. Other tours include horseback riding, ballooning, and much more.

## Walking and hiking tours
**Austin Ghost Tours**
*Tel: 512-853-9826*
**www.austinghosttours.com**
Not for the faint-hearted, these tours offer a chilling spin on local history.

**Grand Canyon Field Institute**
Grand Canyon, AZ
*Tel: 866-471-4435*
**www.grandcanyon.org/fieldinstitute**
This organization leads educational hikes covering geology, archaeology, ecology, and other specialties.

**Discover Houston Tours**
*Tel: 713-222-9255*
**www.discoverhoustontours.com**
Although Houston is not very pedestrian-friendly, guide Sandra Lord has devised several downtown theme tours, such as a pub crawl.

# FESTIVALS AND EVENTS

In addition to the events below, communities in the Southwest celebrate several Mexican holidays, such as Cinco de Mayo (May 5) and Mexican Independence Day (September 16). At Christmas, *las posadas* performances are held, a parade and ritual re-enactment of Mary and Joseph's search for shelter.

## January
**River Walk Mud Festival**
River Walk, San Antonio
**www.thesanantonioriverwalk.com**
Every year, when the river is partially drained for maintenance, parties and parades break out in San Antonio.

## Late Feb–early Mar
**Houston Livestock Show and Rodeo**
Reliant Center, 8334 Fannin Street
**www.hlsr.com**
Well over two million fans pack in for music acts such as Miley Cyrus, barbecue contests, calf scrambles and roping, and a gargantuan livestock show and rodeo.

## March
**South by Southwest (SXSW)**
Austin
**http://sxsw.com**
A vast showcase of up-and-coming musicians, indie films, and the latest tech breakthroughs, this is one of the country's hottest and most creative annual events.

## April
**San Antonio Fiesta**
*Tel: 210-227-5191*
**www.fiesta-sa.org**
With over 100 parades, music shows and other events throughout town, San Antonio's biggest annual festival celebrates the heroes of the Alamo.

## August
**Santa Fe Indian Market**
*Tel: 505-983-5220*
**http://swaia.org**
August is a good time to visit Santa Fe, as hundreds of artisan booths fill the blocks around the Plaza for the country's largest Native American festival and crafts fair.

## September
**Austin City Limits Music Festival**
Zilker Park, Austin
**www.aclfestival.com**
The park throbs with dozens of rock acts – mostly cutting-edge but with a few classic groups mixed in.

# The West

The Western states include some of the country's most exciting playgrounds, catering to the crazy, the easy-going, and everyone in between. Las Vegas blinks and twinkles with casinos, Aspen is home to the ultra-rich and a few intrepid skiers, and the Rocky Mountains dazzle with the beauty of America's back country. This is the place for extreme lifestyles to play well and play hard.

## Las Vegas and Denver

**Population:** Las Vegas: 584,000; Denver: 600,000

**Local dialing codes:** Las Vegas: 702; Denver: 303 and 720

**Local tourist offices:** Las Vegas: 3150 Paradise Road; tel: 702-892-7575; www.visitlasvegas.com. Denver: 1600 California Street, Unit 6; tel: 303-892-1505; www.denver.org

**Main police stations:** Las Vegas: 400 South MLK Boulevard; tel: 702-795-3111. Denver: 1331 Cherokee Street; tel: 720-913-6010

**Main post offices:** Las Vegas: 1001 East Sunset Road; Denver: 951 20th Street

**Hospitals:** Las Vegas: Sunrise Hospital & Medical Center; 3186 South Maryland Parkway; tel: 702-731-8000. Denver: University of Colorado Hospital; 1635 Aurora Court; tel: 720-848-0000

**Local newspapers/listings magazines:** The daily *Las Vegas Review-Journal* covers the news, while *Las Vegas Weekly* is the free alternative newspaper for a racier take on the Strip's antics and events. *The Denver Post* is Colorado's largest daily newspaper; the free magazine-style *Westword* provides reviews of arts events and comprehensive entertainment listings

**Time zones:** Las Vegas: PST; Denver: MST

Since the 19th century, travelers have been awestruck by the Western landscapes, from the sharp ridges of the Rockies to the thrilling canyons in Utah. Yellowstone National Park's fgeysers and hot springs remind visitors of the Earth's forces.

Meanwhile, Las Vegas, the country's most extravagant gambling center, rises up out of the desert in a glittering mass of light and sound.

## Las Vegas

**Las Vegas ❶** is one of those myth-laden towns that everybody should visit at least once. The name conjures up wild nights lit by neon, showgirls and stacks of gambling chips, extravagant dinners, and bargain buffets the morning after. The city has gone through cycles of adults-only decadence and more family-friendly promotions. For now, it's got a foot in both worlds, touting kid-friendly entertainment alongside the naughtier possibilities of 'what happens in Vegas, stays in Vegas'. By contrast, the city's surburbs are becoming popular with retirees, who are attracted by the sunny weather and vacation atmosphere.

### The Strip

Las Vegas Boulevard, otherwise known as **the Strip**, encompasses 4 miles (6.5km) of casinos, hotels, and giant neon signs for girlie shows, concerts, and other splashy headliners.

This is where fortunes are staked, won, and more often lost to the house.

A walk or drive down the Strip takes in the monuments of Vegas. Some casinos recreate the wonders of the world: the Great Pyramid at Luxor, a half-scale reproduction of the Eiffel Tower at Paris; the scaled-down pastiche of the Manhattan skyline at New York–New York. Others serve up historic fantasy – most famously Caesars Palace, with its Ancient Rome theme. Still others go for elegant grandeur. Huge fountains shimmy

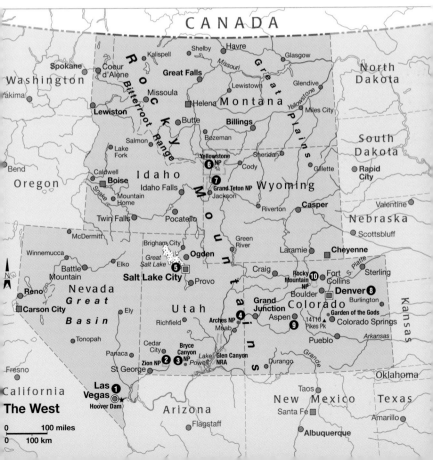

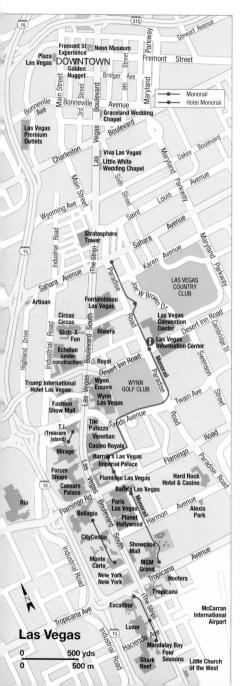

Las Vegas

| Monorail |
| Hotel Monorail |

0 ___ 500 yds
0 ___ 500 m

through a light show at the Italianate Bellagio, and the Wynn Las Vegas includes a man-made lake. It's a name worth remembering, as casino entrepreneur Steve Wynn has had a big hand in Vegas's development. The 'King of the Strip' runs several of the biggest and most lavish properties.

To lure your wallet out even when you're away from the gaming tables, several casinos have luxury shopping arcades. The Via Bellagio, for instance, musters up boutique after boutique of international luxury brands: Gucci, Armani, Prada, Dior. Over at Caesars Palace, the Forum Shops turn shopping into a Romanesque theme park, with a triumphal arch, animatronic fountains, and an aquarium.

### Downtown

Unlike the Strip, downtown Vegas isn't all wall-to-wall resorts, even though it does still offer plenty of casinos and showmanship. The focus is **Fremont Street**, which is otherwise known as 'Glitter Gulch' for its blinding neon. In the lit-up windows along this stretch, people endlessly tug the levers of the one-armed bandit slot machines, hoping to win the jackpot.

Between Main Street and the Strip twinkles the **Fremont Street Experience**, a five-block stretch with food kiosks and craft vendors. Above the street arches is a steel-mesh canopy; during the day, this shoots out a cooling mist, while at night, it blazes with a free sound-and-laser-light show.

Las Vegas's signature signs are now celebrated as an art form, championed by the **Neon Museum** (tel: 702-387-6366; http://neonmuseum.

The glittering lights of Las Vegas Boulevard, otherwise known as the Strip

org). The organization restores classic signs, several of which can be seen along Fremont Street, like the golden Aladdin's lamp. To see the 'neon boneyard,' where old signs are stored out in the desert, contact the museum for a tour.

## Utah

An otherworldly landscape defines southern Utah. Sculpted by wind and water, the reddish sandstone forms arches, spires, and balancing rocks. These stark shapes form the backdrop of beloved national parks such as Zion

### Las Vegas city transportation

 **Airport:** McCarran International Airport (LAS); tel: 702-261-5211; www.mccarran.com; 3 miles (4.8km) from the southern end of the Strip. Shuttle: There are many shuttle services available at McCarran, including Bell Transportation; travel times vary according to the drop-off points for other passengers; $6.50 to $8 per person. Taxi: 8 to 15 minutes to Strip locations but longer to Las Vegas Boulevard, roughly $20

 **Monorail:** The Las Vegas Monorail, tel: 702-699-8299; www.lvmonorail.com, can be the fastest way to get up and down the Strip when traffic is running slow. The Monorail arrives every 5 to 10 minutes and runs until 2am (3am on weekend nights). One-way fares are $5, with one-day ($12) and three-day ($28) passes available at the vending machines at each station. There are also short, free monorail systems between several of the hotel properties on the western side of the Strip

 **Shuttles:** Several hotel/casino properties operate free shuttle services – particularly those not on the Strip. The catch? They depart anywhere from every 20 minutes to every hour and they only connect their sister properties. For example, a shuttle at the Rio can take you to the Strip via Harrah's or Bally's/Paris, while the Hard Rock shuttle can take you to the Forum Shops. Wherever you stay, ask for information regarding any shuttles, as schedules and routes are subject to change

 **Taxis:** These are an exceedingly popular way to get around, and the best way to hail one is from the line in front of the main entrance to any casino or hotel. Fares cost $3.20 for the meter drop, then $2.60 per mile, but fares can mount up quickly when you account for traffic on Las Vegas Boulevard. If you need to call for a pickup, try Yellow Checker Star cabs at 702-873-2000 or Desert Cab at 702-386-9102

## Las Vegas wedding chapels

Las Vegas first gained traction in the early 1900s as a place to get a fast divorce. The flip side of that coin was quickie weddings. Calling itself the 'Wedding Capital of the World', Vegas hosts more than five percent of all American marriages. You can tie the knot in a ceremony led by an Elvis impersonator or get hitched at a drive-through window. Here are two of the Strip's top chapels:

- **Little White Wedding Chapel** (tel: 702-382-5943; www.alittlewhite chapel.com). Famous couples include Bruce Willis and Demi Moore. Pop star Britney Spears had her wee-hours wedding here, too.
- **Graceland Wedding Chapel** (tel: 702-382-0091; www.gracelandchapel. com). Elvis didn't marry here, but the owner was a friend. It became the first chapel to launch weddings officiated by Elvis impersonators.

The best way to 'read the rocks' is to drive into Zion from the west, along Highway 9, following the course of the pretty Virgin River to the park's South Entrance. Along the way, you'll see different shades of vermilion, pink, and orangey-red in the rocks. Not far into the entrance sits the **Zion Canyon Visitor Center** (tel: 435-772-3256; www.nps.gov/zion; Memorial Day–Labor Day daily 8am–7.30pm, late Apr–late May and Sept–Oct daily 8am–6pm, Nov–mid-Apr daily 8am–5pm; free), which is overshadowed by huge rock formations.

Highway 9 then becomes the **Zion-Mount Carmel Highway**, the easiest way to drive through the park. A free shuttle also runs around a scenic route April through October. Look out en route for the massive towers of the **Great White Throne** – the park's signature formation.

Neon lights are a common feature at Las Vegas wedding chapels

and Bryce Canyon. The northern part of the state is more urban. Salt Lake City is now one of the up-and-coming cities of the West, with its easy access to high-quality skiing. It's also the headquarters of the Church of Jesus Christ of Latter-day Saint.

### Zion National Park

This spectacular cliff-and-canyon landscape in southern Utah is full of unexpected sights, including one of the world's largest natural arches. **Zion National Park** ❷ (tel: 435-772-3256; www.nps.gov/zion; daily 24 hours; charge) is nature at its most eloquent, with sandstone monoliths, narrow slot canyons, and areas of dense greenery.

Bryce Canyon's distinctive geological feature are the *hoodoos*, carved by wind erosion

To get a sense of the park's different ecosystems, it's best to do a one-day hike. The **Emerald Pool Trail** leads to waterfalls and lush pools. The easy, paved **Riverside Walk** follows the Virgin River. The pavement ends at the **Gateway to the Narrows**, a tougher trail that involves slogging along the river through narrow canyon walls.

### Bryce Canyon National Park

A geologic fantasyland of technicolored spires, natural stone bridges, and sky-filled windows, carved into the orange-colored cliffs – Bryce has remarkable vistas at every turn. The story goes that Ebenezer Bryce, a 19th-century Mormon settler, complained that this landscape was 'a hell of a place to lose a cow!' That beautiful frustration is now named for him, **Bryce Canyon National Park** ❸ (tel: 435-834-5322; www.nps.gov/brca; daily 24 hours; charge).

Unlike Zion, which was eroded by water, the amphitheaters here were shaped by freeze-and-thaw cycles, and wind erosion. The park is also noted for its *hoodoos* – spires of rock, some of them entirely free-standing. You can view the park's cliffs by driving along the 18-mile (29km) scenic route, **Highway 63**. A free shuttle is also offered from May through early October. The drive follows the edge of the plateau through pine forests.

There are several overlooks and trailheads so that you can look or climb down into the bowls. From the **Sunset Point** overlook, for example, you can clamber down the **Queen's Garden Trail**, giving you a fresh look at formations such as Queen Victoria, which looks like the monarch in profile. This trail connects with the **Navajo Loop Trail**, which leads down to the canyon floor, with views of the Thor's Hammer balancing rock.

## How to make a rock arch

The key to the stone arches is something you have in your kitchen: salt. Thick salt deposits were left below the earth's surface about 300 million years ago, in the area known as Paradox Basin. Slowly, the salt began to bulge upward, through a dozen layers of rock, cracking them and letting groundwater seep in.

Over millennia, water and ice weakened the rock and, eventually, the salt domes began to collapse. Freezing and thawing continued to sculpt the rock, widening joints and molding the sandstone into the curious shapes you see today. At the Cove of Caves, for instance, the back of the largest cave will one day become an arch. Iron in the sandstone gives the rock that reddish tint.

New arches are still forming and rocks sometimes fall. Very occasionally, you hear sharp cracking noises – if so, move away from the rocks quickly!

### Arches National Park

More than 2,000 rock arches spring up at **Arches National Park ❹** (tel: 435-719-2299; www.nps.gov/arch; daily 24 hours; charge). There are more natural sandstone arches here than anywhere else in the world – along with fins, pinnacles, and other fantastic shapes. The park is small enough to explore in a day, thanks to its scenic drive, pullouts, and short hikes, but you can always take longer.

Gen up first on the red-rock giants by stopping at the **Arches Visitor Center** (tel: 435-719-2299; www.nps.gov/arch; Apr–Oct daily 7.30am–6.30pm, Nov–Mar daily 8am–4.30pm; free). From here, embark on the 18-mile (29km) **Scenic Drive**, watching the sunlight tint the rocks

The breathtaking Double Arch at Arches National Park

Salt Lake City is nestled against the mountains

salmon, orange, and rose. You can spot many of the most dramatic arches and other formations from the road, including the Three Gossips, Skyline Arch, and Balanced Rock. From **Panorama Point**, you can see much of the park in one swoop. The **Devils Garden** area, at the end of the road, is the tightest jumble of jagged rocks.

A few popular arches are a short hike away from the road. From the Devils Garden parking lot, for instance, take the **Landscape Arch trail** to the world's longest natural arch, shiny with 'desert varnish'.

### Salt Lake City

Years ago, **Salt Lake City** ❺ had the reputation of a strait-laced pro-vincial town. After the 2002 Winter Olympics, though, its reputation as a vibrant city has grown. New invest-ment and booming winter-sports resorts have swung a spotlight on to SLC. But what makes Salt Lake

unique is that it is the home of the Church of Jesus Christ of Latter-day Saints, also called LDS, whose members are called Mormons. Followers of the spiritual leader Brigham Young settled here in 1847, believing that the salt flats between the Wasatch Mountains and the Great Salt Lake would be the new Zion. That faith still influences many aspects of city life and you'll see locals dressed in conservative clothing.

**Temple Square** is the center of Utah's capital. A high wall surrounds the 10 acre (4 hectare) compound; inside are the core Mormon buildings, including the Temple, Tabernacle, and Visitors' Center. The granite **Temple,** with its sharp towers, is closed to non-believers. However, anyone may visit the **Tabernacle** (tel: 801-240-4872; http://lds.org/placestovisit; daily 9am–9pm; free). The long turtleback dome provides wonderful acoustics for the renowned Mormon Tabernacle Choir.

The Great Salt Lake itself is worth the drive. About 15 miles (24km) west of Salt Lake City, along I-80, you'll reach the entrance to **Great Salt Lake State Park** (tel: 801-250-1898; www.utah.com/stateparks/greatsaltlake.htm; Apr–Sept daily sunrise–sunset, Oct–Mar daily 8am–5pm; charge). This takes you to the marina on the largest saltwater lake in the western hemisphere. The water is so saline that swimmers bob like apples on the surface. It is also home to thousands of birds and contains brine shrimp.

### Lake Powell

A trip to Lake Powell will push your eyeballs into overdrive. The colors are intense, especially under strong sun, with the green water and red rocks above creating a striking contrast.

The lake comes under the umbrella of the **Glen Canyon National Recreation Area** (tel: 928-608-6200; www.nps.gov/glca; daily 24 hours; charge). It's the second-largest man-made lake in the country, and with its dozens of side canyons, it has 1,960 miles (3,154km) of shoreline. The best way to experience the lake is by boat. Six marinas buzz with visitors all year round, though especially so in summer. Of these, Bullfrog and Wahweap have the widest range of services, which even include houseboat rentals. The concession-aire Aramark (tel: 1-888-896-3829; www.lakepowell.com) manages both marinas.

## Yellowstone and Grand Teton National Parks

Yellowstone, the world's first national park, established in 1872, has been famous for well over a century, but still retains the capac-ity to surprise visitors. As one of the most geologically active spots

A houseboat on Lake Powell, which is set within the Glen Canyon National Recreation Area

encompasses the broad valley of Jackson Hole stretching out below.

### Yellowstone National Park

No amount of superlatives or statistics can prepare you for **Yellowstone National Park ❻** (tel: 307-344-7381; www.nps.gov/yell; daily 24 hours; charge). Its 2.2 million acres (890,300 hectares) protect over 10,000 thermal features as well as diverse wildlife, including the last wild bison in America. Most of the park extends across a high plateau, with the Gallatin mountain range to the northwest and the Absarokas to the east. Within those bounds are lakes, rivers, and the steaming, gurgling geysers, hot springs, and mud pots. Sometimes you can follow your nose, as the thermal features can give off a strong sulfur smell.

The main driving route through the park is **Grand Loop Road**,

on earth, it is constantly evolving, with geysers erupting and hot springs bubbling up and changing course. Adjacent to Yellowstone are the soaring, spiny peaks of Grand Teton National Park, which also

---

## Yellowstone's wildlife

Bring your binoculars – Yellowstone's diverse and abundant animal population can have you swiveling at any moment.

The most iconic inhabitant is the **bison,** with its high, shaggy shoulders, curved horns, and dispassionate stare. Nearly wiped out in the early 1900s, the country's only wild herd now numbers around 4,000. They're often seen in the Lamar and Hayden valleys.

**Wolves** were controversially reintroduced to the park in 1995, partially to help reduce the **elk** population in the

natural way. Packs tend to hunt in the Lamar Valley.

Look to the treetops and you might see a **bald eagle's** nest. The eagles' bright-white heads make them relatively easy to spot; they hunt fish in Yellowstone Lake and along the rivers.

Both **black and grizzly bears** also live in the park, sticking to high meadows and forests. If you see one, give it a wide berth, make some noise so that it becomes aware of your presence, move very slowly… and you'll have a great story to tell.

which forms a rough figure of eight. The **Upper Geyser Basin** along the Firehole River is a hotbed of thermal activity, with more than 200 spouters within a range of a couple of miles. The undisputed star of the park is the **Old Faithful Geyser**, which still blows every 60 to 90 minutes. Around this geyser grew the park's first major tourist center, Old Faithful Village. In 2010, a new **Old Faithful Visitor Information Center** (tel: 307-344-7381; www. nps.gov/yell; mid-Apr–May daily 9am–6pm, June–Sept daily 8am–8pm, Oct–early Apr daily 9am–5pm; free) opened, with geyser-eruption predictions and interesting exhibits on how thermal features work.

A few miles north of Old Faithful gleams the brilliantly colored **Grand Prismatic Spring**. Dubbed 'Hell's Half-Acre', it's a psychedelic sight, with brilliant orange edges around a blue pool.

Arizona isn't the only place with a Grand Canyon. The **Grand Canyon of the Yellowstone** is testimony to the awesome power of nature, with its tremendous waterfalls and its depth of 1,200ft (370m). Red Rock Point and Artist Point are the best overlooks of the vertiginous **Lower Falls**.

### Grand Teton National Park

The Tetons is the youngest range in the Rockies. The peaks rise abruptly from the plain to a giddy 13,770ft (4,200m). The steep granite spires

## Denver

_[Map of Denver showing:]_

Coors Field, Wynkoop St, Wazee St, 13th St, 20th Street, Blake Street, Market Street, Larimer St, 22nd Street, 21st Street, 19th St

**LOWER DOWNTOWN (LODO)**

Sakura Square, Arapahoe Street, Lawrence Street, Park Avenue West, Broadway

Denver Bus Terminal, Main Post Office, 17th St Plaza, Denver Place Plaza, Curtis Street, Stout Street, California Street, Welton Street

Tabor Center, SKYLINE PARK, Denver Place, 20th St

Independence Plaza, D&F Tower, US Bank Tower, Equitable Bldg, 1801 California, E. 20th Ave

Federal Reserve Bank, Champa St, 18th/Stout, 18th/California, First Interstate North, E. 19th Avenue

16th/Stout, Dominion Plaza, Wells Fargo

Denver Performing Arts Complex, Denver Conv. & Visitor Bureau, 16th/California, Masonic Bldg, Paramount Theatre, Brown Palace Hotel, E. 18th Ave, Lincoln Street, Grant Street

Temple Buell Theatre, 14th/Stout, Denver Pavilions, 14th/California, Republic Plaza Tower, World Trade Center, E. 17th Ave

Colorado Convention Center, Welton Street, 13th St, Tremont Place, Court Place, Glenarm Place, Curtis Place, Stout Place, Sherman Street

Firefighters Museum, Pioneer Monument, Denver Post Tower, RTD Civic Center Bus Station, E. 16th Ave

W. Colfax Avenue, Galapago St, Speer Blvd, Fox Street, Cherokee St, WAR MEMORIAL PARK, E. Colfax Ave

US Mint, CIVIC CENTER PARK, Bronco Buster, Greek Theater, Colorado Veterans' Monument, State Capitol

W. 14th Ave, Delaware Street, Camera Obscura, Indigos, Bannock Street, Denver Art Museum

W. 13th Avenue, Byers-Evans House, Denver Public Library, E. 13th Ave, Lincoln Street, Sherman Street

Inca St, Native American Trading Company, Clyfford Still Museum, W. 12th Avenue, History Colorado Center, Boulevard

0 — 400 yds
0 — 400 m

### Denver city transportation

✈ **Airport:** Denver International Airport (DIA); tel: 303-342-2000; http://flydenver.com; 23 miles (37km) northeast of downtown. Denver's Regional Transportation District's SkyRide buses (tel: 303-299-6000; www.rtd-denver.com): about 50 minutes to downtown on route AF, runs from 4.45am to 12.45am $9–13 depending on distance. Taxi: at least 45 minutes to downtown, around $55

🚕 **Taxis:** There are four taxi companies authorized to operate within Denver. The easiest to remember is Denver Yellow Cab, tel: 303-777-7777. Meter drop is $2.50, then $2.25 per mile

The San Juan Skyway Scenic Byway in Colorado

overlook the Snake River, Jackson Hole valley, and the rustic-ritzy town of Jackson. Most of this territory is protected as **Grand Teton National Park** ❼ (tel: 307-739-3300; www.nps. gov/grte; daily 24 hours; charge).

The two main routes through the park are **Highway 89**, along the Snake River, and **Teton Park Road**, which runs along the base of the mountains and skims by Jenny Lake. Both are breathtakingly scenic and have plenty of pullouts. Of the glacial lakes in the park, the two popular draws are the broad **Jackson Lake** and the petite **Jenny Lake**, both sapphire-blue and favorites of boaters.

The Grand Teton park has better opportunities for hikers, both serious and semi-serious, than Yellowstone. The Jenny Lake Loop is a classic day hike, with dazzling views of the lake all along its 7 miles (11km).

## Colorado

On a visit to the Rocky Mountain State in 1901, Theodore Roosevelt said, 'the scenery bankrupts the English language.' Those spectacular peaks, aspen forests, and vast grass-lands still dazzle, along with dynamic cities, gold-rush towns, and world-class ski resorts. Colorado is some-times called America's Switzerland, with over 50 peaks topping 14,000ft (3,660m) all crowded together.

### Denver

From humble beginnings as a gold-mining camp, **Denver** ❽ tips its hat to its roots with its State Capitol building, capped with a gold-leaf dome. The Wild West days are long gone, though. The city's architecture is relentlessly modern, beyond of a few historic pockets. What counts instead is the marvelous backdrop of the Rocky Mountains in the Mile-High City's backyard.

A few blocks from the Capitol sparkles the **Denver Art Museum** (tel: 720-865-5000; www.denverart museum.org; Tue–Thur and Sat–Sun 10am–5pm, Fri 10am–8pm; charge),

# CALIFORNIA ZEPHYR THROUGH THE ROCKIES

The *California Zephyr* captivates its passengers as it winds through the Rocky Mountains on one of the most scenic train routes in the whole of the country.

Jack Kerouac wrote about riding it and watching America roll past. Hank Williams and Ben Gibbard have sung about it. You might be inspired, too, by the epic *California Zephyr* train trip, running daily between Chicago and San Francisco, cutting through the Rockies and Sierra Nevada mountains.

Amtrak's *Zephyr* (tel: 1-800-872-7245; www.amtrak.com) takes its name and much of its route from a passenger-train service that was popular after World War II. Just like the original 'Silver Lady', the modern *Zephyr* gives riders an up-close look at dramatic mountain scenery – some of the same landscapes seen by wagon-train pioneers on their way west. (You can even spot Donner Lake, named for the ill-fated Donner Party, who resorted to cannibalism once they became snowbound.) It's also the only passenger train that covers some of the same ground as the first transcontinental railroad.

The full trip from Chicago to San Francisco takes 2.5 days, with 34 stops in seven states. It's possible to climb aboard for just a portion of the ride, though; the 8-hour section between Denver and Grand Junction, Colorado, has some of the most impressive views. The train uses double-decker cars, including a special sightseer lounge car with panoramic windows and comfortable seats.

Union Station in Denver, Colorado

## Tips

- Distance: 273 miles (439km)
- Time: 1 or 2 days
- Take advantage of the **Trails & Rails volunteers** who join the *Zephyr* during this Colorado segment. This initiative brings guides aboard scenic train routes. These knowledgeable folks describe the natural and cultural histories of the landscape as you pass by.

The California Zephyr runs along remote stretches of the Colorado River in the Rockies

On leaving Denver, the *Zephyr* climbs high into the Rockies. Darting in and out of dozens of tunnels, it zips through **South Boulder Canyon** in the Roosevelt National Forest.

The train burrows under the Continental Divide through the 6.2-mile (10km) **Moffat Tunnel**, the longest tunnel in the United States. The steep mountainsides of the Winter Park ski area hug the train tracks on the far side of the tunnel, en route to **Granby,** a gateway town for the Rocky Mountain National Park *(see p.213)*.

Past Granby, the *Zephyr* skims along the Colorado River. In **Gore Canyon,** the river is narrow with churning rapids; this is one of the roughest stretches of white water in the country. Next up: craggy **Glenwood Canyon,** which is especially beautiful in the fall when its aspen trees turn gold.

At **Glenwood Springs**, the Colorado broadens and joins up with the Fork River. Around **Palisade**, you'll start to see the Book Cliffs, rock formations that resemble lined-up shelves of books. By the time you pull in to **Grand Junction**, the landscape morphs into a vista of mesas, including the nearby Grand Mesa, one of the world's highest flattops. Grand Junction is a historic

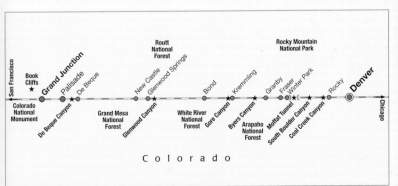

its buildings sheathed in glass tiles and titanium panels. Inside, seek out the Western and Native American art collections, with the artifacts of tribes all over America.

Running through downtown streaks the **16th Street Mall**, a pedestrian zone that has revitalized the area. It's a popular place to stroll, dotted with shops and historic buildings. It cuts northwest toward **Lower Downtown (LoDo)**, a one-time warehouse district that's now a busy restaurant-and-bar zone.

### Boulder

Though only 30 miles (48km) northwest of Denver, Boulder is a world apart. It's decidedly liberal and idealistic, with university-town energy and an enviable quality of life. Often called "the Independent Republic of Boulder", you'll find a variety of lifestyles in town. Rock slabs known as the Flatirons jut up to the west, part of the **Boulder Mountain Parks** system, which make for a great side trip.

Downtown Boulder revolves around the four-block **Pearl Street Mall**, one of the country's first pedestrian zones. It's perennially popular, with cafés, boutiques, street musicians, and great people-watching.

The **Boulder Creek Path** is another local landmark: 5½ miles (9km) of pavement along the namesake creek, shaded by cottonwood trees – perfect for strollers and cyclists.

### Colorado Springs

Unlike the majority of towns in this stretch of the Rockies, Colorado Springs took root as a health resort, not a mining camp. Civil War general William Palmer established the town as a clean-living center during the 1870s, extolling the benefits of the local mineral springs and pristine air. The city still retains a certain fresh-faced appeal.

The Garden of the Gods in Colorado Springs

Aspen was a thriving boom town studded with mansions. After the inevitable bust, the town became nearly deserted. After World War II, though, salvation came out of the blue. Friedl Pfeifer, an Austrian ski instructor, decided to build Colorado's first ski resort.

There's a downtown historic district to explore, where you can see the 1889 Wheeler Opera House. However, Aspen is much more about the atmosphere, the *soigné* resorts, and the skiing than about sightseeing.

### Rocky Mountain National Park

Straddling the Continental Divide, **Rocky Mountain National Park** ❿ (tel: 970-586-1206; www.nps. gov/romo; daily 24 hours; charge) is defined by its sky-scraping peaks, dense forests, and rare Alpine tundra.

**Trail Ridge Road** is the main route through the park; it has many scenic pullouts and it's the easiest way to see the tundra. Drivers also often see elk grazing alongside the road. Stop at **Beaver Meadows Visitor Center** (tel: 970-586-1206; www.nps.gov/romo; Oct–Apr daily 8am–4.30pm, mid-late June and Sept–Oct daily 8am–5pm, mid-June–Aug daily 8am–9pm; free) for park maps and orientation.

For a closer look at the tundra, seek out the **Tundra Nature Trail** near Rock Cut; it's relatively easy to negoti-ate. Exhibits explain how the ecosys-tem's tough plants survive. Some of those short, twisted trees and colorful splotches of lichen are centuries old.

**213**

The West

At the north of town is the **Garden of the Gods** (tel: 719-634-6666; www.gardenofgods.com; Memorial Day–Labor Day daily 8am–8pm, Labor Day–Memorial Day daily 9am–5pm; free). Sandstone blades rise out of the earth, glowing honey or crimson depending on the sun. Trails loop around the base.

Nearby Pikes Peak is part of Rockies lore. Explorer Zebulon Pike saw it and claimed it could never be climbed. He's been proved wrong millions of times over, not least by the **Pikes Peak Cog Railway** (tel: 719-685-5401; www.cograilway.com; trips several times daily; charge).

### Aspen

Aspen ❾ is the prototype of every ghost town-turned-tourist resort. During the silver boom of the 1880s,

# ACCOMMODATIONS

In Las Vegas, hotels count their rooms in thousands. Room rates vary wildly; gaming hotels have all sorts of incentives for gamblers and repeat guests, too. Since the Winter Olympics, Salt Lake City also has plenty of rooms, so finding a bargain is usually not too difficult. National-park lodging, however, is another story. Some parks have only a few lodgings, so visitors need to book months ahead and deals are scarce.

## Las Vegas

### CityCenter Las Vegas
Las Vegas Boulevard, between Tropicana and Harmon Aves.
*Tel: 702-590-8888 for the Mandarin Oriental; 1-866-359-7111 for the Aria; 1-866-745-7111 for the Vdara*
**www.citycenter.com**
MGM went truly gargantuan for this 'urban environment' of hotels, condos, shops, restaurants, and nightclubs. It was one of the most expensive projects in the world when it opened in 2009. Hotels include the Mandarin Oriental, Aria, and Vdara; Cirque du Soleil twists through a special tribute to Elvis. There's a tram just to get around the massive complex. **$$$–$$$$**

### Mandalay Bay
Las Vegas Boulevard at Hacienda Avenue
*Tel: 702-632-7777*
**www.mandalaybay.com**
At the south end of the Strip, this resort is a good bet for families. Its vast Mandalay Beach includes a wave pool, sandy areas, and swimming pools; Broadway's *The Lion King* plays almost every night. **$–$$$**

### MGM Grand Hotel & Casino
Las Vegas Boulevard, at Tropicana Avenue
*Tel: 702-891-7777*
**www.mgmgrand.com**
A prime example of the 'supersize' Vegas mentality: a huge property at a great Strip location. Rooms in the West Wing are the best. Cirque du Soleil performs *Kà* nightly and there's even a lion habitat. **$–$$$**

### Wynn Las Vegas and Encore
Las Vegas Boulevard, between Sands Avenue and E. Desert Inn Road
*Tel: 702-770-7100*
**www.wynnlasvegas.com**
Two curved, bronze towers mark developer Steve Wynn's current stake in Vegas. They emphasize elegance rather than a particular theme, with lavish amenities in each room and glamorous spas. At the Encore, there are even some casino tables that get sunlight. **$$$$**

## Utah

### Bryce Canyon Lodge
Bryce Canyon National Park
*Tel: 1-877-386-4383*
**http://brycecanyonforever.com**
This is the only lodge inside the park's boundaries. It's a 1920s landmark, and offers basic motel rooms and separate cabins with log-beam ceilings and fireplaces. The lodge restaurant – which is the only place to eat in the park – has incredible views. **$$**

### Devil's Garden Campground
Arches National Park
*Tel: 1-877-444-6777*
**www.recreation.gov**
Wake up among the park's greatest concentration of rock arches and fins. **$**

### Hotel Monaco
15 West 200 S., Salt Lake City
*Tel: 801-595-0000*
**www.monaco-saltlakecity.com**

Strong jewel-toned decor and a sense of humor set this hotel apart. You can, for instance, 'adopt' a goldfish for your room. Tall folks can request special rooms with extra-long beds and higher showerheads. **$$–$$$**

### Zion Lodge
Zion National Park
*Tel: 303-297-2757*
**www.zionlodge.com**
This is the only lodge in the park. Rebuilt to mimic its 1920s roots, it includes motel-style rooms as well as historic cabins with fireplaces. **$$**

## Yellowstone and Grand Teton national parks
### Hostel X
3315 Village Drive, Teton Village
*Tel: 307-733-3415*
**www.thehostel.us**
Though called a hostel, this lodge actually offers private rooms along with shared-bunk quarters. A ski-bum standby. **$–$$**

### Moulton Ranch Cabins
Mormon Row, Grand Teton National Park
*Tel: 307-733-3749*
**www.moultonranchcabins.com**
Open Memorial Day through September, these cabins are smack dab among early 20th-century pioneer ranches. A perfect view of the Teton peaks. **$$**

### Old Faithful Inn
Old Faithful Village,
Yellowstone National Park
*Tel: 1-866-439-7375*
**www.yellowstonenationalparklodges.com**
A classic dating back to 1903, with a soaring main hall in the 'Old House'. Rooms with the best geyser views are in this section or the west wing. **$$–$$$**

## Colorado
### Brown Palace Hotel
321 17th Street, Denver
*Tel: 303-297-3111*
**www.brownpalace.com**

Historic to the hilt. When it opened in 1892, it showed the country that the West could match Eastern sophistication. **$$–$$$**

### Hotel Boulderado
2115 13th Street, Boulder
*Tel: 303-442-4344*
**www.boulderado.com**
Just off the Pearl Street Mall, this 1909 palace hotel exudes atmosphere. **$$$**

### Limelight Lodge
355 S. Monarch Street, Aspen
*Tel: 970-925-3025*
**www.limelightlodge.com**
A sleek, eco-friendly lodge with roof terraces and a complimentary ski-guide service. **$$$**

### The Little Nell
675 East Durant Avenue, Aspen
*Tel: 970-920-4600*
**www.thelittlenell.com**
Despite the name, this is a luxurious retreat with rooms and condos just steps away from the Silver Queen Gondola. Rooms are toasty and streamlined, all with fireplaces. **$$$$**

Lobby of the Brown Palace Hotel, Denver

Listings

# RESTAURANTS

Classic Las Vegas hotel buffets do still exist, but they no longer monopolize the dining scene as they once did. In the past decade, major resorts have established outposts of famous restaurants from all over the world, making this one of the most extravagant restaurant towns in the country. In Salt Lake City, it's easier to have a drink with dinner but local laws mean that bartenders must be hidden from public view.

## Las Vegas

### Alizé

Palms Casino Resort, 4321 W. Flamingo Road
*Tel: 702-951-7000*
**http://andrelv.com/alize**
Prized for its sweeping view of the city lights, Alizé is also the rare high-end French restaurant where the star chef stays in the kitchen. Seasonal meals hew to the classics, such as pan-seared foie gras and lobster Thermidor. **$$$$**

### Hash House a Go Go

6800 W. Sahara Avenue
*Tel: 702-804-4646*
**www.hashhouseagogo.com**
The 'twisted farm food' dished up here kicks diner standbys up several notches: half-a-dozen hashes, and eggs Benedict with smoked salmon. There are other branches in the Imperial Palace and M hotels, with late-night hours on Friday and Saturday. **$$**

### L'Atelier de Joël Robuchon

MGM Grand Hotel & Casino
*Tel: 702-891-7358*
**www.mgmgrand.com/restaurants**
Robuchon, one of France's most famous chefs, has been lured to Vegas for a pair of restaurants. L'Atelier is more casual (although that's relative), with a sleek counter and tasting plates of simple yet rich dishes such as lobster salad and whipped potatoes. There's another namesake restaurant, too, with formal service and sky-high prices. **$$$$**

### Lotus of Siam

953 E. Sahara Avenue
*Tel: 702-735-3033*
**www.saipinchutima.com**
Get off the Strip and into a strip mall. It's worth it for this outstanding authentic Thai restaurant that racks up *Wine Spectator* awards. The hot-and-sour soups, curries, and crispy duck draw hordes of fans. **$–$$$**

The elevated dining room at Alizé, at the Palms Casino Resort, Las Vegas

## Utah

**Bit & Spur Restaurant & Saloon**
1212 Zion Park Boulevard, Springdale
Tel: 435-772-3498
www.bitandspur.com
Not far from Zion's South Entrance, this might be called a roadhouse – although the cooking aims higher, with duck *carnitas*, sweet-potato *tamales*, and lots of micro-brews. **$$–$$$**

**Buck's Grill House**
1393 N. Highway 191, Moab
Tel: 435-259-5201
www.bucksgrillhouse.com
After exploring Arches National Park, tuck into a spice-rubbed steak or *chipotle* baby back ribs. **$$–$$$**

**The Copper Onion**
111 E. Broadway, Salt Lake City
Tel: 801-355-3282
www.thecopperonion.com
On the local-and-seasonal bandwagon, in a good way. The small plates and sides are meant for sharing; locals rave about the mussels and ricotta dumplings. **$$**

## Yellowstone and Grand Teton national parks

Xanterra, the concessionaire for Yellowstone, runs formal dining rooms and casual delis in all of its lodges, where day visitors are welcome to dine along with overnight guests.

**Canyon Soda Fountain**
Canyon Village, Yellowstone National Park
Tel: 307-242-7377
A 1950s-style diner inside the general store at Canyon Village. Omelettes, sandwiches, and great root-beer floats. **$$**

**Dornan's Chuckwagon**
Moose, Wyoming
Tel: 307-733-2415
www.dornans.com/dining/chuckwagon
On the edge of Grand Teton, this authentic homestead operation serves up Western-style open-air meals: sourdough pancakes,

Drinks and a chat at the exotic Boulder Dushanbe Teahouse

beef stew, Southern-style biscuits and gravy. Open June through Labor Day. **$$**

## Colorado

**Boulder Dushanbe Teahouse**
1770 13th Street, Boulder
Tel: 303-442-4993
www.boulderteahouse.com
A café with a global outlook. The entire building was shipped from Boulder's sister city, Dushanbe, in Tajikistan. It serves dishes plucked from all over the world, from Thai curry to Hungarian goulash. **$$**

**Craftwood Inn**
404 El Paseo Boulevard, Colorado Springs
Tel: 719-685-9000
www.craftwood.com
Carnivore alert: this restaurant specializes in all kinds of Colorado-raised game, from elk to wild boar to quail. **$$$–$$$$**

**Rioja**
1431 Larimer Street, Denver
Tel: 303-820-2282
www.riojadenver.com
A polished downtown spot for American cooking that includes house-made tortellini or Colorado lamb sausage. A more casual spot with the same owner, Euclid Hall, is just around the corner. **$$–$$$**

# NIGHTLIFE AND ENTERTAINMENT

Las Vegas is the splashiest nightlife hotspot in the West. It showcases divas (Bette! Cher! Celine!) and persuades partiers to splurge on expensive table reservations at nightclubs. Outside Vegas, local microbreweries are gaining legions of fans. Salt Lake City's nightlife is improving now that some restrictive liquor laws are dissolving. When up in the Rockies, remember that elevation will lower your alcohol tolerance.

## Bars

### Double Down Saloon
4640 Paradise Road, Las Vegas
*Tel: 702-791-5775*
**www.doubledownsaloon.com**
'Shut up and drink' orders this wild and woolly honkytonk. Pool, pinball, a great juke-box, and lurid murals.

### Green Russell
1422 Larimer Street, Denver
*Tel: 303-893-6505*
**www.greenrussell.com**
Go in through a pie shop to find this LoDo speakeasy. It's an intimate, serious spot for cocktails old and new.

### Luxe Bar
Hard Rock Hotel & Casino, 4455 Paradise Road, Las Vegas
*Tel: 1-800-473-7625*
**www.hardrockhotel.com**
Odds are good that a real-life rock star will hit this bar. On weekends, partiers also splash into Rehab, the hotel's outdoor pool party.

### Moab Microbrewery
686 S. Main Street, Moab
*Tel: 435-259-6333*
**www.themoabbrewery.com**
If the dry Arches landscape makes you thirsty, stop by to sample some of these local brews with names inspired by the surrounding parkland.

### Squatters Pub
147 W. Broadway, Salt Lake City
*Tel: 801-363-2739*
**www.squatters.com**

This brewpub serves up a couple dozen locally made suds, from year-round ales to seasonal specials such as espresso stout.

## Casinos

### Binion's
128 E. Fremont Street
*Tel: 702-382-1600*
**www.binions.com**
Serious gamblers head Downtown to this longtime gaming hall with its million-dollar display and relatively friendly odds.

### Caesars Palace
3570 Las Vegas Boulevard
*Tel: 1-866-227-5938*
**www.caesarspalace.com**
The height of Vegas kitsch, with its Ancient-Rome decor and cocktail waitresses in mini-togas. An epic gaming area with the city's biggest poker room.

### The Mirage
3400 S. Las Vegas Boulevard
*Tel: 702-791-7111*
**www.mirage.com**

Slot machines at Caesars Palace

Large but not overwhelming, with a comfortable theater for race and sports betting.

## Live shows

### Celine Dion
Caesars Palace, Las Vegas
*Tel: 1-877-423-5463*
www.celinedion.com/return-las-vegas
The singer hits high note after high note in her greatest-hits show.

### Bar-M Chuckwagon Live Western Show and Cowboy Supper
US 191, 7 miles (11km) north of Moab
*Tel: 435-259-2276*
www.barmchuckwagon.com
From April through mid-October, this operation caters to visitors wanting a taste of the Old West, with roping demos, live music, corny jokes, and a whopping meal of roast beef, Southern-style biscuits, baked beans, and cowboy coffee.

### The Joint
Hard Rock Hotel & Casino,
4455 Paradise Road, Las Vegas
*Tel: 702-693-5000*
http://thejointlasvegas.com
Primed for rock. Touring acts rotate through, plus resident artists such as Santana make repeat appearances through the year.

### Penn & Teller
Rio Hotel, 3700 W. Flamingo Road, Las Vegas
*Tel: 1-888-746-7784*
www.riolasvegas.com
These illusionists broke the mold with comedy, history of magic tricks, stunts, and a showgirl. Talkative Penn and silent Teller are in an unbelievable league of their own.

### Red Rocks Amphitheatre
18300 West Alameda Parkway
*Tel: 720-865-2494*
www.redrocksonline.com
This is one of the country's most stunning outdoor concert venues. Red sandstone flanks the bowl, where symphonies and country singers take the stage.

### The State Room
638 S. State Street, Salt Lake City
*Tel: 801-878-0530*
http://thestateroomslc.com
A comfortable, mid-size downtown music venue for everything from country to hip-hop, with lots of up-and-coming bands.

### Wheeler Opera House
4320 E. Hyman Avenue, Aspen
*Tel: 970-920-5770*
www.wheeleroperahouse.com
This historic, crimson-and-gold venue now hosts movies, live-music shows, comedy nights, and an annual John Denver tribute.

## Performing arts

### Denver Arts Complex
Speer and Arapahoe streets
*Tel: 303-893-4100 for theatre, 303-623-7876 for symphony, 303-468-2030 for opera, 303-837-8888 for ballet*
www.artscomplex.com
A glass arch shelters venues and arts groups, including the Denver Center Theatre Company, Colorado Symphony Orchestra, Opera Colorado, and Colorado Ballet.

### Mormon Tabernacle Choir
Temple Square, Salt Lake City
*Tel: 801-570-0080*
http://mormontabernaclechoir.org
The 360 members of this choir are known for their perfect harmonies. Their Tabernacle home base has an 11,623-pipe organ.

## Nightclubs

### Chateau Nightclub & Gardens
Paris Las Vegas, 3655 Las Vegas Boulevard
*Tel: 702-776-7770*
http://chateaunightclublv.com
This Strip megaclub ropes in star DJs and high-energy live acts. Heavy on the hip-hop.

### PURE
Caesars Palace
*Tel: 702-731-7873*
www.purethenightclub.com/pure
This huge, icy-white dance club regularly shows up in the gossip columns.

# SPORTS AND ACTIVITIES

Outdoor sports aren't just a pastime in this region – they're a way of life for the locals. The best time for most outdoor activities in the desert is spring or fall, since the summers get so brutally hot. The Rocky Mountains become a winter-sports paradise from late fall to early spring.

## Adventure sports

**Zion Adventures**
Zion National Park
*Tel: 435-772-1001*
**www.zionadventures.com**
This outfitter racks up adrenaline-rush activities, including slickrock biking, canyoneering, and rock climbing.

## Biking

**Poison Spider Bicycles**
497 N. Main Street, Moab
*Tel: 435-259-7882*
**http://poisonspiderbicycles.com**
Moab, just south of Arches National Park, is one of the greatest mountain-bike areas in the country. You can rent all kinds of tough bikes here, plus maps and tips.

**Zion Cycles**
868 Zion Park Boulevard, Springdale
*Tel: 435-772-0400*
**http://zioncycles.com**

Deep powder at Snowbird, in Utah

This is the best source for rental bikes, maps, and advice.

## Hiking

Stop by the visitor's center at each National Park for information on popular hiking trails. Always bring plenty of water, as the temperatures and/or elevation can make your head spin.

## Horseback riding

**Canyon Trail Rides**
*Tel: 435-679-8665*
**www.canyonrides.com**
Get a close-up, pioneer-style look at the rock formations in Bryce and Zion with one of these short rides.

## Skiing and snowboarding

**Aspen Skiing Company**
Aspen, Colorado
*Tel: 970-925-1220*
**www.aspensnowmass.com**
This company oversees Aspen's four ski areas: Aspen Mountain, Aspen Highlands, Buttermilk (best for beginners), and the biggest, Snowmass.

**Jackson Hole Mountain Resort**
Teton Village, Wyoming
*Tel: 307-733-2292*
**www.jacksonhole.com**
The red aerial tram scoots up and down Rendezvous Mountain, a magnet for powderhounds.

**Snowbird Wasatch-Cache National Forest, Utah**
*Tel: 1-800-232-9542*
**www.snowbird.com**
With an average snowfall of 500in (1270cm) (just think of all that dry powder), Snowbird has the longest ski season in Utah.

# TOURS

In addition to the options below, check with national-park visitor centers for ranger-led walks or hikes.

### Boat tours
**Lake Powell Boat Tour**
Wahweap Marina, Lake Powell
*Tel: 928-645-2433*
www.lakepowell.com/tours
Glide into canyons or cruise to the Rainbow Bridge stone arc.

### Bus tours
**Historic Yellow Bus Tours**
Yellowstone National Park
*Tel: 1-866-439-7375*
www.yellowstonenationalparklodges.com
Bright-yellow vintage tour buses trundle through the park, with itineraries ranging from a half-day highlights route to photo safaris.

The Rainbow Bridge in Arches National Park is a favorite photo opportunity

### Helicopter tours
**Sundance Helicopter**
McCarren International Airport, Las Vegas
*Tel: 702-736-0606*
www.sundancehelicopters.com
Get an eye-popping aerial view of the Strip and Glitter Gulch; a sunset option also swings by the Hoover Dam.

# FESTIVALS AND EVENTS

In addition to all the sporting events (marathons, bike races, and suchlike), communities in the Rockies often have exciting summer music festivals.

## May
**Elkfest**
Jackson Hole, Wyoming
*Tel: 307-733-5935*
http://elkfest.org
Every year, elk shed their antlers and local Boy Scouts gather them up, then auction them – the highlight of this festival.

## June–July
**World Series of Poker**
Rio Hotel & Casino, Las Vegas
*Tel: 1-800-342-7724*
www.wsop.com
Anyone can watch the tournament but it costs $10,000 to buy in and play.

## June–August
**Aspen Music Festival**
*Tel: 970-925-9042*
www.aspenmusicfestival.com
One of the country's premier summer music events, with orchestral performances, recitals, and masterclasses.

**Colorado Music Festival**
Boulder
*Tel: 303-449-1397*
www.coloradomusicfest.org
Symphonies and chamber-music ensembles perform regularly all summer long.

## July
**Days of '47**
Salt Lake City
*Tel: 801-250-3890*
www.daysof47.com
SLC celebrates Utah's settlement with a rodeo, horse parade, a heritage festival, and a sunrise service at the Mormon Tabernacle.

# California

For millions of people, California is the apotheosis of the American dream – whether that dream involves celebrity in Hollywood, urban cool in San Francisco, or natural wonders in Yosemite, the Mojave Desert, or Death Valley. The West Coast is the ultimate fantasyland, a dream stoked by thousands of movies and songs, and the real-world delights of an extraordinary landscape and plenty of sun.

## Los Angeles and San Francisco

**Population:** Los Angeles: 3.8 million; San Francisco: 815,000

**Local dialing codes:** Los Angeles: 310 and 323; San Francisco: 415

**Local tourist offices:** Los Angeles: 685 S. Figueroa Street; tel: 213-689-8822; www.discoverlosangeles.com. San Francisco: 900 Market Street; tel: 415-391-2000; www.onlyinsanfrancisco.com

**Main police stations:** Los Angeles: 251 East 6th Street; tel: 213-485-3294. San Francisco: 766 Vallejo Street; tel: 415-315-2400

**Main post offices:** Los Angeles:

406 East 2nd Street. San Francisco: 170 O'Farrell Street

**Hospitals:** Los Angeles: Cedars-Sinai Medical Center, 8700 Beverly Boulevard, West Hollywood, tel: 310-423-3277. San Francisco: University of California San Francisco Medical Center, 505 Parnassus Avenue, tel: 415-476-1000

**Local newspapers/listings magazines:** The main daily papers are *The Los Angeles Times* and the *San Francisco Chronicle*. For listings, see the alt-weekly *L.A. Weekly* and monthly *Los Angeles* and *San Francisco*

**Time zone:** PST

The novelist Wallace Stegner once described California as 'America only more so.' Everything here seems to be so much bigger, brighter, more dramatic, more intense. Ever since the mid-19th century Gold Rush and the building of the transcontinental railroad, people gravitated to the Golden State in the hope that their lives would be better than before. When California joined the Union in 1850, it promised a glorious final frontier, drenched in riches and sunshine.

Even more than most states, California was – and continues to be – defined by waves of immigrants. Each population makes its own significant mark: the dust-bowl families fleeing the Midwest during the Great Depression; Chinese workers recruited for the railroad; a constant stream of Mexican and Central American arrivals; the wave of Vietnamese immigrants starting in the late 1970s; and so on. In 2011, census numbers showed that

The rooftop bar of The Standard, an upmarket hotel in downtown Los Angeles

The city is knitted together by freeways and iconic routes such as Sunset Boulevard. Distinct neighborhoods thrive between the overpasses, defined by cultures imported (Chinatown) or created ('the people's republic of Santa Monica').

### Downtown

Downtown LA, with its skyscrapers, state-of-the-art concert hall, run-down movie palaces, and Skid Row, exposes the old and new faces of the city. Over the past several years, real-estate developers have latched on, turning neglected buildings into gleaming condo towers. The Music Center performing-arts complex and a few

California's population increased by 10 percent from the previous decade. In great ways, and with great challenges, California is decidedly multicultural.

There's also an age-old divide between the northern and southern sections of the state. Southern California nurtures a playground feeling, fueled by the film industry. Northern California clings to its counter-cultural identity while also feeding the tech community.

## Los Angeles

Angelenos believe that **Los Angeles** ❶ is more of a state of mind than a city. A state of mind that sprawls over hundreds of miles, attracting myths like a magnet. It is bounded by the Pacific on the western shore, and the San Gabriel and Santa Monica mountains to the east. With its fabulous weather, it's little wonder that everyone is drawn outdoors.

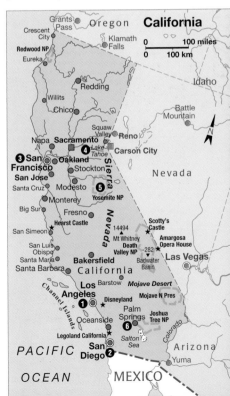

museums draw culture aficionados, while a starkly modern cathedral overlooks the intersection of the 110 and 101 freeways.

The construction of the **Walt Disney Concert Hall** (tel: 323-850-2000; www.laphil.com), opened in 2003, helped to turn the rough neighborhood around. Designed by hometown star architect Frank Gehry, its silvery curves always catch the eye.

Across the 101 freeway stands a striking architectural contrast: the **Cathedral of Our Lady of the Angels** (tel: 213-680-5200; www.ola cathedral.org; Mon–Fri 6.30am–9pm, Sat 9am–6pm, Sun 7am–6pm; free). José Rafael Moneo designed an angular, sand-colored house of worship, its alabaster windows turning the sunshine a creamy gold.

The **Museum of Contemporary Art** (MOCA, tel: 213-626-6222; Mon and Fri 11am–5pm, Thur 11am–8pm, Sat–Sun 11am–6pm; charge) has two downtown locations filled with works dating from 1940 to the present day. Rotating shows touch on everything

from Robert Frank's photography to new currents in graffiti art.

The cluster of historic buildings called **El Pueblo de Los Angeles** (tel: 213-485-6855; www.elpueblo.lacity.org; hours vary; free) could be considered downtown L.A.'s first tourist attraction. Its hub, **Olvera Street,** was turned into a Mexican marketplace in 1930, drawing visitors and saving old adobe structures from ruin. Now Olvera Street is a hokey alley of vendors, with graceful old buildings to either side and the occasional mariachi outbreak.

## Hollywood and the West Side

Hollywood became synonymous with the American movie industry back when the talkies first took off. Now it's more a symbol than an active part of this company town, as the film studios have moved east. But after decades in a slump, Hollywood is climbing back as splashy movie theaters, bars, and restaurants bring new life to this neighborhood.

The **Walk of Fame** runs through the tourist heart of Hollywood, on Hollywood Boulevard, west of Vine

# ★ BEHIND THE HOLLYWOOD CURTAIN

'Hollywood is a place where they'll pay you a thousand dollars for a kiss and 50 cents for your soul,' claimed Marilyn Monroe. Tinseltown, Hollyweird, the Dream Factory – whatever you call it, this neighborhood is linked with movie production. Although most studios moved to the San Fernando Valley, the Hollywood glow permeates Los Angeles. You can get an insight into the myths and glory of the silver screen by visiting the places where the stars work and play.

To see a working lot, head to the last major studio in Hollywood proper, **Paramount Pictures** (tel: 323-956-1777; www.paramount.com; tours Mon–Fri at 10am, 11am, 1pm and 2pm; charge). The behind-the-scenes tour shows you where classic TV and films were made, as well as new movies in the making.

To get the lowdown on Hollywood's Golden Era, hightail it to the **Hollywood Museum** (tel: 323-464-7776; www.thehollywoodmuseum.com; Wed–Sun 10am–5pm; charge). Fittingly, it occupies the Art Deco building owned by Max Factor, the make-up artist who transformed cosmetics and created the iconic looks of Bette Davis, Rita Hayworth, and dozens of other stars. The movie memorabilia here spans the period from the silent era to recent blockbusters.

Grauman's Chinese Theater

The red carpet is regularly rolled out for film premieres at Hollywood's classic theaters. But the biggest frenzy centers around the **Academy Awards** (tel: 310-247-3000; www.oscars. org), in late February. At time of printing, some 2,701 statuettes had been awarded since the first ceremony in 1929. You can try for a viewing spot in the bleachers in front of the Kodak Theater by entering an online lottery in late summer – see the Academy's website for details.

Seeing a celebrity get his or her star on the Hollywood **Walk of Fame** is a snap. The public is welcome to watch from the sidelines when a famous name becomes a permanent part of the streetscape. Ceremonies are usually scheduled a week or two in advance. Or your trip might coincide with a footprint ceremony at **Grauman's Chinese Theater.**

VIP ropes make it hard to stumble across celebs in nightclubs, but when actors have a movie to promote or awards to jockey for, they do the rounds with interviewers and studio executives. The Chateau Marmont, Beverly Hills Hotel, and Regent Beverly Wilshire hotel all draw major wattage. If you think you can get past the rope, many famous faces prefer to dance the night away at Ritual and the Sky Bar. Of course, you might also just get lucky and spot a starlet across a crowded restaurant. Try reserving a table at The Ivy, Koi, or Mr Chow, where the beautiful people order beautiful food, but only take a bite or two.

Golden Oscar statuettes measure 13ins (34cm) and weigh 8½lbs (3.9kg) each

Behind the Hollywood curtain

Marilyn Monroe's star on the Hollywood Walk of Fame

The view over Los Angeles from the Griffith Observatory, which crowns Griffith Park

Street. Stars embedded in the sidewalk symbolize the strange place that is Hollywood, with great stars and forgettable names positioned cheek by jowl. This is a rare part of LA where walking is considered normal.

**Grauman's Chinese Theater** (tel: 323-464-6266; www.manntheaters.

com/chinese; free forecourt) is a stalwart piece of Old Hollywood, a 1927 movie palace done up as a Chinese temple. In the entryway, famous hand- and footprints dent the cement. Nowadays, Grauman's is practically dwarfed by its neighbor, the **Kodak Theater** and the Hollywood

## Los Angeles transportation

 **Airport: Los Angeles International Airport (LAX)**; tel: 310-646-5252; www.lawa.org/lax; 16 miles (26km) from downtown. Free shuttle buses run to the Metro Green Line station every 12 to 15 minutes, 24 hours a day. SuperShuttle and Prime Time Shuttle: about a half-hour to downtown L.A., $15 to $35 per person, depending on your destination. Taxi: about a half-hour to downtown L.A., roughly $42

 **Subways: Los Angeles County Metropolitan Transit Authority (MTA)**; tel: 213-922-2000, www.mta.net, runs the L.A. subway system – a system many people don't know exists, since the city is so identified with cars. The Red and Gold lines, the most useful for sightseeing, run 24 hours a day. The Red Line begins at Union Station and travels west into Hollywood. The Gold Line links Union Station with stops in Old Pasadena. The base Metro fare is $1.25 for all lines. A Metro Day Pass is $5 and weekly passes are $17. Passes are available at Metro Customer Centers and local convenience stores

 **Taxis:** L.A. cab fares are high – even a short trip can cost $20 or more. Unless you're downtown, cabs will not usually stop when hailed. You can find cabstands at airports, at Union Station, and at major hotels. Taxis charge $2.85 at the start of the meter plus $2.70 per mile. Try Checker Cab, tel: 310-330-3720, or United Independent Taxi, tel: 213-483-7660 or 310-821-1000. Report any issues by contacting the Taxi Franchise Office, tel: 213-928-9732

& Highland complex, where the Academy Awards are held in late February *(see pages 226–7)*. Up in the hills, if it's not too smoggy, you can see the cheery white letters of the **Hollywood' sign**.

While Hollywood Boulevard nets the Golden Age gawkers, Wilshire Boulevard claims the **Miracle Mile's Museum Row**. The **Los Angeles County Museum of Art** (LACMA, tel: 323-857-6000; www.lacma.org; Mon–Tue and Thur noon–8pm, Fri noon–9pm, Sat–Sun 11am–8pm; charge) is the big deal here. The art campus accommodates a number of buildings, which hold impressive collections of art from all over the world. A serene pavilion displays Japanese art and crafts. The Broad Contemporary Art Museum has sensational large-scale installations, including the hulking metal shapes of Richard Serra.

Across Wilshire, the **Petersen Automotive Museum** (tel: 323-930-2277; www.petersen.org; Tue–Sun 10am–6pm; charge) celebrates a crucial aspect of Angeleno culture:

cars. Rotating exhibits display gleaming rarities, dragsters, and the latest supercars.

Turn up the bass when driving on Sunset Boulevard into West Hollywood. This city-within-a-city includes **Sunset Strip**, the stretch of Sunset that's lined with music clubs, bistros, giant billboards, and a few cool hotels, before plunging into **Beverly Hills**, where mansions with landscaped grounds close ranks.

Look up near the 405 freeway and you'll spot a pale, stony outcrop on the slopes of Bel-Air. The **Getty Center** (tel: 310-440-7300; http://getty.edu; Tue–Fri and Sun 10.30am–5.30pm, Sat 10am–9pm; free but charge for parking) is an art-filled castle on a hill, its collection matched by stunning gardens and coastal views. The permanent displays of pre-20th-century European art are complemented by traveling shows.

### The coast

Taking the 10 freeway west through the city will zip you straight to a

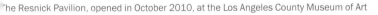

The Resnick Pavilion, opened in October 2010, at the Los Angeles County Museum of Art

## Rodeo Drive

For many, Rodeo Drive in Beverly Hills is shopping experience. In just a few short, carefully manicured blocks, the top luxury brands glitter. It's here that Prada has its 'epicenter,' designed by Rem Koolhaas. Louis Vuitton and Hermès compete for the attention of handbag lovers, while Bulgari and Tiffany & Co. wink with gems and gold. The clothes and accessories at Chanel, Gucci, Dolce & Gabbana are a shopper's dream.

The blocks around Rodeo (pronounced row-*day*-oh) Drive are known as the Golden Triangle; here you'll find shops with a lower profile. Note that the one bargain you can't find around here is parking for your car.

Santa Monica itself, a separate city, is a low-key but pricey bastion of liberalism. Immediately south along the Pacific Coast Highway (PCH), things get scruffier as you pass into **Venice**. For generations, the **Venice Boardwalk** has been the place to let your freak flag fly. Bodybuilders pump iron at the 'Muscle Beach' outdoor workout area, while skaters, joggers, and rainbow-haired dreamers wander along by the sand, stopping off at cafés to watch the world go by.

North of Santa Monica, things go from posh to *very* posh, as the PCH curves into **Malibu**. The highway skims along right by the water; mansions and gated communities lie hidden in the hills beyond. One welcoming destination, however, is the **Annenberg Community Beach House** (tel: 310-458-4904; http://beachhouse.smgov.net; daily 8.30am–8.30pm; free). The complex has a pool (closed in winter), café, playground, and volleyball courts, plus the historic cottage of Marion Davies, mistress

picture-postcard scene: the **Santa Monica Pier** (tel: 310-458-8901; www.santamonicapier.org; daily 24 hours; free), which stretches into the Pacific. With its carousel, junk-food vendors, mini-amusement park, and Ferris wheel, it's a classic family draw.

Biking along the beach's boardwalk

Looking back along Santa Monica Pier

of newspaper magnate William Randolph Hearst. Moving north, **Surfrider and Zuma beaches** lure sunbathers and surfers.

### Disneyland Resort

Roughly 45 minutes' drive south of L.A., in Orange County, beckons the original Happiest Place on Earth. No matter how many new parks sprout up in Florida, there's nothing like the original Magic Kingdom.

Even the original theme park has had its growth spurts, though. By now, the **Disneyland Resort** (tel: 714-781-4565; http://disneyland. disney.go.com; Mon–Thur 9am–8pm, Fri–Sun 8am–midnight, with exceptions; charge) includes a second theme park, **California Adventures**, and plenty of attendant hotels and visitor facilities. It encompasses so much that it's impossible to visit in just one day.

Disneyland rolls out the welcome mat with the squeaky-clean **Main Street**. From here, guests usually rush to the rides or 'lands' they crave most. **New Orleans Square**, for instance, offers the Pirates of the Caribbean (now including Johnny Depp-like animatronics) and the Haunted Mansion. **Adventureland** draws hordes for the classic Jungle Cruise and the slick Indiana Jones Adventure, while everyone screams on the Space Mountain indoor roller-coaster in **Tomorrowland**. **Fantasyland** has many of the traditional rides for younger children, tapping into early Disney films such as *Snow White*. The towering **Matterhorn** looms over everything, while a coaster spirals inside its slopes. Check the park calendars for parades and 'character experiences', where costumed cast members greet visitors and pose for photographs.

# San Diego

The region of California became known to Europe here, where Portuguese captain Juan Rodríguez Cabrillo first landed in 1542, and in 1769, Father Junípero Serra founded his first mission on what is now Presidio Hill. Today, **San Diego** ➋ is known as a family vacation hotspot, with its kid-friendly beaches, parks, and zoo.

## Old Town and Sea World

The six-block area known as Old Town, at the foot of Presidio Hill, is full of old adobes and Victorian

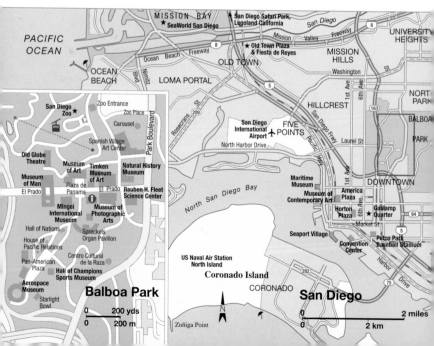

Shamu is among the stars to be seen at San Diego's SeaWorld

homes. **San Diego Avenue**, the main drag, has an esplanade of gift shops and souvenir vendors; where the avenue edges the **Old Town Plaza**, it's pedestrian-only. Just north of the plaza on Juan Street, the **Fiesta de Reyes** focuses on the region's Hispanic roots, with Mexican restaurants and crafts.

Just north of Old Town, on the other side of the 8 freeway, stretches the park and waterways of **Mission Bay**. The big lure here is **SeaWorld San Diego** (tel: 619-226-3901; www.seaworld.com; late May–early Sept Mon–Fri 10am–7.30pm, Sat 9am–11pm, Sun 9am–10pm, early Sept–mid-May Mon–Fri 10am–6pm, Sat 9am–10pm, Sun 10am–7.30pm, with exceptions; charge). With vast aquariums, a walk-through 'shark encounter' tube, and (literally) splashy shows featuring sea lions, dolphins, and killer whales, this park provides visitors with a crash course in ocean ecology and zoology.

### Balboa Park

At the northeast end of town beats the city's cultural heart. Over 1,000 acres, **Balboa Park** (www.balboapark.org) gathers together 15 museums, the Old Globe Theatre, and the much-loved San Diego Zoo.

The towering, Moorish-style **Museum of Man** (tel: 619-239-2001; www.museumofman.org; daily 10am–4.30pm; charge) illuminates the story of ancient peoples with anthropological exhibits ranging from Egyptian mummies to ancient Mayan artifacts. Meanwhile, the **San Diego Museum of Art** (tel: 619-232-7931; www.sdmart.org; Tue–Sat 10am–5pm, Sun noon–5pm; charge) has a particularly rich store of Baroque and Renaissance paintings, along with arts particularly related to California, including Arts-and-Crafts design. The **Mingei International Museum** (tel: 619-239-0003; www.mingei.org; Tue–Sun 10am–4pm; charge) teems with folk art from all over the world, hopscotching from Scandinavia to Japan to the Pacific Northwest.

The star of the park, though, is the **San Diego Zoo** (tel: 619-231-1515; www.sandiegozoo.org; late June–early Sept daily 9am–9pm, early Sept–early Oct and mid-Dec–mid-June, daily 9am–6pm, mid-Oct–mid-Dec daily 9am–5pm; charge). One of the world's best and most progressive zoos, it goes to great lengths to create natural-looking environments for its animals, from the koalas' eucalyptus grove to the polar-bear pool. The zoo has been particularly successful in giant-panda conservation; if a new cub is born, make a beeline for the panda enclosure to catch a glimpse of the cute black-and-white bundle.

### Downtown

San Diego's **Gaslamp Quarter** (www. gaslamp.org) is a prime example of urban revitalization. Starting in the late 1970s, dilapidated Victorian buildings were renovated, gaslamp-style streetlights lit up, and galleries, cafés, and cool shops quickly gravitated to the picturesque streets between Broadway and Harbor Drive. Now the historic district is one of the city's busiest restaurant and nightlife zones.

On the bayfront, **Seaport Village** (www.seaportvillage.com; daily 10am–9pm; free) is done out in New England style. Its weathered-wood buildings are mostly filled with shops and cafés; it's also the departure point for several cruise-tour boats.

### North of San Diego

Within half an hour's drive north of San Deigo proper are two excellent family attractions. The **San Diego Safari Park** (tel: 760-747-8702; www. sdzsafaripark.org; July–Aug daily 9am–7pm, June daily 9am–6pm, Sept–May daily 9am–5pm, with exceptions; charge), partner to the San Diego Zoo, has open-air environments for its wildlife, including many species from Africa. Giraffes, zebras, and rhinos roam the 'African Plain' while tigers, elephants, gorillas, and lions have their own enclosures. Some areas have to be explored on a safari tour.

San Diego's historic Gaslamp Quarter is now a hotspot with a buzzing nightlife

The view of San Francisco from snaking Lombard Street, on Telegraph Hill

Up in Carlsbad, toy bricks reach unbelievable heights at **Legoland California** (tel: 760-918-5346; http://california.legoland.com; June–late Aug daily 10am–8pm, Sept–May Mon and Thur–Sun 10am–5pm with exceptions; charge). There are easy-going rides, mini golf, and amazing models made of Lego, but what really rev kids' engines are the free-play areas where they can get their hands on thousands of blocks.

## San Francisco

Tony Bennett sang it like it is. The City by the Bay steals visitors' hearts effortlessly and locals seem almost exaggeratedly in love with their city. The setting of **San Francisco ❸**, on a thumb of land pushed into San Francisco Bay, ridged with steep hills, offers view after spectacular view. Foghorns and bridges, pastel-painted Victorian houses and cable cars – the city's signatures cohere in a wonderfully romantic atmosphere. With its famously liberal lifestyle, the city has long been a welcome haven for all sorts of communities and subcultures.

### Union Square, Chinatown, and Market Street

At some point, everyone comes through **Union Square,** the downtown plaza bordered by Geary, Powell, Post, and Stockton streets. It's ringed with boutiques and department

---

**Riding the cable cars**

Even if San Francisco's cable cars are jammed with tourists, the experience is unbeatable. The clanging bells and knockout views make the $6 fare worthwhile on those steep hills.

Of the three lines, the Powell-Hyde line gives the best bay views. The California line is less touristy and runs through Chinatown. Riders can hop on and off anywhere along the route at the official stops. Grab a seat on an outside bench for the best sightlines.

stores, including Neiman-Marcus, and an Apple store. Beyond the perimeter, grand hotels pepper the area.

Going uphill on Grant Avenue from Union Square plunges you into the gritty, bustling world of **Chinatown**. This is one of the largest Asian communities outside Asia, and in some ways, an unexpected by-product of the Great Quake. After the city was devastated in 1906, a businessman proposed that Chinatown be rebuilt to attract tourists, with pagoda roofs and dragon carvings. Grant Avenue is the main corridor, chock-a-block with tchotchkes, tea vendors, antique stores and herb shops.

Situated just south of Union Square is **Market Street**, one of the city's main thoroughfares, where vintage trolleys rumble towards the waterfront. On the far side of the street, in the SoMA (South of Market) neighborhood, is the eye-catching **San Francisco Museum of Modern Art** (SFMOMA, tel: 415-357-4000; www.sfmoma.org; Mon–Tue and Fri–Sun 11am–5.45pm, Thur 11am–8.45pm; charge), with its

The food market at the Ferry Terminal

striped central round tower. Its collections range from Ansel Adams to Jeff Koons. Climb up to the rooftop sculpture garden for large-scale works.

Around the corner looms the **Contemporary Jewish Museum** (tel: 415-655-7800; www.thecjm.org; Mon–Tue and Fri–Sun 11am–5pm, Thur 1–8pm, closed on Jewish holidays; charge). This dramatic structure mashes together a graceful 1907 brick building with an angular blue-steel extension inspired by the Hebrew letters for *chai* or 'life.' Rotating exhibits showcase Jewish artists and cultural figures.

When Market Street reaches the waterfront Embarcadero, things get really tasty. The transit hub **Ferry Terminal** (tel: 415-983-8030; www. ferrybuildingmarketplace.com; Mon–Fri 10am–6pm, Sat 9am–6pm, Sun 11am–5pm; free) is also a marketplace filled with food vendors and restaurants, plus a major farmers' market on Tuesday, Thursday, and Saturday. Come with an appetite, as you'll be tempted by everything, from artisanal cheeses to delicate pastries.

### North Beach

In spite of its name, North Beach has no beach. It's the district where the city's Italian community took root and some of its greatest writers and deepest thinkers bloomed.

Cafés, restaurants, and stores line **Columbus Avenue**; it's an ideal place to sip an espresso and people-watch. The landmark **City Lights Books** (tel: 415-362-8193; www.citylights.com; daily 10am–midnight; free) buzzes with browsers who follow in the steps of the Beat writers such as Allen Ginsberg, who was championed by City Lights when *Howl* was banned.

From here, you can also look up the steep Telegraph Hill to see the white cylindrical **Coit Tower**, funded by a fabulously eccentric San Francisco heiress in the 1930s.

### San Francisco's great quake

When you hear San Franciscans talk about 'the big one,' they're usually looking back to 1906. On April 18 at 5.12am the city changed forever when a severe earthquake struck, starting dozens of fires that reduced most of San Francisco to ruins. More than 3,000 people died in the disaster and well over half of the population was left homeless. Downtown neighborhoods, including Chinatown, SoMA, and North Beach, were utterly destroyed, with just a few landmark buildings, such as the US Mint, left standing. A commemorative ceremony is held every April 18 at the intersection of Market and Kearny streets, where a fountain survived the quake.

# 🚶 GOLDEN GATE PARK AND HAIGHT ASHBURY

Spend a day exploring the eastern end of the vast Golden Gate Park, where you can walk or cycle between lush gardens and outstanding museums.

Start at the **de Young Museum**, a stark, copper-clad building. Though public opinion is divided about the architecture, the panoramic view from its observation tower is undeniably beautiful. The galleries display important collections of American, African, and Oceanic art, including works by stellar 20th-century artists such as Georgia O'Keeffe. Major international touring exhibits also stop here.

Just west of the de Young, along Hagiwara Tea Garden Drive, is the **Japanese Tea Garden**. This serene setting of bonsai conifers and curved wooden bridges is the oldest public Japanese-style garden in the country. The best time to visit is April, when its cherry trees burst into bloom.

Cross the Music Concourse to reach the **California Academy of Sciences**, the world's most eco-friendly museum. Under the wavy living roof, you'll find an aquarium filled with exotic fish; a planetarium; a live coral reef; a steamy rainforest environment; and interactive natural-history exhibits. There's also an excellent restaurant, the Moss Room.

Continue heading south on Martin Luther King Jr. Drive to reach the **San Francisco Botanical Garden at Strybing Arboretum**. The 7,500 species found here come from all around the globe, from tropical cloud forests to the most arid of Australian deserts. The arboretum is one of the best places to picnic.

Walk east on the loop road for about a mile. (If you're hungry, turn right on 7th Avenue for lunch options in the Inner Sunset neighborhood.) When you pass the baseball diamonds on Martin Luther King Jr. Drive, look for the nearby **Koret Children's Quarter**.

The dome of the Conservatory of Flowers

## Tips

- Distance: 3 miles (5km)
- Time: A full day
- The 5 and 44 buses stop at 8th and Fulton streets, just outside the park.
- The loop road is car-free on Sundays.
- Carry a map and stick to well-marked trails, since posted maps are rare.

The aquarium at the California Academy of Sciences

This public playground, built in 1887, is the oldest in the US, and has kept its colorful 1912 carousel.

Head north along Bowling Green Drive; at its intersection with Middle Drive East is the main entry to the **National Aids Memorial Grove.** These peaceful woods are a living tribute to those who have been affected by Aids.

Walk up Middle Drive East and cross John F. Kennedy Drive to reach the elegant, glass-domed **Conservatory of Flowers.** Built in the late 1870s, it's filled with nearly 2,000 plant species. Roam among the vivid tropical flowers, high-altitude orchids, and giant water lilies. In spring, 850 varieties of rhododendron bloom in the McLaren Memorial Rhododendron Dell, to the west of the conservatory.

Walk east on John F. Kennedy Drive to exit the park, turning right on Stanyan Street and left on to Haight Street. **The Haight** is still counterculture central after all these years. The Upper Haight, roughly from Stanyan to Masonic streets, presents a mishmash of funky boutiques, cheap eateries, and friendly bars. Amoeba Music, a top independent music store, and the anarchic Bound Together Books are classic places to browse. Finish your day with dinner at one of the Haight's low-key restaurants, such as Cha Cha Cha, and a fringe movie at the Red Vic Movie House.

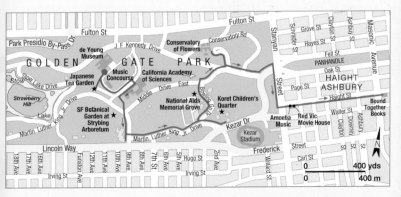

**Airports:** San Francisco International Airport (SFO); tel: 650-821-8211; www.flysfo.com; 14 miles (22km) from downtown San Francisco. BART: about 35 minutes to downtown, $8.10, runs until midnight daily. SuperShuttle, up to an hour to downtown, $15. Taxi: about 35 minutes to downtown, $40. Oakland International Airport (OAK); tel: 510-563-3300; www.oaklandairport.com; 14 miles (22km) from downtown. BayPorter Express: door-to-door service, over an hour to downtown, $34 (each additional person $15). SuperShuttle: vans to San Francisco and Oakland, $27 (each additional person $15). AirBART: about 15 minutes to connect to BART, $3, runs until midnight daily

 **Subway:** Bay Area Rapid Transit (BART); tel: 415-989-2278; www. bart.gov; the city's subway system

operates daily until midnight. Tickets from BART stations and many retailers throughout the Bay Area. Intracity San Francisco fares start at $1.75. Total fares are based on miles traveled

 **MUNI:** The San Francisco Municipal Transportation Agency (MUNI); tel: 415-673-6864; www.sfmuni.com. Muni's system of buses, trolleys, and vintage cable cars operates 24 hours a day. Basic fare for buses, streetcars, and trolleys is $2 one-way; cable-car is $6 one-way. Tickets from Muni vending machines

 **Taxis:** A taxi can be hard to find. Fares start at $3.10 with an additional .45¢ for each additional fifth of a mile. Dispatchers: Veteran's Cab; tel: 415-648-4444; or Luxor Cabs; tel: 415-282-4141. For any issues: San Francisco Municipal Travel Authority; tel: 415-701-2311

### Fisherman's Wharf and Alcatraz Island

Columbus Avenue shoots straight up to one of the city's most touristy spots: **Fisherman's Wharf** (www. visitfishermanswharf.com). A few fishing boats do still dock here, but now the main trade is sightseeing. Plump sea lions bark from floating docks, waterfront restaurants

Alcatraz was once the most feared prison in the US

Walking along the beach at the Presidio provides great views of the Golden Gate Bridge

dish up chowder, and vendors hawk kitschy souvenirs and tickets to the wax museum. There are a couple of historic vessels, too: the USS *Pampanito* and the SS *Jeremiah O'Brien*, both from World War II.

From one of the piers, ferries set off for **Alcatraz Island** (tel: 415-981-7625 for ferry; www.nps.gov/alca; mid-March–mid-Oct daily 9am–8.45pm, late Oct–early March daily 9.30am–4.30pm, with exceptions; charge for ferry). Otherwise known as The Rock, this was America's most feared federal prison. Notorious criminals such as Al Capone and George 'Machine Gun' Kelly served time on the Rock, with San Francisco glittering across the bay. An audio guide provides commentary on the empty cellblocks, telling stories of attempted escapes and desperate riots.

### Presidio and the Golden Gate Bridge

Yearning for a walk in the woods? Head to the **Presidio** (tel: 415-561-4323; www.nps.gov/prsf; daily 24

### Wine Country spas

Ready to be bathed in wine inside and out? Some beauty experts believe that the antioxidants and oils in grapes benefit the skin – and several Wine Country spas have jumped to take advantage of the grapes at their door. Many spas offer grapeseed scrubs and masks, even wine-infused hot-tub soaks. The town of Calistoga, in Napa, also touts its natural hot springs and mineral-rich mud baths.

Top spas include:

- Calistoga Spa Hot Springs (tel: 707-942-6269; www.calistogaspa.com).
- Fairmont Sonoma Mission Inn and Spa (tel: 707-938-9000; www.fairmont.com/sonoma).
- Kenwood Spa (tel: 707-833-1293; www.kenwoodinn.com).
- Spa Villagio (tel: 1-800-351-1133; http://villagio.com).

hours; free), a former military post that's now a lush park studded with historic buildings. It also offers stunning views of the bay.

The Presidio is an unusual national park in that it mixes commercial and residential projects along with the public attractions. For instance, filmmaker George Lucas has a studio here, and, at the time of writing, a Walt Disney museum is being built.

Down at the water stretches **Crissy Field**, once an airstrip and now a favorite place for locals to jog, walk dogs, and cycle. From here, you'll get a wonderful view of that SF icon, the **Golden Gate Bridge** (tel: 415-455-2000; www.goldengatebridge.org; daily 24 hours; free for pedestrians, charge for vehicles). Glowing in its coat of International Orange paint, the graceful span is considered one of the world's loveliest suspension bridges. There are walkways along its length, so walkers and cyclists can cross the bridge to the Marin County side, and back.

## The rest of California

Outside of its major cities, California offers almost every kind of vacation inspiration. In northern California, oenophiles cruise Napa and Sonoma counties, tasting some of the world's best wines. Nature lovers head to Yosemite National Park, with its jaw-dropping rock formations and towering sequoia trees. The Pacific Coast Highway skirts stunning coastal scenery as it winds along the southern half of the state, where inland deserts have an extreme beauty of their own.

### Lake Tahoe

Over in the crook where California and Nevada meet, **Lake Tahoe ❹** glistens an otherworldly shade of blue. The largest Alpine lake in the US (and second-deepest) is high up in the Sierra Nevada mountains, and is ringed with peaks. It is roughly four to five hours' drive from San Francisco.

In summer, waterfront vacation cottages fill with families and the lake comes alive with boats, Jet-skis, and parasailers braving the cold water. In winter, the ski slopes sweep into action. **Squaw Valley** (tel: 1-800-403-0206; www.squaw.com), on the northwest side of the lake, is one of the top ski resorts in California.

The Merced River flows toward Yosemite National Park's granite Half Dome

Relaxing at the peaceful Hyatt Regency Resort in Lake Tahoe

## Yosemite National Park

**Yosemite National Park** ❺ (tel: 209-372-0200; www.nps.gov/yose; daily 24 hours; charge) is still one of the most remarkable places in the world. Giant rock formations, towering sequoias, and rainbow-laced waterfalls have kept visitors in thrall since the park's founding in 1890 (*see pages 40–7*).

Several of the most breathtaking sights can be found in **Yosemite Valley**. Driving to the valley along Highway 41, pull over at **Tunnel View** for a postcard-perfect vista, with the valley stretching out at your feet. To the left rises the granite monolith **El Capitan**. To the right shimmers **Bridalveil Fall**, which plummets 620ft (190m). In the background looms the curved back and sheer granite face of **Half Dome**.

In Yosemite village, stop by at the **Yosemite Valley Visitor Center** (Memorial Day–Labor Day daily 9am–7.30pm, Labor Day–Memorial Day daily 9am–5pm; free) for its ranger-led hiking programs, bookstore, and ecology exhibits.

California

### Great Yosemite day hikes

The best way to see Yosemite is to get off the highway and hit a hiking trail. There are options for all abilities; here are a few of the most popular routes.

- **Valley Loop Trail.** Gentle route, 13 miles (21km) around. Views of Bridalveil and Yosemite waterfalls.
- **Four Mile Trail.** Actually closer to 5 miles (8km). Steep switchback route from Glacier Point into Yosemite Valley.
- **Lembert Dome Trail.** A steep, 3-mile (5km) hike round-trip, with a summit above the lovely Tuolumne Meadows.
- **Sentinel Dome Trail.** Just over 2 miles (3km) round-trip, moderately easy. Sweeping valley views and a good alternative to Half Dome.
- **Half Dome.** A bragging-rights hike and one to take seriously. At least 14 miles (22km) round-trip, including a summit leg for which climbers use metal cables. Views from the top are awe-inspiring.

Julia Pfeiffer Burns State Park, in Big Sur, has a small waterfall and private cove

Following Highway 41 south leads to the Wawona area, where the surreal **Mariposa Grove** of giant sequoias reaches for the sky. The so-called Grizzly Giant is the largest of them all, and is estimated to be 1,800 years old.

## Napa and Sonoma Wine Country

Although grapes are grown all over the state, the term 'Wine Country' usually refers to Napa and Sonoma counties, with the parallel valleys that produce some of the greatest vintages in the world.

Roughly an hour's drive northeast from San Francisco, the Mayacamas Mountains push up between the Napa and Sonoma valleys. Napa is the glitzier of the two, boasting high-profile vineyards and a global reputation. Sonoma is unpretentious, and is known for its smaller wineries. Both are exquisitely beautiful to drive through – head along Route 29 in Napa and Route 12 in Sonoma.

Pull into **Yountville**, in Napa Valley, to wander round a scenic small town with an extraordinary number of outstanding restaurants, including several run by Chef Thomas Keller. Nearby **Stag's Leap Wine Cellars** (tel: 707-944-2020; www.cask23.com; daily 10am–4.30pm; charge for tasting) put California wine makers on the international map, when it won the Judgment of Paris tasting in 1976. Its Cabernets still win accolades today.

At the northern end of the valley, scruffy but historic Calistoga is the home base for **Schramsberg** (tel: 707-942-4558; www.schramsberg.com; tour by appointment; charge for tasting), a venerable winery that is renowned for its sparkling wines.

Over in Sonoma Valley, you can get a bird's-eye view along with luscious wines at the **Kunde Family Estate** (tel: 707-833-5501; www.kunde.com; daily 10.30am–4.30pm; charge for tasting). Sign up for a mountain-top tasting and you'll quickly understand how the landscape and climate influence the grapes. **Sonoma** itself is the oldest town in Wine Country, with a stately town square surrounded by adobes and shops.

Of the many celebrities who have turned their hands to wine-making, the director of *The Godfather* is perhaps one of the most successful. His **Francis Ford Coppola Winery** (tel: 707-857-1400; www.francis coppolawinery.com; daily 11am–9pm; charge for tasting) has a Hollywood level of style and polish, with chic restaurants, movie memorabilia displays, a pool, and Italian bocce ball (similar to British bowls or French *boules*).

### Monterey Bay to Big Sur

When driving down the PCH, otherwise known as **Highway 1**, it can be hard to keep your eyes on the road, with the cliffs and ocean off to one side. The road's curves, though,

A wine maker tests the barrel at the Sebastiani Winery in Sonoma County

demand attention, at least until you pull into one of the charming towns that punctuate the route.

At the northern end of Monterey Bay is **Santa Cruz**, a laid-back beach town with a strong left-wing activist community spirit. Its beach boardwalk is a timeless spot, with an arcade, carousel, and the smell of cotton candy in the air. This is one of the sunnier stretches of coastline, so those eager to swim should hit the beach. Things get chillier further south.

At the bottom of the bay's curve sits Monterey, once a tough working town for fishing and canning. Now people get excited about the fish in the **Monterey Bay Aquarium** (tel: 831-648-4800; www.montereybay aquarium.org; mid-Sept–late May daily 10am–5pm, June–early Sept Mon–Fri 9.30am–6pm, Sat–Sun 9.30am–8pm; charge). The building, with outdoor pools overlooking the ocean, took over the site of what had once been a sardine cannery. The kelp-forest tanks are mesmerizing and you might see a Southern sea otter cracking open shellfish for a tasty snack.

One of the most scenic sections of the coastal route has a toll, as it crosses land owned by the Pebble Beach golf resort. Still, the **17-Mile Drive** merits its $9 charge as it meanders around the Monterey Peninsula, past the warped cypress trees clinging to the cliffs.

The PCH gets foggier as it winds south to **Big Sur**, arguably California's most beautiful stretch of coastline. The town itself is a small huddle of houses and shops but the scenery is wonderfully photogenic.

### Hearst Castle

Another 60 miles (96km) further south stands the fantastical, Baroque-style **Hearst Castle** (tel: 1-800-444-4445; www.hearstcastle.org; call for tour times; charge). The so-called 'little hideaway' of newspaper magnate William Randolph Hearst, the castle is stuffed with antiques and art.

### Palm Springs

Driving inland along the I-10 from Los Angeles, the landscape becomes more and more arid. **Palm Springs** ❻ glitters a couple of hours away, a palm-fringed oasis town with a distinctly retro feel. Its mid-century modern homes and reputation as a Rat Pack getaway draw thousands of tourists who would like some of that 1950s style to rub off on them. The primary leisure activities – golf, sunbathing, shopping, and swimming in hotel pools before a sunset cocktail – haven't changed.

**North Palm Canyon Drive** is a magnet for art galleries, clothing boutiques, and vintage furniture stores. On Thursday evenings, several blocks turn into VillageFest, bustling with outdoor vendors and unique food booths.

Get high with a ride up Mount San Jacinto on the **Palm Springs Aerial Tramway** (tel: 1-888 515-8726; www.pstramway.com; Mon–Fri 10am–8pm last tram up, Sat–Sun and holidays 8am–8pm last tram up; charge). The large, rotating cars provide spectacular views over the town and valley.

### Death Valley and the Mojave Desert

Deep into southern California, near the Nevada border between Highway 395 and I-40, lies some of the most desolate, challenging terrain in

A kelp-forest tank at the Monterey Bay Aquarium

The outlook from the spectacular vantage point of Death Valley's Dante's View at sunset

America. The Mojave (pronounced 'moh-hahv-ee') is relatively easy to explore between November and April, but in summer the heat is formidable. Situated within the Mojave Desert is Death Valley, the very hottest and driest location in North America, with a daily average high temperature of over 116°F (47°C). The valley acquired its name during the 1849 Gold Rush – although only one death in the area was recorded at the time. Wherever you drive today, be sure to bring plenty of water, food, and sunscreen.

Much of Death Valley is now contained within the **Death Valley National Park** (tel: 760-786-3200; www.nps.gov/deva; daily 24 hours; charge). Its **Badwater Basin**, a vast, gleaming salt flat, is the lowest place in North America, at 282ft (86m) below sea level. Stop by at the **Furnace Creek Visitor Center** (tel: 760-786-3200; www.nps.gov/deva; daily 8am–5pm; free) for natural-history exhibits, maps, and other information resources.

One of the more surreal sights in Death Valley is **Scotty's Castle** (tel: 760-786-2392; www.nps.gov/deva; Nov–Apr daily 8.30am–5.30pm, May–Oct daily 9am–4.30pm; charge). In the 1920s, Chicago millionaire Albert Johnson got suckered into a hunt for gold here by a local character dubbed 'Death Valley Scotty.' Although no gold came to light, Johnson fell for the desert and built a Spanish-style castle among the dunes.

The other surreal sight in the area is the **Amargosa Opera House** (tel: 760-852-4441; www.amargosa-opera-house.com) in Death Valley Junction, just outside the park limits. This venue, built in the Spanish Colonial Revival style, and decorated with elaborate murals painted in the late 1960s and early 1970s, still hosts plays and other dramatic performances.

# ACCOMMODATIONS

Whether you're traveling in northern or southern California, to a major city or to a quiet retreat, you will probably need to book at least three weeks in advance. And for Yosemite's lodges, make that several months. As a major vacation destination, the state is constantly flooded with travelers. In L.A., consider your hotel location carefully, since the city is so spread out and involves a lot of driving. If you plan to spend most of your time at the beach, for instance, stay on the West Side. For trips to Wine Country or Palm Springs, look for packages (wine-tasting and golf, respectively).

## Los Angeles

### Chateau Marmont
8221 Sunset Boulevard, Hollywood
*Tel: 323-656-1010*
**www.chateaumarmont.com**
Perched above the Sunset Strip, this is the discreet hideaway beloved of film stars and rock gods. If you're sitting in the bar, keep your eyes peeled to spot the celebrities. **$$$$**

### Figueroa Hotel
939 S. Figueroa Street, Downtown
*Tel: 213-627-8971*
**www.figueroahotel.com**
A onetime YWCA has been transformed, Hollywood-style, into an exotic, Moroccan-inspired reverie. Happily, it's also a bargain by L.A. standards. Rooms have wrought-iron beds and there's a pool out back for enjoying the California sun. **$$**

### Hotel Erwin
1697 Pacific Avenue, Venice Beach
*Tel: 310-452-1111*
**www.jdvhotels.com**
Situated just off the Venice boardwalk, the Erwin has a beach-party feel, with casual-chic guest rooms, a rooftop bar, and an all-round relaxed vibe. **$$$**

## San Diego

### Gaslamp Plaza Suites
520 E Street
*Tel: 619-232-9500*
**www.gaslampplaza.com**
At 11 stories high, this was San Diego's very first skyscraper – completed back in 1913. When booking, be sure to ask for a bay-facing room – and a higher floor, to ensure that you escape the night-time buzz of the Gaslamp neighborhood. Guest rooms are traditionally and comfortably furnished. **$$**

A room at the Hotel Erwin in Los Angeles

San Diego's Hotel del Coronado, the behemoth that inspired L. Frank Baum's *Wizard of Oz*

## Hotel del Coronado
1500 Orange Avenue
*Tel: 619-435-6611*
www.hoteldel.com
How about a stay in the hotel that inspired the City of Oz? On an island in San Diego Bay, this grand Victorian hotel sparked an idea in author L. Frank Baum. The 'Hotel Del' still feels fantastical, with its wide stretch of beach and red-roofed turrets. **$$$$**

## San Francisco
### The Fairmont
950 Mason Street
*Tel: 415-772-5000*
www.fairmont.com/sanfrancisco
Perched at the top of Nob Hill, this giant, white palace hotel has sweeping city views from every guest room. The kitsch-tastic Tonga Room tiki bar is renowned. **$$$$**

### Inn Above Tide
30 El Portal
*Tel: 415-332-9535*
www.innabovetide.com
The only hotel actually perched on the waters of San Francisco bay, the Inn Above Tide is the perfect place to watch the sunrise. **$$$–$$$$**

### Sir Francis Drake Hotel
450 Powell Street
*Tel: 415-392-7755*
www.sirfrancisdrake.com
Located just off Union Square, and with a 'beefeater' doorman, the 1928 Drake combines historic public areas with modern guest rooms. **$$$**

## Elsewhere in California
### The Ahwahnee
Yosemite Village
*Tel: 801-559-5055*
www.yosemitepark.com
The epitome of a gracious, historic lodge with an upscale restaurant. There are views of Half Dome from the back porch and valley views from the top-floor rooms. **$$$**

### Auberge du Soleil
180 Rutherford Hill Road, Napa Valley
*Tel: 707-963-1211*
www.aubergedusoleil.com
For a touch of the South of France in California's Wine Country, head to this smart hotel, which offers private terraces, lush grounds, and a posh restaurant. **$$$$**

### Curry Village
Curry Village, Yosemite National Park
*Tel: 801-559-4884*
www.yosemitepark.com
Curry Village offers large, canvas-sided tents on platforms down by the Merced River in Yosemite Valley. **$–$$**

**H2Hotel**
219 Healdsburg Avenue, Sonoma Valley
*Tel: 707922-5251*
**www.h2hotel.com**
Eco-friendly from the 'living roof' down to the bamboo floors. There's a great restaurant and bar, too. **$$$**

**Post Ranch Inn**
47900 Highway 1, Big Sur
*Tel: 831-667-2200*
**www.postranchinn.com**
Perched on oceanfront ridges, sometimes swathed in mist, this inn feels otherworldly. The cottages are built around pre-existing trees; guest rooms have spa tubs and fireplaces. **$$$$**

**River Ranch Lodge & Restaurant**
Highway 89 and Alpine Meadows Road, Tahoe City
*Tel: 530-583-4264*
**www.riverranchlodge.com**
Right along the Truckee River, this lodge is near the Squaw Valley ski resort. Homey to the hilt, with pine furniture and puffy down comforters. **$$**

**Viceroy Palm Springs**
415 S. Belardo Road
*Tel: 760-320-4117*
**www.viceroypalmsprings.com**
Ring-a-ding-ding! Channel a Rat Pack lost weekend in this Greco-Hollywood boutique hotel. **$$–$$$**

# RESTAURANTS

Food is a passion here – from the farm-to-table devotees in San Francisco to the celebrity-chefs in Los Angeles. There's also a lively food-truck and hole-in-the-wall crowd, always chasing the latest ethnic spot. Outside the main cities, Wine Country is a particularly good place to indulge, with local produce and artisanal treats accompanying the region's wine.

**Restaurant price categories**

Prices are for a main course meal for one, excluding alcoholic drinks:

**$** = less than $15
**$$** = $15–$25
**$$$** = $25–$50
**$$$$** = more than $50

## Los Angeles

**Animal**
435 N. Fairfax Avenue
*Tel: 323-782-9225*
**www.animalrestaurant.com**
Angelenos may be famously health-conscious, but this popular restaurant proves they also relish all kinds of meat, from pig tails to foie gras. **$$$**

**La Serenata**
1416 4th Street,
Santa Monica
*Tel: 310-656-7017*
**www.laserenataonline.com**
Classic Mexican dishes such as fish enchiladas and chile rellenos taste fabulously fresh here. **$$–$$$**

**Pizzeria Mozza**
641 N. Highland Avenue
*Tel: 323-297-0101*
**www.mozzarestaurantgroup.com**
Nancy Silverton made her name as a baker; her next act involves massive ovens turning out addictive pizzas, with toppings such as house-made sausage, Gorgonzola, and squash blossom. The fancier Osteria Mozza is just next door. **$$–$$$**

**Umami Burger**
500 Broadway,
Santa Monica
*Tel: 310-451-1300*
**http://umamiburger.com**
Did you know that the cheeseburger was invented in L.A.? This fast-growing chain

pays homage to this fast-food classic with its own gourmet version: house-ground meat and toppings such as green chiles and truffled cheese. **$**

## San Diego
**Cucina Urbana**
505 Laurel Street
*Tel: 619-239-2222*
**www.cucinaurbana.com**
A loose, Cal-Italian, family-friendly joint right near Balboa Park. Speck, mozzarella, and dried pineapple on a pizza? It's southern California, after all. **$$**

**Nine-Ten**
910 Prospect Street, La Jolla
*Tel: 858-964-5400*
**www.nine-ten.com**
Beautifully presented seasonal cooking with impeccably fresh local produce. The Jamaican jerk pork belly, though, stays put on the menu. **$$$$**

## San Francisco
**La Espiga de Oro**
2916 24th Street
*Tel: 415-826-1363*
San Francisco burritos are a special breed: they tend to be oversize, stuffed with rice and tons of condiments. This expert *taqueria* in the Mission District makes its own tortillas and is generous in piling on the *pico de gallo*. **$**

**Ton Kiang**
5821 Geary Boulevard
*Tel: 415-752-4440*
**www.tonkiang.net**
This dim-sum palace stands out from Chinatown competitors by virtue of its creative menu, tender dumplings, and additional Hakka specialties. **$$–$$$**

**Zuni Café**
1658 Market Street
*Tel: 415-552-2522*
**www.zunicafe.com**
A local legend. The simple, Mediterranean-influenced menu changes according to the

season, but the famous roasted chicken with bread salad is a fixture. **$$$**

## Elsewhere in California
**Bouchon**
6534 Washington Street, Napa Valley
*Tel: 707-944-8037*
**www.bouchonbistro.com**
The middle child of Thomas Keller's empire perfectly replicates a Parisian bistro, right down to its late-night menu. Just down the street is Keller's more casual spot, Ad Hoc (**$$**), while up the street sits his 'kingmaker', the innovative French Laundry (**$$$$**). **$$$**

**Bovolo**
106 Matheson Street, Sonoma Valley
*Tel: 707-431-2962*
**www.bovolorestaurant.com**
Calling this a sandwich and pizza shop doesn't nearly do it justice. Among the specialties are house-made bacon and sausage, local cheeses, and super-tender pork cheeks. **$–$$**

**Stokes Restaurant**
500 Hartnell Street, Monterey
*Tel: 831-373-1110*
**www.stokesrestaurant.com**
A 19th-century adobe house is filled with the homey smells from the wood-burning oven. The menu is a bit skewed towards the Mediterranean, with grilled fish and pizza. **$$**

A hearty American-style lunch for two

# NIGHTLIFE AND ENTERTAINMENT

East Coast types may joke about California culture involving suntan oil and popcorn flicks, but the performing-arts scene here is actually a force to be reckoned with, especially in Los Angeles and San Francisco. Rock and pop acts bounce out of Los Angeles as frequently as movie blockbusters, while Death Valley even has its own opera house if you prefer your culture of a higher calibre. Both San Francisco and LA nurture quite a cocktail culture, and San Diego area is known for experimental microbreweries.

## Bars and pubs

### The Abbey
692 N. Robertson Boulevard,
West Hollywood
*Tel: 310-289-8410*
**www.abbeyfoodandbar.com**
The mainstay of WeHo's busy gay scene buzzes all day long, starting with coffee in the morning and ending with drag nights and cocktails. There's a shrine to Elizabeth Taylor, who often came here later in her life.

### Father's Office
3229 Helms Avenue, Los Angeles
*Tel: 310-736-2224*
**www.fathersoffice.com**
With a big patio, cocktails as well as micro-brew beers, and the famous blue-cheese-topped burger, this pub is a favorite with locals, and is even better than the Santa Monica original.

### Stone Brewery
1999 Citracado Parkway, Escondido
*Tel: 760-294-7866*
**www.stonebrew.com**
Situated about 30 miles (48km) north of downtown San Diego, this is one of the area's top brewpubs, home of the Arrogant Bastard ale.

### Top of the Mark
1 Nob Hill, San Francisco
*Tel: 415-392-3434*
**www.intercontinentalmarkhopkins.com/
top_of_the_mark/**
Generations of sweethearts have toasted each other at this romantic perch, 19 stories up, enjoying spectacular views of the city all around.

### Twin Peaks Tavern
401 Castro Street
*Tel: 415-864-9470*
**www.twinpeakstavern.com**
Sometimes called the 'gay *Cheers*' bar, this long-established watering hole is a great spot for people-watching as the Castro's daily parade goes by.

## Classical music

### San Francisco Symphony
Civic Center, at Van Ness and Hayes streets,
San Francisco
*Tel: 415-864-6000*
**www.sfsymphony.org**
Celebrating its centennial in 2011, the San Francisco Symphony continues its world-renowned performances of both classical and modern music.

### Walt Disney Concert Hall
Music Center, N. 1st and S. Hope streets,
Downtown Los Angeles
*Tel: 323-850-2000*
**www.laphil.com**

The Abbey bar in Hollywood

Frank Gehry's curvaceous Walt Disney Concert Hall, Los Angeles

The L.A. Philharmonic performs in the silvery curls of its Frank Gehry building, an acoustically perfect space. The hall also hosts choral groups, jazz, and performances of world music.

## Film

### The Arclight
6360 Sunset Boulevard, Hollywood
*Tel: 323-464-1478*
www.arclightcinemas.com
It wouldn't be a trip to L.A. without a flick. Besides the classic movie palaces in Hollywood, check out the Arclight's huge Cinerama Dome, where special premieres and film events are held.

### Grauman's Chinese Theater
6925 Hollywood Boulevard
*Tel: 323-461-3331*
www.chinesetheaters.com
Located on the Hollywood Walk of Fame, many actors and actresses have stepped through this gate for premieres and award shows. There are nearly 200 hand- and footprints in the courtyard.

### Castro Theatre
429 Castro Street, San Francisco
*Tel: 415-621-6120*
www.castrotheatre.com
This 1920s movie palace shows new releases but the real fun is had at the retro

nights, showing camp classics such as *Mommie Dearest*. A Wurlitzer organ opens each show.

## Live music

### Boom Boom Room
1601 Fillmore Street, San Francisco
*Tel: 415-673-8000*
www.boomboomblues.com
Founded by legendary bluesman John Lee Hooker, Boom Boom still rocks the blues.

### Largo
366 N. La Cienega Boulevard, Los Angeles
*Tel: 310-855-0350*
www.largo-la.com
Rapt audiences listen to sets by guitarist-singers as well as enjoying comedy nights by TV stars such as Sarah Silverman.

### Whiskey A Go Go
8901 W. Sunset Boulevard, West Hollywood
*Tel: 310-652-4202*
www.whiskyagogo.com
Still rocking after all these decades, this Sunset Strip legend pounds with hard rock and alternative bands, plus a few tributes to great bands past, including the Doors.

## Theater

### Ahmanson Theatre and Mark Taper Forum
135 N. Grand Avenue, Downtown L.A.
*Tel: 213-972-7211*
www.centertheatregroup.org
Part of the Music Center performing-arts campus, the Ahmanson mounts everything from heavy dramas to Broadway musicals, while the smaller, round Taper is known for contemporary plays.

### Old Globe Theatre
Balboa Park, San Diego
*Tel: 619-234-5623*
www.theoldglobe.org
Modeled after Shakespeare's Globe in London, this round theater naturally hosts an annual festival of the Bard's works. It produces classic and modern plays, even musicals, on its three stages.

Listings

# SPORTS AND ACTIVITIES

The legend is true: in California you can start the day surfing and be skiing by the afternoon. With its long coastline, good surf, and dramatic mountain ranges, the state offers dozens of reasons to get outside and play.

## Baseball

**Los Angeles Dodgers**
1000 Elysium Park Avenue
*Tel: 866-363-4377*
http://losangeles.dodgers.mlb.com
Munch a 'Dodger dog' while watching a game. The Dodgers' biggest rivals are the San Francisco Giants and the New York Yankees.

**San Francisco Giants**
24 Willie Mays Plaza
*Tel: 415-972-2000*
http://sanfrancisco.giants.mlb.com
The waterfront AT&T ballpark makes for a fun game when players make a 'splash hit.'

## Basketball

**Los Angeles Lakers**
1111 S. Figueroa Street
*Tel: 213-742-7340*
www.nba.com/lakers
You might see stars cheering on Kobe Bryant from the courtside seats at the Staples Center.

## Golf

**Classic Club**
75200 Classic Club Boulevard, Palm Desert
*Tel: 760-601-3600*
This top-notch club racks up awards for its Arnold Palmer design.

**Pebble Beach Resort**
1700 17 Mile Drive, Pebble Beach
*Tel: 1-800-654-9300*
www.pebblebeach.com
Legendary set of courses in a stunning coastal setting; Spyglass Hill is one of the toughest in the world.

La Jolla Beach in San Diego is famous for great waves

## Hang-gliding
**The San Francisco Hang-gliding Center**
*Tel: 510-528-2300*
www.sfhanggliding.com
Leap from the peak of Mt Tamalpais, just north of the city, and catch a current that will land you gently on the sands of Stinson Beach. You can jump alone or with a guide, depending on your daring.

## Hiking
Hiking up in the Hollywood Hills or Santa Monica Mountains is a great way to offset hours in Los Angeles traffic. The trails in Griffith Park, Runyon Canyon, and Will Rogers State Historic Park are especially popular; you might even see a celebrity working off a power lunch. Check the L.A. Trails website, http://latrails.com, for details.

Yosemite National Park is a hiker's wonderland. (*See the box on p.243 for top day hikes.*) Ranger-led hikes are offered regularly, and most leave from the park's main visitor centers.

## Skiing

Squaw Valley (see the Lake Tahoe section on p.242) is one of the biggest ski resorts in the US. The other well-known resort around Lake Tahoe is Heavenly (tel: 970-496-4500; www.skiheavenly.com), on the south shore. It's considered especially family-friendly since it offers childcare and ski-school options for young children.

## Surfing

**Learn to Surf L.A.**
Tel: 310-663-2479
http://learntosurfla.com
Test the waves and learn to pop up along several L.A. beaches. With lessons for beginners and the more experienced, you'll be out on a board and catching waves in no time.

**San Diego Surfing Academy**
Tel: 1-800-447-7873
www.surfsdsa.com
Sign up for lessons at South Carlsbad State Beach, just north of downtown San Diego.

# TOURS

Skip the star maps – tour guides in California offer all sorts of angles on the state's pleasures and adventures past and present. With wine and beer tours, there's the extra benefit of being able to taste without having to drive afterwards.

## Boat tours

**Hornblower Cruises**
1066 North Harbor Drive, San Diego
Tel: 1-888-467-6256
www.hornblower.com
Go on a Hornblower Cruise and spot seals on a harbor cruise, or take a longer voyage and head out to sea for whale-watching in season.

## Driving tours

**Hollywood Tours**
Tel: 1-800-789-9575
www.hollywoodtours.us
This company offers over a dozen different tours, including a ride in a vintage Cadillac, as well as night-time drives and a route that takes you past a roster of film-star and celebrity homes.

## Food, wine, and beer tours

**Beau Wine Tours**
Napa and Sonoma
Tel: 707-938-8001
http://beauwinetours.com
Buses or limousines meander between the vineyards, either following your requested itinerary or suggesting wineries to try. This is a good option for a group vacation or special event.

**Brew Hop**
San Diego
Tel: 858-361-8457
www.brewhop.com
Sample some of the best beer from San Diego's bubbling microbrewery scene. Tours hit three or four specialty breweries, or can be customized at your request.

Sonoma County Vineyard

### Sonoma County Vineyard Adventures
*Tel: 707-522-5860*
**www.sonomavineyardadventures.com**
On any day, and with no advance booking required, visitors can take free, self-guided tours at nine of the most popular Sonoma wineries. The vineyard tours vary in length (the longest are just over a mile long), and are created for all ages to enjoy. After strolling past the vines to get an all-around impression of the vineyard, you can visit the vineyards' tasting rooms (charges may apply for tastings).

## Walking tours
### San Francisco City Guides
*Tel: 415-557-4266*
**www.sfcityguides.org**

Lace up some comfortable shoes (remember those hills!) and join one of these excellent tours offered by the public library. Themes range from neighborhood explorations to ghost walks.

### Local Taste of the City Tours
*Tel: 1-888-358-8687*
**www.localtastesofthecitytours.com**
These are the best tours if you have some time to spend and you're looking to indulge in a sampling smorgasbord. The tour leaders really do know all the locals, and recommend the best samples from a range of shops, including coffee, chocolate, pastries, pizzas, and olive oil. Tour options include North Beach and Little Italy, Chinatown, or a customized tour.

# FESTIVALS AND EVENTS

California's immigrant communities see to it that festivals such as Cinco de Mayo and Chinese New Year are celebrated lavishly. In agricultural or viticultural areas, there are also plenty of events centered around harvests or local specialties; check with local visitor bureaus for details.

## January
### Rose Parade
Jan 1
Pasadena
**www.tournamentofroses.com/the-rose-parade**
Every New Year's Day, a parade of marching bands, horseback riders, and floats entirely covered in flowers travels through the streets of Pasadena, just east of Los Angeles.

### Palm Springs Arts Festival
Palm Springs
**www.palmspringsartsfestival.com**
A gathering of 125 acclaimed artists in the desert town of Palm Springs. Includes a separate Indian Market with arts and crafts.

## January–mid-March
### Whale-watching
San Diego
**www.whaledays.com**

The San Diego area is a great place for spotting Pacific grey whales during their annual migration between Alaska and Baja California. You can watch from the shore at Cabrillo Point or sign up for a whale-watching cruise for a closer look. A Whale Days weekend celebrates the season, usually in late January.

## February
### Chinese New Year
San Francisco
**http://chineseparade.com**
San Francisco's Chinatown parade and festival is one of the biggest Chinese New Year celebrations in the US

### Palm Springs Modernism Week
**www.modernismweek.com**
Modernism Week is devoted to mid-century design in this desert-resort town, with architecture tours, lectures, and parties in some of the smartest homes.

## April

### Coachella

Indio, near Palm Springs

www.coachella.com

Not much more than a hipster-packed, indie rock weekend out in the desert, but all the famous names show up at some point. The dress code is super casual and the mood is anything-goes.

## May

### Bay to Breakers

San Francisco

http://zazzlebaytobreakers.com

This 12km (7.5 mile) race is a serious effort for some – but it's really more of a long-standing fun run, complete with a costume contest and Footstock, a post-race concert and beer garden.

## June

### Los Angeles Film Festival

www.lafilmfest.com

Major showcase for international and American independent films.

### San Francisco Pride

www.sfpride.org

The high-profile Pride organization throws the biggest LGBT event in the country each summer, with parades, concerts, outreach efforts, and more. Brings together leather, glitter, and political activism.

### Monterey Bay Blues Festival

www.montereyblues.com/festival

With multiple stages and the biggest headline acts, this is the place to get your blues on. The main arena holds almost 6,000 people, but the smaller stages are more intimate affairs and have seating.

## July

### Mendocino Music Festival

Mendocina

www.mendocinomusic.com

Fully staged operas, intimate chamber-music concerts, and international debuts are a key feature of this festival. With a concert hall overlooking the Pacific Ocean, you'll have beautiful views to match the music.

### Willits Frontier Days

Willets

www.willitsfrontierdays.com

California explores its past in the Wild West, as cowboys and girls participate in rodeos, parades, and contests. The oldest rodeo in the state provides the perfect backdrop for celebrating the Fourth of July.

## October

### Sonoma County Harvest Fair

http://harvestfair.org

Toast the annual grape harvest with tastings from over 100 local wineries, chef demos, art shows, and much more.

The starting line at San Francisco's Bay to Breakers race draws all kinds of characters

# The Pacific Northwest

The spirit of the Pacific Northwest is a watery one. The region is saturated with rain, snow, lakes, salmon-filled rivers, inlets, and, of course, the ocean. It's also saturated with a maverick spirit, an independence shared by Native American communities, farmers, musicians, and internet entrepreneurs.

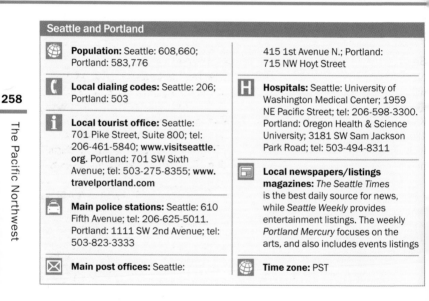

## Seattle and Portland

**Population:** Seattle: 608,660; Portland: 583,776

**Local dialing codes:** Seattle: 206; Portland: 503

**Local tourist office:** Seattle: 701 Pike Street, Suite 800; tel: 206-461-5840; www.visitseattle. org. Portland: 701 SW Sixth Avenue; tel: 503-275-8355; www. travelportland.com

**Main police stations:** Seattle: 610 Fifth Avenue; tel: 206-625-5011. Portland: 1111 SW 2nd Avenue; tel: 503-823-3333

**Main post offices:** Seattle:

415 1st Avenue N.; Portland: 715 NW Hoyt Street

**Hospitals:** Seattle: University of Washington Medical Center; 1959 NE Pacific Street; tel: 206-598-3300. Portland: Oregon Health & Science University; 3181 SW Sam Jackson Park Road; tel: 503-494-8311

**Local newspapers/listings magazines:** *The Seattle Times* is the best daily source for news, while *Seattle Weekly* provides entertainment listings. The weekly *Portland Mercury* focuses on the arts, and also includes events listings

**Time zone:** PST

Among the many attractions of Portland and Seattle are breathtaking scenery, great restaurant and music scenes, and innovative businesses. These two cities have both their histories and futures in pioneering. It started with the pioneers of the Oregon Trail in the 1840s, seeking gold or farmland in the raw West. Now these urban centers attract trailblazers in software, microprocessing, and biotechnology.

The so-called Silicon Forest companies, such as Microsoft, Amazon, and Intel, have drawn plenty of satellite enterprises. For all the business booms, locals appreciate and protect the region's small towns and natural areas. Quality of life is a high priority, with outdoorsy 'tech heads' eager to hit the Cascade Mountains or Columbia River. If it weren't quite so rainy, everyone might want to live here.

## Washington

Playing hard is serious work. Ask Washingtonians what they do, and they might describe their favorite hike or kayaking spot, their wine-tasting weekends, or a new rock club. (Only later will they mention their day job.) There are constant reminders of the fun to be had outdoors; from Seattle, you can see the glorious slopes of glacier-topped Mount Rainier.

### Seattle

Nestled on Puget Sound, and awash with successful businesses, **Seattle** ❶ first hitched its fortunes to the Klondike Gold Rush back in the late 1800s and has had several strokes of luck since. Most recently, its prominence comes from beans and bytes:

the city is home to the coffee giant Starbucksand Bill Gates's Microsft.

The webbed-foot stories are mostly true. It generally rains for more than 150 days each year, and when it's not raining, it's often drizzly, foggy, or just plain overcast.

**Pioneer Square**, a 17-square block area south of downtown, is Seattle's oldest neighborhood. Galleries, boutiques, bars, and cafés now fill its red-brick 1890s buildings, especially around the intersection of 1st Avenue and Yesler Way. Yesler was the original 'skid row', so called because trees were 'skidded' down a steep slope towards the waterfront.

Along the waterfront north of Yesler, up to Broad Street, swarm souvenir vendors and seafood shacks. One must-see is the **Pike Place Market** (tel: 206-682-7453; www. pikeplacemarket.org; Mon–Sat 9am– 6pm, Sun 9am–5pm; free). Opened

A fishmonger at Pike Place Market in Seattle

The Pacific Northwest

in 1907 so that farmers could sell directly to customers, it quickly became a city institution. Hundreds of vendors sell everything from locally grown vegetables to fresh flowers to wind-up toys. A briny smell draws visitors to the Pike Place fishmongers, who put on a show by throwing huge salmon between each other with never a slip. At the time of writing, the market was being renovated section by section, with work continuing until 2013.

Seattle's iconic building, the Eiffel Tower of the Rainy City, is the **Space Needle** (tel: 206-905-2100; www.spaceneedle.com; Mon–Thur 9.30am–11pm, Fri–Sat 9am–11-.30pm, Sun 9am–11pm; charge). Built for the 1962 World's Fair, it stands at 605ft (184m), topped with a flying-saucer-ish observation deck at 520ft (158m). You'll get a panoramic view from the 360° viewing area, making this a handy way to get oriented. There's also a restaurant that rotates slowly in the halo. The Needle pierces the **Seattle Center park**, which groups museums, gardens, and performance venues.

At the base of the Needle is the colorful mass of the **Experience Music Project** (EMP; tel: 206-770-2700; www.empmuseum.org; daily 10am–5pm; charge). Designed by Frank Gehry, the psychedelic building is said to evoke either the inner ear or a smashed guitar. The brainchild of tech billionaire Paul Allen, it focuses on music, science fiction, and pop culture, with cutting-edge interactive exhibits.

For another architectural showpiece, turn to the **Central Library**

The Space Needle viewed from Seattle's Olympic National Park

(tel: 206-386-4636; www.spl.org/locations/central-library; Mon–Thur 10am–8pm, Fri–Sat 10am–6pm, Sun noon–6pm; free). The main branch of the city's public-library system can be found in an angular building designed by Rem Koolhaas.

A huge steel figure pounds silently outside the **Seattle Art Museum** (SAM; tel: 206-344-5275; www.seattle artmuseum.org; Wed and Sat–Sun 10am–5pm, Thur–Fri 10am–9pm; charge). Its collection of Northwest Native American art is particularly strong, ranging from modern carvings to turn-of-the-20th-century basketry.

## Seattle city transportation

 **Airport:** Seattle-Tacoma International Airport (SEA); tel: 206-433-5388; **www.portseattle.org/seatac**; 14 miles (23km) south of downtown. Link Light Rail: about 35 minutes to downtown, $2.50 fare, runs daily from 5am to 1am. Taxi: between 20 and 30 minutes to downtown, roughly $35

 **Buses:** Seattle's Metro Transit, tel: 206-553-3000, **http://metro. kingcounty.gov**, offers a terrific deal by allowing riders to travel throughout downtown Seattle for free, 6am to 7pm daily. If you travel outside the Ride Free Area, fares run between $2.25 and $3, depending on peak hours and distance. Exact change is required on the bus, but bills are accepted. When you pay, make sure to ask for a transfer, which will allow you back on any Metro bus within a few hours. Locals purchase an ORCA card online, at Link Light Rail vending machines, or at some drugstores, to use on all forms of public transportation. Most bus routes are operational between 5am and 1am daily, although a few 'Night Owl' buses cover the remaining four hours

 **Monorail:** Seattle Monorail Services, tel: 206-905-2620; **www.seattle monorail.com**, operates the nation's oldest commercial monorail system on a short, 1-mile (1.6km) track between the Seattle Center (across from the Space Needle) and the Westlake Center Mall. The trip takes just a couple of minutes and runs between 7.30am and 11pm daily. One-way $2 fares can be purchased from the monorail cashier

 **Taxis:** It can be hard to find a cab, especially outside downtown, so call Yellow Cab, tel: 206-622-6500, for a pick up. Taxis charge $2.50 once the meter drops, then $2.50 per mile

# ★ NATIVE AMERICAN ARTS AND CRAFTS

Ceramics, baskets, jewelry, and other crafts by Native American artisans are not only attractive, but also provide a window into an ancient way of life. While beauty is in the eye of the beholder, it is important carefully to watch for authentic workmanship, so that you can be sure of supporting a tribal artist rather than a con artist.

### Masks

Carved wooden masks fashioned by Northwest Coast peoples have been prized since the days of the English explorer Captain James Cook (1728–79). Carved from cedar or alder, then vividly painted, these masks often represent spirits or animals; they may be worn during ceremonial dances.

If you're interested in buying a mask, check to make sure it does not have hairline cracks, indicating that it was carved from green wood. Steer clear of any mask with pink, blue, or orange paint, which are not traditional colors. Masks made by Alaskan Native artists are certified with a Silver Hand seal of authenticity.

### Pottery

Traditional ceramics are made by hand on a wheel, painted with natural dyes, and then fired over an open flame. Pottery vessels

Indians traditionally used materials that were very specific to them when making baskets

from the Southwest are among the most famous and styles between tribes vary considerably. The Hopi, for instance, are known for bold, geometric designs in red and black, while the renowned Pueblo 'black on black' look, with its matte and glossy combination of glazes, is a modern invention from the 1920s. Look for symmetrically shaped vessels with relatively thin, smooth walls.

## Jewelry

Metalwork and beadwork are the two main categories for this craft. Since jewelry-making was not significantly interrupted by colonization, and since metal, shells, and semiprecious stones were commonly traded goods, there is a certain continuity of style between various regional tribes. Jewelry made after the 1800s tends to be more elaborate, such as the 'squash blossom' silver necklaces made by the Navajo in the Southwest. In the Pacific Northwest, look out, too, for copper bracelets, which became popular during the early 1900s when trading ships brought supplies of the metal.

## Basketry

Handmade baskets are becoming increasingly rare. The materials vary according to location – tribes on the Northwest Coast traditionally use cedar bark or spruce root, while the Cherokee, in the Southeast, turned to river cane. For either coiled or woven baskets, look for a tight, smooth, and even construction. Again, reputable dealers will provide certificates of authenticity.

Carved, painted wooden masks, made from cedar or alder, are highly prized objects

Beadwork, along with metalwork, is one of the main types of traditional craft jewelry

Native American arts and crafts

Seattle's coffee scene

Starbucks may have originated in Pike Place Market, but the green mermaid doesn't monopolize the local caffeine scene. Far from it – locals are passionate about their independent cafes. Here are a few of the best:

**Ancient Grounds** (tel: 206-749-0747; no website). Strong espresso in a coffeehouse-slash-gallery.

**Caffe Vita** (tel: 206-652-8331; www.caffevita.com). The Pioneer Square branch of this small local chain has an attached pizzeria, in case you need a base layer for the potent coffee from its own roasters.

**Espresso Vivace** (tel: 206-860-2722; www.espressovivace.com). This roaster and coffee bar has a stand-up counter, sidewalk tables (for when it's not raining), and a mural painted in coffee.

## Olympic National Park

Often called 'three parks in one', **Olympic National Park** (tel: 360-565-3130; www.nps.gov/olym; daily 24 hours; charge) has three distinct ecosystems: glacier-capped mountains; pristine Pacific coastline; and the world's largest intact temperate rainforest.

Covering most of the Olympic Peninsula, this park is not only diverse but also remarkably undeveloped. Highway 101 skirts around three sides of the park. To get oriented, start at the **Olympic National Park Visitor Center and Museum** (tel: 360-565-3130; www.nps.gov/olym; daily

9am–4pm, extended hours in summer; free), on the north side of the park. Drive up to the nearby **Hurricane Ridge**, where you can get a good look at the park's mightiest peaks. **Mount Olympus**, the tallest at 7,965ft (2,428m), gleams with seven glaciers.

Deep in the interior, the **Hoh Rainforest** sponges up rain and mist. The moss-draped trees, including huge hemlocks, cast an emerald twilight. Black bears are occasionally spotted.

Over on the western coastline, hikers gravitate to the wild beaches. Harbor seals loll on the rocks; bald eagles soar overhead; and otters look for shellfish in the kelp beds.

## Mount Rainier

The greatest single-peak glacier system in the United States pours

The Hall of Moss in the Hoh Rainforest, part of Olympic National Park

The snowcapped Mount Rainier, with a summit elevation of 14,411ft (4,392m)

from the summit of the namesake peak of **Mount Rainier National Park** (tel: 360-569-2211; www.nps.gov/mora; daily 24 hours but limited vehicle access in winter; charge). The tallest mountain in the Cascade Range shines in the (all-too-rare) sun with dozens of glaciers.

Like Mount St Helens, Rainier is still an active volcano, although it hasn't erupted for more than a century. Its slopes form a perfect cone shape, and its lush, protected forest is laced with cascading waterfalls.

Most drivers arrive at the glacier through the Nisqually Entrance, approximately two hours' drive south of Seattle, taking the incredibly scenic Route 706 to Paradise village. The **Henry M. Jackson Memorial Visitor Center** (tel: 360-569-6036; www.nps.gov/mora; daily, mid-May–mid-June 10am–6pm, late June–Labor Day 10am–7pm, fall and winter hours more restricted; free) includes displays on local ecology. For the more energetic, there are several hiking trails that branch off nearby.

## Oregon

Oregon is a state divided by the Cascade mountains but not by ideas. There may be a 'wet' (west) and 'dry' (east) side, but Oregon residents universally appreciate the natural beauty around their cities.

### Portland

'The dream of the '90s is alive in Portland… Portland is a city where young people go to retire,' quips a number from the TV show *Portlandia*. True, life in **Portland ❷** can seem pretty easy, with tech-industry stars, a beautiful setting on the Willamette River, and a low-key attitude. Little wonder it's also called 'the city of beers, bikes, and blooms.'

**Pioneer Courthouse Square**, downtown by the intersection of Southwest

## Portland city transportation

 **Airport:** Portland International Airport (PDX); tel: 503-460-4234; **www.flypdx.com**; 10 miles (16km) northeast of downtown. TriMet's MAX Red Line: 38 minutes to downtown, $2.35 fare, runs from 4.45am to 11:50pm daily. Taxi: between 20 and 30 minutes to downtown, around $40

 **Buses:** Portland's TriMet, tel: 503-238-7433; **www.trimet.org**, operates an extensive bus system that carries passengers for free within the Fareless Square, an area that covers 300 blocks of downtown Portland. Outside of the Fareless Square, adult fares are either $2.05 or $2.35 depending on the distance traveled. Purchase your ticket on the bus with exact cash fare and ask for a transfer receipt, or purchase tickets and multi-day passes at TriMet's MAX stations or at some grocery stores.

This bus service technically runs 24 hours a day, but in fact, only a few routes are in operation between 1am and 4am

 **Streetcars:** Portland Streetcar, tel: 503-238-7433; **www.portlandstreetcar.org**, is integrated with TriMet and mostly operates within the Fareless Square area. If you leave the area, adult fares are a daily $2.05. All TriMet tickets and passes can be used on the streetcar, or else a streetcar ticket can be purchased on board. Streetcars run between 5.30am and 11.30pm daily

 **Taxis:** Looks for cabs outside major hotels or give them a call to be picked up. Two options are Radio Cab, tel: 503-227-1212, and Broadway Cab, tel: 503-227-1234. Taxicab rates are $2.50 for the first passenger, then $2.50 per mile

Pioneer Courthouse Square , Portland

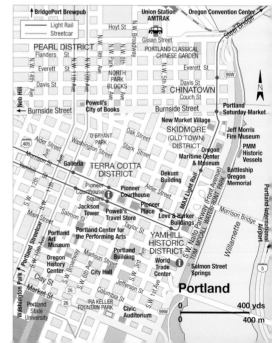

Portland's Japanese Garden is an oasis of peace and calm in the city

Broadway and Yamhill Street, is the city's living room. Civic events coalesce on the brick-paved plaza and locals flock to Powell's Bookstore here.

Nearby are several historic neighborhoods. The Yamhill and Skidmore districts, for instance, border the Willamette River, with a wealth of 19th-century buildings. The **Tom McCall Waterfront Park** unspools a lush ribbon of lawn, studded with sculptures and fountains, along the river.

And up by the Burnside Bridge, the **Portland Saturday Market** (tel: 503-222-6072; www.portlandsaturdaymarket.com; Sat 10am–5pm, Sun 11am–4.30pm; free) heats up every weekend with hundreds of artisan booths, food vendors, and live music.

Just west of downtown rise the slopes of West Hills, which are bristling with evergreens. This residential area includes the expansive

The Pacific Northwest

---

**Portland's food carts**

Mobile food trucks rumble through many US cities, but in Portland they are encouraged to join a permanent 'pod' in a parking lot rather than drive around town. Some of the city's most inventive cooking now happens on four wheels.

Check the Food Carts Portland website (www.foodcartsportland.com) for updates on who's cooking what where.

The vibe is relaxed and bike-friendly. Everyone from office workers to daytrippers congregate around the vendors, trying out pad Thai or Korean barbecue.

---

**Washington Park** (www.washingtonparkpdx.org; daily 5am–10pm; free), with its cluster of gardens, a children's museum, and a zoo.

For the most transporting experience, however, head to the **Portland Japanese Garden** (tel: 503-223-1321; http://japanesegarden.com; Mon noon–7pm, Tue–Sun 10am–7pm; charge). Five serene areas recreate traditional Japanese-garden styles, such as the Zen raked-sand garden and a Tea Garden. On a clear day, you can see Mount Hood.

The **International Rose Test Garden** (tel: 503-823-7529; www.rosegardenstore.org; daily 7.30am–9pm; free) is another standout. The garden was planted during World War I; now more than 400 varieties of roses perfume the air.

# ACCOMMODATIONS

Seattle and Portland both have plenty of easy-going hotels and bed and breakfastss – and luxury here almost always goes hand-in-hand with eco-friendliness. To overnight in one of the national-park lodges, try to reserve several months in advance; space is limited and the best lodges are prized for their views.

## Seattle

**Ace Hotel**
2423 1st Avenue
*Tel: 206-448-4721*
**www.acehotel.com/seattle**
This hotel is recommended for its eco-homey-hipster decor, vintage Modernist furniture, cool café, and low prices. There's an outpost in Portland, too. **$$**

**The Edgewater**
2411 Alaskan Way, beside Pier 67
*Tel: 206-728-7000*
**www.edgewaterhotel.com**
The city's only true waterfront hotel. The best rooms have views over Elliott Bay and, on clear days, the Olympic Mountains. An urban-rustic look, with pine furniture, plaid bedspreads, and fireplaces. **$$$**

**Gaslight Inn**
1727 15th Avenue
*Tel: 206-325-3654*
**www.gaslight-inn.com**
A bed and breakfast on Capitol Hill, an artsy neighborhood northeast of downtown. The

Craftsman bungalow has a pool out back and earth-toned guest rooms. **$$**

## Olympic National Park

**Kalaloch Campground**
Highway 101
*Tel: 360-962-2283*
**www.nps.gov/olym**
The park's only campground that takes reservations – from mid-June through Labor Day. It's got 170 sites and offers access to the wild coastline. **$**

**Kalaloch Lodge**
157151 Highway 101
*Tel: 360-288-2900*
**www.olympicnationalparks.com**
Kalaloch has both lodge rooms and separate cabins with sweeping ocean views. Guest rooms have fireplaces but no phones or TVs. **$$**

## Mount Rainier National Park

**Paradise Inn**
Paradise
*Tel: 360-569-2275*
**www.mtrainierguestservices.com**
The 1916 landmark gets a boost from hand-carved woodwork, including a wooden bear holding up a 'mail' sign. Some guest rooms are tucked under the rafters. The biggest attraction, though, is the glorious location. **$$**

## Portland

**The Lion and the Rose**
1810 NE 15th Avenue
*Tel: 503-287-9245*
**www.lionrose.com**

A standard room at the Ace Hotel, Seattle

This bed and breakfast is Victorian to the hilt. One room has a turret, another has a claw-foot tub. **$$**

### The Nines
525 SW Morrison
*Tel: 1-877-229-9995*
**www.starwoodhotels.com**
Portland's first modern-luxe hotel. Fine art everywhere, a well-stocked lending library, and plush guest rooms. Perfect for shoppers as it perches above a Macy's department store in the historic terracotta Meier & Frank Building. **$$$**

### RiverPlace Hotel
510 SW Harbor Way
*Tel: 503-228-3233*
**www.larkspurhotels.com**
Downtown's only riverfront hotel is set next

The atmospheric lending library at The Nines, in Portland

to the Tom McCall Waterfront Park. The plush modern rooms are decorated in sand-tones, and make the most of the wonderful views. **$$$**

# RESTAURANTS

The increasingly hot restaurant scenes in Portland and Seattle rely on locally sourced produce, meat, and seafood. Local salmon and oysters are particular treats. Asian and European cooking influences are very popular. Coffee is taken very seriously.

| Restaurant price categories |
| --- |
| Prices are for a main course meal for one, excluding alcoholic drinks: |
| **$** = less than $15 |
| **$$** = $15–$25 |
| **$$$** = $25–$50 |
| **$$$$** = more than $50 |

## Seattle
### Etta's
2020 Western Avenue
*Tel: 206-443-6000*
**http://tomdouglas.com**
Combining two Seattle institutions: Pike Place Market and restaurateur Tom Douglas. Etta's showcases seafood, such as grilled wild coho salmon. In 2010, Douglas bookended the market with Seatown, a casual seafood bar and rotisserie. **$$$**

### Le Gourmand
425 NW Market Street
*Tel: 206-784-3463*
**http://legourmandrestaurant.com**
Le Gourmand combines exquisite French technique with a Pacific Northwest grocery list. The sophisticated menu rotates season-ally; you might find halibut in sorrel sauce infused with fir, for instance. For a taste of the chef's more informal French cook-ing, stop in at the (less expensive) Sambar lounge next door. **$$$$**

### Salumi
309 3rd Avenue S
*Tel: 206-621-8772*
**www.salumicuredmeats.com**
This perennial Seattle favorite, set in the heart of the Pioneer Square district, offers sandwiches and delicious cured meats by celebrity TV chef Mario Batali's dad, Arman-dino. **$–$$**

### Wild Ginger
1401 3rd Avenue
*Tel: 206-623-4450*
**www.wildginger.net**
A pan-Asian local favorite, serving everything from curries to Malaysian fish stew in a sleek dining room. **$$–$$$**

## Portland
### Blueplate
308 SW Washington Street
*Tel: 503-295-2583*
**www.eatatblueplate.com**
An old-fashioned downtown lunch counter and soda fountain, with souped-up classics such as meatloaf, pot roast, and house-made sodas (try the Purple Haze, with hibiscus and star anise). **$**

### Clyde Common
1014 SW Stark Street
*Tel: 503-228-3333*
**www.clydecommon.com**
Tucked into the ever-hip Ace Hotel, the Common serves uncommonly good seasonal Euro-American fare, in which chicken wings get dolled up with a pomegranate sauce. **$$$**

### Toro Bravo
120 NE Russell Street
*Tel: 503-281-4464*
**www.torobravopdx.com**
It's hard to resist the parade of tapas (salt cod fritters, grilled shrimp) before devouring Moroccan-and-Spanish-inflected dishes like paella or butternut squash with harissa. **$$**

# NIGHTLIFE AND ENTERTAINMENT

Ever since the 1990s, Seattle has specialized in inward-gazing rock; these days, Portland's music scene is also gaining traction. Portland soaks up microbrewery accolades, too, with some of the country's best craft brewers manning the taps. Besides the bars noted below, look for a local brewpub chain called McMenamins

## Bars
### Bar Ferd'nand
1531 Melrose Avenue, Seattle
*Tel: 206-623-5882*
**www.ferdinandthebar.com**
An airy, pretention-free wine bar in Capitol Hill, with dozens of vintages by the glass. If you get hungry, the owner's restaurant, Sitka & Spruce, is right next door.

### BridgePort Ale House
3632 SE Hawthorne Boulevard, Portland
*Tel: 503-233-6540*
**www.bridgeportbrew.com**
Said to be Portland's oldest craft brewery, BridgePort runs a pub where you can sample its signature India pale ales.

### Brouwer's Café
400 N. 35th Street, Seattle
*Tel: 206-267-2437*
http://brouwerscafe.blogspot.com

Brouwer's Café is a former warehouse-turned-spacious beerhall, with roughly 65 international brews on tap, nearly as many whiskies to pour, and hundreds of bottled beers to sample (just not all at once).

### Rogue Distillery
1339 NW Flanders Street, Portland
*Tel: 503-222-5910*
**www.rogue.com**
One of Oregon's most successful micro-breweries, Rogue sets up shop here with over 30 of its ales, stouts, and lagers on tap Distillery tours offered, too.

### Zig Zag Café
1501 Western Avenue, Pike Street Hill Climb, Seattle
*Tel: 206-625-1146*
http://zigzagseattle.com
Tucked away behind Pike Place Market, this cocktail haven shakes up over a dozen

house specialties with evocative names such as Satan's Soulpatch.

## Live music

### Aladdin Theater
3017 SE Milwaukie Avenue, Portland
*Tel: 503-234-9694*
**www.aladdin-theater.com**
Once a movie palace, now a top venue for roots music, jazz, and country.

### The Crocodile
2200 2nd Avenue, Seattle
*Tel: 206-441-4618*
**http://thecrocodile.com**
The 'Croc' was a breeding ground for the grunge scene, shaping the Seattle Sound with Nirvana, Pearl Jam, and more. It still rounds up good indie rock, both local acts and international tours.

### Doug Fir Lounge
830 E. Burnside Street, Portland
*Tel: 503-231-9663*
**www.dougfirlounge.com**
Carved out of the Jupiter Hotel, this rock hotspot brings in everything from high-energy electronic music to folk-pop.

### The Showbox
1426 1st Avenue and 1700 1st Avenue S., Seattle
*Tel: 800-745-3000*
**www.showboxonline.com**
A pair of top-notch venues with music from rock to hip-hop. The Market location at

1426 dates back to 1939; further south, Showbox SoDo hums in an old warehouse.

### The Triple Door
216 Union Street, Seattle
*Tel: 206-838-4333*
**www.thetripledoor.net**
A cabaret-style venue for all kinds of acts, from burlesque to chamber pop. It's especially good for quieter acts, such as singer-songwriter guitarists.

## Classical music, opera, and ballet

### Benaroya Hall
200 University Street, Seattle
*Tel: 206-215-4747*
**www.seattlesymphony.org/benaroya**
Two downtown performance spaces, including the home of the Seattle Symphony, which performs from September to July. Summer brings jazz concerts.

### Marion Oliver McCaw Hall
321 Mercer Street, Seattle
*Tel: 206-733-9725*
**www.seattlecenter.com**
The Pacific Northwest Ballet and the Seattle Opera, a company with a special talent for Wagner, share this Seattle Center venue.

### Portland Center for the Performing Arts (PCPA)
SW Broadway and Main Street
*Tel: 503-248-4335*
**www.pcpa.com**
A trio of performance venues: the Antoinette Hatfield Hall for theater, the Arlene Schnitzer Concert Hall for the Oregon Symphony, and Keller Auditorium, home of the Portland Opera and the Oregon Ballet Theater.

## Theater

### Seattle Repertory Theater
155 Mercer Street, Seattle
*Tel: 206-443-2222*
**www.seattlerep.org**
Over at the Seattle Center, the Rep uses two stages for Broadway-tested plays and new works that it helps to develop.

Seattle has a great microbrewery scene

# SPORTS AND ACTIVITIES

To look like a local, climb on a bike (especially in Portland), go for a hike, or grab a kayak paddle. Unless it's raining, the Pacific Northwest's dramatic scenery pulls everyone off the sidewalks sooner or later.

## Bicycling

**Montlake Bicycle Shop**
2223 24th Avenue E., Seattle
*Tel: 206-329-7333*
**www.montlakebike.com**
Rental bikes are available daily. The shop is situated near the connected Burke-Gilman and Sammamish River trails – over 20 miles (32km) of paved pathway that follows an old railroad route.

**Waterfront Bicycles**
10 SW Ash Street, Portland
*Tel: 503-227-1719*
**www.waterfrontbikes.com**
Portland's largest rental-bike dealer, with easy access to the namesake strip of river-side park.

## Hiking

Olympic and Mount Rainier national parks are threaded with dozens of hiking trails, which often connect up so that visitors can put together their own routes. When hiking on Olympic's coastline, be sure to check tide timetables so you don't get caught during high tide.

In Seattle proper, many visitors make their way to Discovery Park (tel: 206-386-4236; www.seattle.gov/Parks/environment/discovparkindex.htm; daily 6am–11pm; free), which is the city's biggest park. Trails wind their way between beaches on Puget Sound, areas of dense forest, and swaths of beautiful meadows.

## Kayaking

**Moss Bay**
1001 Fairview Avenue N., Seattle
*Tel: 206-682-2031*
**www.mossbay.net**
Paddle out on to Lake Union or join a guided kayaking tour that includes a run through gravity locks.

# TOURS

The Pacific Northwest offers a great range of tour options – whether they're based on the history of the Gold Rushes or the region's impressive food scenes.

## Day trip

**Tillicum Village Tour**
Leaves from Pier 55, Seattle
*Tel: 206-623-1445*
**www.tillicumvillage.com**
Like the Space Needle, Tillicum was built for Seattle's 1962 World's Fair. Nowadays, you can take a boat ride out to Blake Island for a salmon dinner in a traditional longhouse, followed by Salish tribal masked dances.

## Food and beer tours

**Portland BrewBus**
*Tel: 503-647-0021*
**www.brewbus.com**
Climb aboard the BrewBus for a crash course in Portland's brewing history. Slake your thirst as the bus stops at three or four breweries along the way.

**Savor Seattle Food Tours**
*Tel: 1-888-987-2867*
**www.savorseattletours.com**
Guides toting pink umbrellas lead groups on food tours that take you through Pike Place Market, via several top chocolatiers, and around the numerous ethnic restaurants in Capitol Hill.

## Walking tours

**Portland Walking Tours**
*Tel: 503-774-4522*
**www.portlandwalkingtours.com**
Half-a-dozen terrific theme tours, including a downtown culture stroll, a chocaholic route, and an in-depth tour of the International Rose Test Garden.

**See Seattle**
*Tel: 425-226-7641*
**www.see-seattle.com**
A good, thorough introduction to Seattle, touching on history, architecture, colorful local characters, and more.

**Underground Tour**
Pioneer Square, Seattle
*Tel: 206-682-4646*
**www.undergroundtour.com**
Get to know the buried history of Seattle: downtown's original roads and store fronts are hidden below street level. Guides take you through the warren of walkways beneath Pioneer Square, with lively tales of the city's bawdy Gold Rush days.

# FESTIVALS AND EVENTS

In addition to the celebrations below, check the schedule for the widely acclaimed Oregon Shakespeare Festival (tel: 541-482-4331; www.osfashland.org). More of a full season than a festival, this annual event in Ashland, Oregon, presents 11 plays over 8.5 months.

## May

**Northwest Folklife Festival**
Memorial Day weekend, Seattle
*Tel: 206-684-7300*
**www.nwfolklife.org**
All sorts of ethnic communities participate in this event, showcasing dance and music by local performers.

## June

**Portland Rose Festival**
*Tel: 503-227-2681*
**www.rosefestival.org**
One of Portland's nicknames is the City of

The Portland Rose Festival Parade

Roses; this celebration lives up to that accolade, with rose displays, fireworks, and a floral-float parade.

## July

**Oregon Brewfest**
Last weekend in July
Waterfront Park, Portland
*Tel: 503-778-5917*
**www.oregonbrewfest.com**
Thousands of beer lovers converge on the city to taste well over 80 craft brews from Oregon, and other states as well. Be sure to bring a designated driver.

## September

**Bumbershoot**
Labor Day weekend
Seattle Center
*Tel: 206-281-7788*
**http://bumbershoot.org**
A free-spirited music and arts festival with a wide-ranging roster of musicians – think Bob Dylan, the Decemberists, and Mary J. Blige all on one bill. It's sometimes a bit of a risk with the weather, but it's well-worth wearing the wellies.

# PRACTICAL ADVICE

# Accommodations

Accommodations in the US run the whole spectrum – from historic palace hotels to campgrounds in remote back country. And as for all those hotels that boast celebrity guests – Oscar Wilde, George Washington, or even Buffalo Bill – you never know, they might even be telling the truth.

High seasons for accommodations are shaped by the weather as well as school vacations, major local festivals, and popular sports. Winter means that ski resorts and the Sun Belt southern states get busy; in summer, northern beach towns and theme parks are mobbed *(see also pages 12–13)*. If you are staying in a major vacation destination or are hitting town during a popular festival, such as New Orleans for Mardi Gras, try to book several months in advance. In some locations, most hotels will close during low season, but a few will stay open year-round with reduced rates.

## HOTELS

American hotels come in all varieties, with regionally influenced tweaks in addition to the usual categories. History buffs seek out centuries-old properties in New England, for instance, while modern-architecture fans can find stylish new hotels on the west coast. There are no US-wide official grading systems for hotels, but national travel publications such as *Travel + Leisure* give annual awards for outstanding properties.

It's always sensible to make reservations in advance, which you can do over the phone or online, either via the hotel's own website or perhaps through an aggregator such as Expedia.com. American hotels usually charge by the room, not by the number of occupants; sometimes a child's bed or sofa bed can be included. The advertised rates do not normally include the state and city sales taxes or daily

The Stanley Hotel in Estes Park, Colorado was the inspiration for Stephen King's novel *The Shining*

occupancy tax. Hotel rooms generally have air-conditioning, a private bathroom, and a television. Many resort hotels offer special rates to guests who take their meals on the premises.

There are several hotel chains with properties across the country, offering a consistent quality of accommodations. Major companies such as Starwood or Marriott have tiered systems, with brands at different price points.

If you're interested in unique historic lodgings, review the members of the **Historic Hotels of America** (www.historichotels.org). The **Small Luxury Hotels of the World** association (www.slh.com) rounds up high-end boutique properties. To quickly find an eco-friendly hotel, try online directories such as **iStayGreen** (www.istaygreen.org) or the **Green Hotels Association** (http://greenhotels.com).

## BUDGET OPTIONS

Motels are America's classic bargain accommodations. They offer basic amenities such as in-room bathrooms and TVs, but are otherwise no-frills. Two of the major national chains are Super 8 and Motel 6. Motels are often targeted at drivers or travelers staying just one night, with franchises near major freeways or on the outskirts of towns. Outside cities, motels cost around $60 a night; urban locations hover around $80 to $100. Travelers who stay multiple nights with a particular chain often get discounts.

**Hostelling International** (www.hiusa.org) has a US chapter and affiliated hostels in over 20 states. There's a dearth of HI hostels in the Midwest and the South, but along both coasts

A chain hotel can provide you with a reliable level of quality at a reasonable price

and in Texas you will find numerous options. Dorm-room rates can be as low as $20 in suburban or small-town locations. In major cities, dorm beds cost $60 to $70. Hostels do have a maximum number of nights for overnight stays.

**YMCA** and **YWCA** hostels (http://ymca.net) are another popular option, with lodgings across the country and rates similar to HI-affiliated hostels. Membership is not necessary but demand is high, so reserve in advance.

## OTHER ACCOMMODATIONS

Bed-and-breakfast inns are quite popular in some parts of the US. Often converted from historic private homes, with just a few guest rooms, they provide a more intimate lodging experience. They usually offer breakfast in a common dining room and innkeepers are able to offer recommendations on area attractions.

Camping is a good option for travelers on a tight budget, but book early for popular sites

Intimate doesn't always mean bargain, though. While some bed and breakfasts are informal, family-run properties, others are polished, expensive showcases, stuffed with antiques, costing $200 or more a night. Bed and breakfasts tend to proliferate in smaller towns and holiday centers. Major cities such as Boston and New York City have very few bed and breakfasts. There are several associations that offer directories of properties and reservation services. Try **Bed & Breakfast Inns Online** (www.bbonline.com) or **Bed & Breakfast America** (www.bedandbreakfastamerica.net).

Dude ranches are an especially American phenomenon – a chance to ride the range and chow down on cowboy steaks around a campfire. These range from luxury spreads, with plush rooms and swimming pools, to straightforward working ranches, where guests take part in daily chores.

## CAMPING

Many of the best campgrounds are in or near national or state-run parks. Some have pitches for tents and RVs; others are tent-only. You can expect at least pit or flush toilets and some type of grill or cooking area. Some sites also have showers, laundries, and other amenities. Parks specify which sites can run generators and sometimes impose a limit on the size of RVs or trailers. Campgrounds also vary in their policies towards pets. For remote, bare-bones back-country sites, visitors may need a special wilderness permit for hiking and camping.

Campsites generally cost $30 a night or less. National parks often have some campgrounds at which you can reserve in advance, plus other sites on a first-come, first-served basis. For the most popular parks, try to book at least a few months in advance. Concessionaires manage campgrounds in some parks. **Xanterra Parks & Resorts** (www.xanterra.com), for example, operates campsites at several national parks, including Yellowstone, Zion, and the Grand Canyon's South Rim.

Depending on the local weather, campgrounds may close in the off-season. For instance, at Yellowstone, only one campground stays open year-round; the rest close in winter.

For more information on private campgrounds, consult the **National Association of RV Parks and Campgrounds** (www.gocampingamerica.com). The website includes a database of campsites, reviews, suggested trips, and more. Individual states also have camping associations.

# Transportation

## GETTING TO THE US
### By air
**American Airlines:** www.aa.com
**British Airways:** www.ba.com
**Continental Airlines:** www.continental.com
**Qantas:** www.qantas.com.au
**Virgin Atlantic:** www.virgin-atlantic.com

Dozens upon dozens of airlines serve the US on domestic and international routes. Websites for the largest and most popular companies are detailed above. Every major American city has an airport. Two of the biggest international hubs are New York City's JFK International Airport and Los Angeles International Airport. Within the US, there are several non-stop flights every day between major cities. From Europe, the UK usually has the best airfares to the US, so some Europeans fly to London and then on to New York, to take advantage of the lower rates. *See regional chapters for contact details of major airports across the US.*

### Average flying times
**Los Angeles:** to San Francisco, 1 hour 15 minutes; to New York City, 6 hours; to Sydney, Australia, 14 hours
**New York:** to Chicago, 2 hours 20 minutes; to Miami, 3 hours 15 minutes; to London, 6 hours; to Sydney, Australia, 22 hours

## GETTING AROUND THE US
As the US is such as large country, air travel is the quickest and easiest way to travel between major centers. Once you're in a given region or city, though, driving is often the most convenient way to get around. In some cities, especially in the Northeast, public transit is the most efficient (and cheapest) way to explore. *See regional chapters for in-depth information on local transportation.*

### Domestic flights
**American Airlines:** tel: 1-800-433-7300; www.aa.com
**Continental Airlines:** tel: 1-800-523-3273; www.continental.com
**Delta:** tel: 1-800-221-1212; www.delta.com
**JetBlue:** tel: 1-800-538-2583; http://jetblue.com
**Southwest Airlines:** tel: 1-800-435-9792; www.southwest.com

Traveling by air is the quickest way to cross the vast US – often with amazing views

Rail service is best in the Northeast Corridor, between Washington, DC and Boston

## Trains

Train services in the US are uneven. Many of the most reliable routes are those that are popular with daily commuters, such as the Northeast Corridor line between Boston and Washington, DC. There are also good services along popular scenic routes, such as the Coast Starlight from LA to Seattle. Otherwise, intercity train travel is far more limited than in Europe. Services are also not very frequent and are often plagued by delays.

**Amtrak** (tel: 1-800-872-7245; www.amtrak.com) is the national rail provider. Tickets can be bought online, via the hotline, or at train stations from an agent or an automated kiosk. The cheapest tickets are usually reserved several weeks in advance. Indicative fares include: $50 one-way between Boston and New York City; $100 one-way between Chicago and New York City; $200 one-way between L.A. and Seattle.

Amtrak also offers several rail-pass options: the USA Rail Pass and the California Rail Pass. These passes cover multiple days of travel over a set time period. In addition to having a pass, you must reserve a seat for each leg of your journey.

## Inter-city coaches

Bus networks crisscross the entire country. **Greyhound Lines** (tel: 1-800-231-2222; www.greyhound.com) is the largest national company, with services around the clock. In addition to single-journey tickets, Greyhound offers a Discovery Pass for unlimited travel within a certain time frame – for 7, 15, 30 or 60 days.

There are over half-a-dozen airlines that provide extensive coverage of domestic routes in the US. The largest and most popular are listed above. In addition to the major urban airports, there are smaller regional hubs and airports for most popular vacation destinations. This network enables you to get to almost any corner of any state by plane.

It takes roughly six hours to fly non-stop between east and west coasts. Flights running north and south between coastal cities, such as routes between L.A. and San Francisco, or Boston and Miami, take anywhere from one to four hours.

Aggregator websites for discounted airfares are an easy way to simultaneously search several airlines for their best prices. Some, such as Momondo and Kayak, act as search engines just to review prices. Online travel agencies such as Orbitz, Travelocity, and Expedia let you compare costs and book tickets directly.

Regional companies include **Peter Pan Bus Lines** (tel: 1-800-343-9999; www.peterpanbus.com), which provides services between New England and Mid-Atlantic cities. For destinations that are a few hours apart, bus fares can run at less than $30.

Some discount bus lines have recently sprung up in regions with heavy commuter traffic. For instance, **BoltBus** (tel: 1-877-265-8287; www.boltbus.com) runs between New York City, Boston, Philadelphia, Newark, and Washington, DC, with tickets costing less than $20.

# DRIVING

The allure of the open road has a special power for Americans. For traveling between destinations, or for enjoying the scenery, driving is often the best way to travel. Despite the rising cost of gas, it can also be one of the cheapest ways to get around.

A few cities are known for being difficult to drive in because of their confusing street systems and aggressive drivers. Boston, New York,

Philadelphia, and Dallas are perhaps the worst. L.A. has notoriously bad traffic. but since this sprawling city is built around freeways, it is almost impossible to get around without driving.

## Road conditions

The interstate highway system is extensive, well-signposted, and well-maintained. Odd-numbered highways run north to south, while even-numbered highways run east to west. There are also large networks of state and county routes. Many, but not all, highways or turnpikes are toll-free. Gas stations stay open late or 24 hours along main arteries.

## Regulations

Drive on the right. Intersections are usually marked with stop or yield signs to indicate who has priority. Making a right-hand turn on a red signal may or may not be legal, depending on where you're driving; look for signage.

Speed limits vary from state to state and depend on the type of road. Some interstates in rural areas have 75mph (120kmh) limits, while busy downtown roads may have 35mph (57kmh) limits. Look out for yellow school signs; in school zones, the speed limit drops to 15mph (24kmh).

The average minimum driving age in the US is 16, but this limit is determined by individual states. Foreign driver's licenses are generally accepted in the US if they are in English; otherwise, it is best to get an international driver's license before your visit.

A few states, including California and New York, do not allow the use

Long, straight, empty roads characterize cross-country driving

of handheld mobile phones while driving; over 30 states do not allow texting while driving. All states have adopted .08 as the legal limit of blood alcohol content (BAC) for drivers.

### Motoring associations

If you have a breakdown on a freeway, pull over on to the right-hand shoulder, turn on your hazard lights, raise the hood (bonnet), and either use your cellphone to call for help or wait in the car for assistance.

The **American Automobile Association** (AAA; tel: 1-800-222-4357, www.aaa.com) offers information on traveling in the US as well as roadside assistance to motorists. International visitors who are members of an affiliate auto association in their home country, including the UK's Automobile Association, are eligible for these benefits, too.

Some states, including California, also operate a freeway service patrol for stranded drivers.

### Vehicle hire

National car-rental agencies include: **Alamo** (tel: 1-877-222-9075; www.goalamo.com), **Avis** (tel: 1-800-331-1212; www.avis.com), **Budget** (tel: 1-800-527-0700; www.budget.com), **Dollar** (tel: 1-800-800-3665; www.dollar.com), **Enterprise** (tel: 1-800-261-7331; www.enterprise.com), **Hertz** (tel: 1-800-654-3131; www.hertz.com), **National** (tel: 1-877-222-9058; www.nationalcar.com), and **Thrifty** (tell 1-800-847-4389; www.thrifty.com).

Most car-rental companies offer a flat rate with unlimited mileage. Charges, taxes, and policies vary

Multiple lanes of traffic on San Francisco's Golden Gate Bridge

considerably, so it pays to consider your needs and shop around carefully.

When it comes to insurance coverage, ask your credit-card company about any automatic coverage they may provide when you use the card for a rental. Note that even credit cards don't cover liabilities if you hurt another party or damage something other than the rental car. Car-rental companies offer loss/damage waivers (LDWs) for $15 to $20 per day, which is a reasonable price to pay for coverage and peace of mind.

## ACCESSIBILITY

The **American Disabilities Act** (www.ada.com) requires equal access for the disabled at most places that cater to the public, including all government facilities. The **Society for Accessible Travel and Hospitality** (SATH; tel: 212-447-7284; www.sath.org) offers numerous resources for travelers with disabilities, including an informative website.

# Health and safety

## MEDICAL CARE

No vaccinations are required for travel to the US, though you should make sure that you are up to date with your polio and tetanus vaccinations. If you're traveling during 'flu season, from late fall to early spring, it may be a good idea to get a flu shot.

Health-care provision in the US is generally of a good standard, but it doesn't come cheap. Free medical services are not available in the US and a visit to a doctor or hospital can be very expensive. Federal law obliges emergency rooms to admit and care for any patient, but hospitals may balk at international-insurance carriers. Holiday medical insurance is a good idea. *See regional chapters for contact details of hospitals in major cities.*

For relatively minor health problems, such as coughs and colds, seek out a walk-in health clinic. Many pharmacy chains are adding these inexpensive treatment counters. The Walgreens chain, for example, offers Take Care Clinics, staffed by nurse practitioners, in over 300 drugstores across the country.

Pharmacies are readily available throughout the US. While there is no general indicating symbol, you will soon become familiar with the national drugstore chains such as Rite-Aid, Walgreens, and CVS. Some large grocery stores also have their own in-store pharmacies. In larger cities, you can usually find a 24-hour pharmacy or drugstore with late-night hours. In smaller communities, pharmacies may only stay open from 8am to 6pm or 7pm.

Drugstores fill prescriptions and sell over-the-counter remedies. Note that some medicines you may buy over the counter in another country must be filled by a prescription in the US. If there's any doubt about getting a necessary medicine, be sure to bring your own supply.

If you need to contact a travel health specialist in the US, check the national directory of the **Centers for Disease Prevention and Control** (wwwnc.cdc.gov/travel). Another information resource worth consulting is the **International Association of Medical Assistance to Travellers** (www.iamat.org).

The ban on HIV-positive travelers entering the US was lifted in 2010.

Travelers are strongly advised to take out private medical insurance when in the US

HEAT 'KILLS

DON'T LEAVE
PETS IN
PARKED VEHICLES

BCMC 7-3-9F NRS 574.19C
COPYRIGHT BY AMERICAN HUMANE SOCIETY

DONATED BY THE
BOULDER CITY
COMMUNITY CLUB
AND DESI ARNAZ JR

Beware of soaring temperatures and take
precautions to avoid heatstroke

## NATURAL HAZARDS

If you are traveling in an area known
for its extreme summer temperatures,
such as the Southwest, be wary of
heatstroke. Be sure to wear a hat,
slather on the sunblock, and drink
plenty of fluids.

Large swaths of the US, including
the Midwest, Northeast, and South,
suffer from swarms of mosquitos in
summer. Lyme disease, carried by
ticks, is a concern in wooded areas.
Repellent sprays and lotions are readily available in pharmacies.

The South – and particularly
Florida – is prone to hurricanes in
summer. The National Hurricane
Center (www.nhc.noaa.gov) tracks
tropical storms. California and the
Southwest are particularly vulnerable
to wildfires in summer and fall. Any
type of fire may be illegal in these
areas, even at campsites.

## FOOD AND DRINK

Tap water is safe to drink in the US.
Non-potable water may be in use at
campgrounds, though, and it's not a
good idea to drink water from lakes,
streams, or rivers, as Giardia, E. coli
and other bacteria may be present.

There are few major food concerns
in US, though you should take the
usual precautions. (Discounted sushi
in a deli at midnight? Steer clear.)
Street-food vendors are common in
cities and their snacks and hot meals
are generally safe for consumption.

You must be 21 or older to purchase
or consume alcoholic drinks. You may
be asked to show a legal form of identi-
fication to prove your age.

## CRIME AND SAFETY

American police officers are generally fair and friendly. Don't hesitate
to approach one for assistance or
information. City police handle local
crime and traffic violations. Highway
patrol officers or state troopers ensure
road safety and watch for people
speeding or driving while under the
influence of alcohol.

If you have been the victim of a crime, seek out the nearest police precinct station to file a report. If you need emergency assistance, dial 911.

Since September 11, security checks have been stepped up at airports and other transportation hubs. In large cities, you may see armed security officers in train stations, subways, and other transit centers. Bags may be searched. Government buildings, museums, and other institutions usually run basic security checks as well.

Tourist-centric areas are generally safe – though the risk of pickpockets is ubiquitous. Large cities inevitably have their less-salubrious neighborhoods and outbreaks of petty crime, so use the same precautions you would at home. Ask your hotel concierge or other local contact about any neighborhoods that may be risky to walk or drive through.

Don't leave valuables in your car; keep your wallet in a closed bag or concealed pocket; and avoid dark, deserted streets, parks, or public areas late at night. Always keep bags on your lap or tucked between your feet, not hung on the back of a chair or otherwise unattended. Stay awake and alert on public transportation.

Gay travelers will find the US increasingly tolerant of same-sex couples, especially the larger cities or long-time gay-friendly destinations such as Provincetown, Massachusetts, and Palm Springs, California. The **International Gay & Lesbian Travel Association** (www.iglta.org) provides a directory of gay-friendly hotels and other businesses.

States have varying, but usually strict, laws about driving under the influence or having open containers of alcohol in vehicles.

Health and safety

City police deal with crime and traffic issues; highway patrol officers with road safety

# Money and budgeting

Tipping around 20 percent is standard in most US restaurants

## CURRENCY

The US dollar is divided into 100 cents. Coins: 1 (penny), 5 (nickel), 10 (dime), 25 (quarter), 50 (half-dollar), and $1. Bills: $1, $2 (rare), $5, $10, $20, $50, and $100. Larger denominations ($500 and $1,000) are not in general circulation. All denominations of bills are the same size and primarily green in color. Newer $5, $10, $20, and $50 bills are easier to read, with large numbers and purple accents.

At the time of writing, one American dollar equals €0.71 and £0.62. Travelers arriving and departing are required to report currency or checks that exceed a total of $10,000.

### Currency exchange

Only major banks in larger cities or at international airports will change foreign money or foreign-currency traveler's checks, so it's important to carry cash or traveler's checks in dollars. If you're cashing traveler's checks in a bank, be sure to take your passport. It's a good idea to have a supply of $1–$10 bills on hand for taxis, tipping and small purchases.

## CASH AND CARDS
### ATMs

Automated teller machines are often the easiest way to get cash, as they are so widely available. You can find them at banks, convenience stores, some pharmacies, and some shopping malls. A transaction fee is usually charged, which varies from location to location. (Tip: avoid using casino ATMs.) You might also incur a currency-conversion fee.

Before your trip, ask your bank about their withdrawal policies abroad. If your bank is a member of the Global ATM Alliance, it won't charge you a withdrawal fee for taking out money from another bank in the network. At the time of writing, banks in the alliance included Bank of America, Barclays, and Westpac.

### Credit cards

Credit cards play an even greater role in the US than in Europe. Most Americans have several credit or debit cards; the latter deduct money directly from bank accounts. The major credit cards, such as MasterCard and Visa, are accepted almost everywhere; American Express is also widely accepted. When paying for goods or services, including hotel and restaurant checks, you will usually be asked, 'cash or charge?' In Las Vegas and some other towns, you may be asked to show ID when using your credit card.

### Traveler's checks

Overseas visitors will find traveler's checks drawn on American banks, or checks issued by American Express, far easier to deal with than those issued by banks in their home country. Traveler's checks are technically accepted in stores, restaurants, and hotels, but since they are increasingly rare, staff may be reluctant to process them. Only carry small amounts of cash at a time, and, if possible, keep the rest of your checks in the hotel safe. Keep a record of your traveler's checks numbers in a separate place, in case you need to replace them if they are lost or stolen.

## TIPPING

Tipping is a very common practice in the US. Service charges are generally not included in bills. Shelling out gratuities to all kinds of service staff, from hotel workers to coffee-shop baristas is the norm.

Taxi drivers are usually tipped 15 to 20 percent. Porters and doormen are slipped a couple of dollars per bag; hotel cleaning staff should get a few dollars per day of your stay. Waiters are tipped 15 to 20 percent of the total restaurant bill, though at higher-end restaurants 20 percent is standard. At bars, leave the bartender a dollar or two per drink. Tour guides may suggest, implicitly or explicitly, 15 percent or so. While tipping is expected, it is also considered a reward for a job well done, so round upward if you have been given top service.

## TAXES

There is no federal sales tax in the US but instead, sales taxes are levied by individual states or counties. Most states have sales taxes ranging from 4 percent to 8.25 percent; a few states, such as Oregon and New Hampshire, do not have sales taxes.

Money and budgeting

Families on tight budgets should find options to suit them on vacations in the States

## Budgeting costs

**Top-class/boutique hotel:** $250–300 and upwards for a double
**Standard-class hotel:** $120–150 for a double
**Bed and breakfast:** $80–150 for a double
**Motel:** $70–100 for a double
**Youth hostel:** $20–40 per person
**Campsite:** $12–30 per tent

**Domestic flight:** $250–500 to fly between coasts one-way
**Inter-city coach ticket:** $20–35 between New York City and Boston, or between New York City and Washington, DC
**Inter-city train ticket:** $68–100 between New York City and Boston
**Car hire:** $25–100 per day
**Airport shuttle bus:** $15–35

**Breakfast:** $8–15
**Lunch in a café:** $8–15
**Coffee/tea in a café:** $3–6
**Main course, budget restaurant:** $8–14
**Main course, moderate restaurant:** $15–24
**Main course, expensive restaurant:** $25–35
**Bottle of wine in a restaurant:** $15–50
**Beer in a pub:** $4–7

**Museum admission:** $10–20
**Theme-park admission:** $50–105 adult ticket
**Movie:** $8–12
**Theater/concert ticket:** $20–80
**Nightclub entry:** $10–30
**Souvenir T-shirt:** $10–25

In most, but not all, states food and medicine are not taxed. Hotel rooms usually get their own extra tax, which can be as high as 12 percent. Travelers also have to pay a $16.30 international transportation tax on any international flight arriving in or departing from the US, Puerto Rico, or the US Virgin Islands.

## BUDGETING FOR YOUR TRIP

With a huge choice of accommodations, nightlife, and places to eat, it's easy to satisfy most budgets in the US. Of course, major cities and popular resort destinations are more expensive, but reasonably priced options are available.

Flights from the UK to the US are most expensive in July and August, when a round-trip ticket to LA can easily cost £800. Savvy savers visit key locations during their shoulder seasons. For instance, early autumn can be a lovely time to visit beaches on either coast. New York City is a good deal in early December, when the city blazes with holiday lights and the shops have plenty of sales. Some low seasons carry a certain amount of risk, though. Hurricane season in Florida, for example, leads to discounted room rates – but you might have to postpone your trip if a storm hits. Discounted airfares are available online for roughly half the high-season rates.

In destinations where driving is the norm, such as California, car hire is inexpensive; in cities such as New York City and Boston, however, rates creep up. Fly-drive packages are usually a good bargain. US gasoline prices have gone up significantly in

The elevated train in Chicago is an easy way to get a bird's eye view of the city below

the past few years, but are still cheap by European standards. At the time of writing, gas was averaging $3.70 per gallon. The American Automobile Association website (http://fuel-gaugereport.aaa.com) keeps tabs on national, state, and local gas prices.

Most major museums and attractions charge admission of around $12 to $20. However, the Smithsonian Institution museums (most in Washington, DC) offer free admission.

America's glorious national parks and monuments are the country's best bargains. Historic attractions, such as the Alamo in Texas, are free, while entry charges for the parks themselves are minimal. California's Yosemite, for example, charges $20 per family car, with unlimited access for seven days; Arizona's Grand Canyon is $25 per car. If you plan to visit several parks, invest in an America the Beautiful National Parks and Federal Lands Annual Pass, for only $80. See the National Park Service website, www.nps.gov/finda-park/passes.htm, for details.

## Money-saving tips

- Try to fly mid-week. Flights on Tuesdays and Wednesdays are usually less crowded, giving you a better chance of securing a discounted rate. Airlines also tend to post sales early in the week.
- Many airlines now charge a fee for checking in luggage. Whenever possible, pack a carry-on size bag and make sure its contents will pass security inspection.
- If you are intending to use public transit repeatedly, look for multi-use or flat-rate tickets or passes.
- Most museums have a free-entry period, either on a weekly evening or one day a month.
- If you are staying in one place for more than a few days, consider a vacation rental. Renting an apartment or home can be less expensive on a per-night basis than even a motel. Having a kitchen also lets you cook meals. Homeaway.com and vrbo.com are two popular rental brokers.

Money and budgeting

# Responsible travel

If you plan on using an electric car, plan ahead to find charging locations

## GETTING THERE

Short of an ocean voyage, flying is the only way to reach the US from overseas. Use an online carbon-footprint calculator to assess the amount of carbon resulting from your flight. A non-stop flight between New York City and London, for example, would emit nearly 2,700lbs (1,224kg) of CO2. Travelers can offset these emissions by purchasing a 'carbon offset,' which directs money to planting trees, funding sustainable energy, or other eco-friendly initiatives.

Several airlines, including Delta and Virgin, have launched in-house programs, offering customers the carbon offset directly from their websites. Other independent organizations sell offsets, too, but their standards vary. **TerraPass** (tel: 1-877-210-9581; www.terrapass.com) is a well-established organization. Another reputable choice is **ClimateCare** (tel: 1865-207-000 in the UK; www.jpmorganclimate care.com).

## GETTING AROUND

Reducing carbon emissions from car travel is an important consideration in the US, since reliance on cars is so widespread. Many car-rental agencies – Enterprise and Budget, for example – now offer hybrid or fully electric vehicles. To book one of these eco-friendly vehicles, be sure to reserve several weeks ahead, since these cars are in the minority in an average rental fleet. In a similar way to airlines, rental agencies are also now starting to provide direct links to carbon-offset programs.

## ECOTOURISM

Doing some advance research on your hotels, outfitters, and other travel services will steer you to businesses with environmentally friendly practices. The **Green Key Eco-Rating Program** (www.greenkeyglobal.com) allows hotels to self-assess and then awards them on a one- to five-key rating. The Green Key website includes a property directory and descriptions of their eco-efforts. **Green America** (www.greenamerica.org) lists restaurants, hotels, and other vacation providers with an eco-friendly bent.

**Responsible Vacation** (tel: 1273-600-030 in the UK; www.responsible vacation.com) is a British company that sells holidays with a positive environmental and local economic impact. It offers several US itineraries, focusing on hiking, national-park exploration, and camping tours.

# Family holidays

## PRACTICALITIES

Childcare supplies such as diapers and baby food can be found at drugstores and grocery stores across the country. Diaper-changing areas are available at some public restrooms, but their standards of hygiene are not to be relied upon.

Throughout the US, children must be in a special car seat or buckled in for their safety in vehicles. You can bring your own car seat as long as it meets federal safety requirements, or request one for an extra fee from a car-rental company.

On US-based airlines, babies under the age of two may be held on your lap. Airlines recommend, however, that you purchase a separate seat for the child and use a government-approved car seat. If traveling with a stroller, check your airline's policy about checking in or carrying on the stroller.

It is possible to rent strollers, cribs, and other baby gear while traveling. One national organization that hires out useful kit is **Baby's Away** (www. babysaway.com), which has branches in most major cities.

## ACCOMMODATIONS

It's usually easy to find child-friendly lodgings around the US. Major hotel chains often have swimming pools or other distractions.

Hotels around resorts or theme parks have the most elaborate family options. These might include special kids' activity clubs, babysitting, separate children's pools, and guest rooms that can be easily configured for children.

Bed and breakfasts and country inns are sometimes not child-friendly and may have an age limit of 16 or 18 years. Some historic hotels may not have elevators and may have fewer facilities for families with children.

## ATTRACTIONS AND ACTIVITIES

With its beaches, water parks, and zoos, the US has no shortage of child-friendly destinations. Southern California and Florida, for example, are perennial draws for beach-loving families. Families with older children often gravitate to national parks or adventure-sports havens. And after everything else, America remains the birthplace and home of the theme park; a Disney trip is practically a rite of passage.

California has some great beaches that will make for fun, stress-free family downtime

# SETTING THE SCENE

# History

North America has been inhabited by mankind for at least 25,000 years. Mongolian hunters, probable ancestors of later Indian tribes, crossed into what is now Alaska. Over the centuries, some made their way down the Pacific Coast and east across the continent. Between 500BC and AD500, the Hopi and Zuni settled in farming communities in adobe-walled pueblos in New Mexico and Arizona. Tribes along the East Coast were skilled farmers but they had no wheels, no metal tools, and no horses.

## THE EUROPEANS ARRIVE

On October 11 1492, Christopher Columbus, a Genoese captain acting for the Spanish monarchy, caught sight of an island in what is now known as the Bahamas, just 380 miles (612km) from today's Miami Beach. Columbus is credited with the discovery of America, but it was another Italian explorer, Amerigo Vespucci, whose name was used by a mapmaker to identify both northern and southern continents.

The first European contact with the future United States mainland came in 1513, when Spanish explorer Juan Ponce de León was searching for the Fountain of Youth and stumbled upon the coast of Florida. In 1565, the Spaniards built a fort nearby, at what is now St Augustine, the first permanent settlement.

The English began to explore seriously in 1607. They established their first settlement at Jamestown, Virginia. Then on November 11 1620, some 100 people fleeing from religious persecution in Europe in a small ship, *Mayflower*, sighted Cape Cod, Massachusetts. On settling in the New World, the so-called Pilgrim Fathers made a covenant, the Mayflower Compact, which sowed the seeds of American democracy, and established that laws accepted by the majority would be binding on all.

In 1626, the Manhattan Native Americans sold their island to the Dutch West India Company for the legendary price of $24-worth of trinkets. New Amsterdam soon sprung up as a typical seaman's town of taverns and seedy hangouts. The Dutch didn't invest much in their American property, though, and ceded the area to the British in 1664.

An idealistic portrayal of the first Thanksgiving

## TOWARD REVOLUTION

As the British empire expanded in the mid-18th century, the monarchy demanded that the American colonies contribute more to its upkeep and defense. While accepting royal authority in foreign affairs, the colonists assumed that they would enjoy the same privileges as other Englishmen. But between 1764 and 1767, a series of special taxes and import duties made them realize that they weren't just Englishmen abroad.

Groups known as the Sons of Liberty formed in New York and Boston. As unrest mounted, the British sent two regiments to Boston. In March 1770, a mob snowballed guards in front of the Boston Customs House. The British fired, killing four Bostonians.

## REVOLUTIONARY WAR

The American colonies called their First Continental Congress in Philadelphia in 1774 to coordinate opposition. Again, Massachusetts took the lead, declaring itself a free state and preparing to resist any British offensive with weapons stored at Concord. The British moved 12,000 troops to Boston and, in 1775, a contingent marched out to deal with the rebels. Paul Revere, as legend has it, rode ahead to warn the rebel militia of the British advance on Concord.

Despite the Second Continental Congress's push for independence – led by Massachusetts' John Hancock, Virginia's Thomas Jefferson, and Pennsylvania's Benjamin Franklin – many colonists were still reluctant to sever ties with Britain. Even so, on July 4 1776, the Declaration of

A statue in Boston reminds the city of its revolutionary history

Independence was signed, proclaiming the right to 'life, liberty and the pursuit of happiness.'

War dragged on for seven years, with patriots engaging the British in morale-sapping skirmishes of attrition. French support finally helped the Revolutionaries to win the decisive Battle of Yorktown. On October 17 1781, Lord Cornwallis's British soldiers surrendered. After two years of negotiations led by Benjamin Franklin, the Revolutionary War ended on September 3 1783.

## THE NEW REPUBLIC EXPANDS WESTWARD

New York was the first capital of the new United States of America. On a balcony overlooking Wall Street in 1789, George Washington, commander-in-chief of the Continental Army, was inaugurated

The battle of Fredericksburg in the US Civil War

as the nation's first president. He surrounded himself with politically astute men, among them Thomas Jefferson as Secretary of State.

As champion of a new democracy, Jefferson was disturbed by a shadow on his own doorstep. The United States' first census (1790) showed a population of nearly 4 million, of whom 700,000 were black slaves. Himself a slave-owner on his Virginia farm, Jefferson expressed hopes for 'a total emancipation', fearing trouble for the union of the states.

Jefferson was elected president in 1800 and early the next year was the first to be inaugurated in the new capital Washington. One of the major triumphs of the Jefferson presidency was the Louisiana Purchase of 1803, under the terms of which the French leader Napoleon Bonaparte sold territory for $15 million. The land stretched from the Mississippi River to the Rocky Mountains, and its addition more than doubled the size of the United States.

## PUSHING WEST

Under President Andrew Jackson (1829–37), the American frontier was pushed further west. In canvas-covered wagons known as prairie schooners, thousands set out for California and Oregon, spurred by the glittering news of gold strikes. America's drive to the Pacific Ocean was proclaimed to be the nation's 'manifest destiny'.

## THE CIVIL WAR

Throughout the era of western expansion, the slavery issue festered. As long as cotton was king, representing two-thirds of US exports, the South felt it could justify working slaves on the cotton plantations. When slave rebellions broke out in South Carolina and Virginia, repression was ruthless.

In the North, meanwhile, the Abolitionist movement gained thousands of supporters. And by the 1850s, the purely political issue of states' rights also came to the fore. The slave-owning states insisted on the right to decide their own affairs without the interference of the federal government.

In 1860, after a tumultuous election, Abraham Lincoln won the presidency. Seeing him as 'a man whose opinions and purposes are hostile to slavery,' South Carolina led Mississippi, Alabama, Florida, Georgia, Louisiana, and Texas into secession. Followed by Arkansas, Tennessee, Virginia, and North Carolina, they declared a new Confederate States of America. But Lincoln's aims were not so simple; his priority was to preserve the Union.

On April 12 1861, South Carolina troops opened fire on the US military base of Fort Sumter, launching the Civil War. The four-year war was a horror – a disease-ridden, guerrilla-style conflict resulting in some of the bloodiest losses of American history.

The South had proud military traditions, superior officers, and training, but the North had overwhelming supremacy in heavy industry, railways, arms, and population. It triumphed despite often incompetent military leadership. The South finally surrendered at Appomattox on April 9 1865. Just five days later, Lincoln was assassinated at Ford's Theater in Washington by Confederate sympathizer John Wilkes Booth.

## RECONSTRUCTION

The ravaged South ended the war with its major cities reduced to rubble and a shattered economy. Over 800,000 immigrants streamed into the North during the war; over 3 million more followed in the next decade.

African-Americans, 4 million freed by the Union's victory, faced more hardship. After initial euphoria, they woke to the embittered South's new 'black codes,' under which they could not vote, testify against whites, bear arms, or frequent public places reserved for whites. The federal government set up new hospitals and schools, but many African-Americans faced greater violence than they had ever known as slaves.

## THE WORLD STAGE

By 1914, America had established itself as the world's leading industrial power. From 1860 to 1920, the population more than tripled, from 31 million to 106 million. This was a period of massive immigration: 4 million British, 4 million Irish, 6 million Germans, over 2 million Scandinavians, plus Italians, Poles, and Russian Jews arrived. Northern Europeans went West, to the farmlands; Southern and Eastern Europeans and the Irish mainly stuck to the big Eastern and Midwestern cities. The Chinese worked in the mines and on the railways – and suffered from harsh discriminatory laws.

America bought Alaska from Russia in 1867 and absorbed Hawaii by negotiating trading and military privileges with the strategically vital Pacific islands.

As older nations fought on the battlefields of Europe, America prepared for the world stage. After helping the Allies to victory over Germany in World War I, president Woodrow Wilson played a major role at the peace negotiations at Versailles. These laid the ground for the League of Nations, a forerunner of the United Nations (UN).

Dr Martin Luther King, Jr made his famous 'I have a dream' speech in 1963

## BOOMTIME AND THE GREAT DEPRESSION

After the Russian Revolution, America took fright at the threat of Communism. But the 1920s were also when the good times rolled: jazz, radio, silent movies, big business, and cars all transformed American life. Prohibition of alcohol in 1920 was justified with moral argument but, far from upholding morality, the ban allowed gangland crime to thrive.

In 1929 came the crash of the New York Stock Exchange, and America slumped into the Great Depression. One-third of the population was either unemployed by 1933, or was part of a family whose breadwinner was out of work. America was stunned by the failure of its classic virtues: leadership, organization, and efficiency.

In 1933, president Franklin D. Roosevelt embarked on a whirlwind 'Hundred Days' of economic and social measures to conquer the catastrophe, sweetened by ending Prohibition. FDR's New Deal did beat back the disaster of the Depression, but economic recession did not end until World War II began.

## WORLD WAR II

As vicious fighting broke out in Europe again, Congress supplied arms and aid to its allies – but still resisted conscription. The Japanese raid on Pearl Harbor, on December 7 1941, ended all hesitation; the US declared war.

Roosevelt was re-elected to an unprecedented fourth term in 1944, but died in 1945, before the final victory. His successor, Harry Truman, made the decision to use an atom bomb to end the war with Japan.

After World War II, America emerged as the only major power undamaged by the conflict. In fact, the US economy had grown, with American corporations becoming stronger than ever.

## CIVIL RIGHTS

War flared up again in the early 1950s, when the US backed South Korea against an invasion from the North. Domestically, however, the decade was charactersied by a brash confidence, prosperity, and a sense of new possibilities. Cars were big, clothes were sharp, and disc jockey Alan Freed coined the term 'rock'n'roll' to make black rhythm and blues accessible to white audiences.

In 1955, President Eisenhower sent the first 'military advisors' to Vietnam. The same year, Dr Martin Luther King, Jr, led the first black bus boycott, and the next year, the Supreme Court outlawed segregation on buses. Protests for equal rights for black people took shape, inflamed by school desegregation and other pressing issues. In 1963, King delivered his famous 'I have a dream' speech to a huge crowd in front of the Lincoln Memorial in Washington, DC. The Civil Rights Act was finally passed in 1964, but real change came slowly.

## THE KENNEDY ERA

In 1961, John F. Kennedy was elected president. As a gesture of American can-do grit, he committed the US to putting a man on the Moon by the end of the decade. His presidency hit rough waters quickly when, perhaps acting on poor advice, Kennedy invaded Cuba with CIA-trained insurgents. They were easily defeated.

Soon after, Russia stationed nuclear missiles at bases in Cuba. They were detected by American reconnaissance flights and on April 22 1962, Kennedy demanded that they be withdrawn. The world held its breath for six days, facing nuclear annihilation. In exchange for a face-saving promise not to invade Cuba, Russia removed the missiles.

## LOVE AND DEATH

The 1960s spun into cultural revolution, fueled by the hippie free-love philosophy and the invention of the birth-control pill. The years were marred by political violence. JFK was shot dead in Dallas, Texas, on November 22 1963. Martin Luther King was killed in Memphis, Tennessee, on April 4 1968, prompting riots in more than 100 US cities.

Richard Nixon stepped into the White House in 1968, promising an end to American participation in the Vietnam War. Like presidents before him, he found it a tough promise to deliver. Still, Nixon was able to deliver on one of Kennedy's dreams: on July 20 1969, Neil Armstrong stepped on to the surface of the Moon.

Nixon's second term of presidency was mired in a scandal and criminal proceedings from a burglary at the Watergate building in Washington, DC. He resigned, the only American president ever to do so. The Vietnam War finally ground to a halt in 1973.

## THE REAGAN ERA

President Ronald Reagan took the helm for the roller-coaster of the 1980s. The economic slump of the early years were soon replaced by the swagger of Wall Street 'corporate raiders'. The Cold War between the US and the Soviet Union shifted a gear as Reagan put new pressure on the USSR to move away from its hard-line

On July 20 1969, the US space program put the first man on the Moon

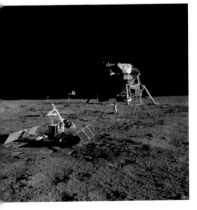

Barak Obama made history in 2008 by becoming the first African-American US president

## INTO THE 21ST CENTURY

On September 11, 2001, terrorists hijacked four commercial aircraft mid-flight. One plane was flown into the Pentagon in Washington DC, and two more hit the World Trade Center in New York. The fourth plane came down on open ground in Pennsylvania. Close to 3,000 people were killed and President George Bush declared a 'war on terrorism.'

The international terrorist network al-Qaeda, led by Osama bin Laden, claimed responsibility for the attack. Soon thereafter, the US began military operations in Afghanistan, believing bin Laden to be hiding there. In 2003, American and British forces attacked Iraq, after claiming that it was harboring weapons of mass destruction.

In 2005, Hurricane Katrina ripped through the southern Gulf Coast states, causing devastation and the deaths of thousands of people. Americans were horrified by how ill-prepared their country was for a large-scale emergency.

Communist stance. Scandal hit again, however, in 1986, as Reagan admitted to secretly selling arms to Iran.

The next decade began with the Gulf War, with UN forces led by the US fending off Iraq's invasion of Kuwait. Over by 1991, the tensions remained. While the headlines were filled with these events, a new revolution was brewing, a surprising legacy from the Cold War missile program.

## THE AGE OF THE INTERNET

In the 1980s, American computer scientists figured out how to link computers almost anywhere using public phone lines. This was the birth of the Internet.

By the 1990s, during the Bill Clinton presidency, investors poured billions of dollars into thousands of dot-com dreams. Seattle, Portland, San Francisco, and the Silicon Valley boomed. Expectations rose, results were slow, and a crash was inevitable.

## THE AUDACITY OF HOPE

In late 2008, a Chicago senator, Barack Obama, became the first African-American to be elected to the US presidency. Amid the widespread jubilation, however, was the recognition that Obama's task was monumental: a global financial crisis had plunged the US into a downward economic spiral.

Starting in 2010, Obama oversaw the slow withdrawal of troops from Iraq and Afghanistan. In May 2011, American special forces achieved a major symbolic victory by finding and killing bin Laden in Pakistan.

## Historical Landmarks

**1492**
Christopher Columbus discovers America.

**1620**
Pilgrims aboard the *Mayflower* arrive at Cape Cod.

**1773**
The 'Boston Tea Party': tea crates are pitched over the sides of three ships in Boston Harbor to protest against taxes.

**1776**
On July 4, the Continental Congress in Philadelphia adopts Thomas Jefferson's Declaration of Independence.

**1789**
George Washington becomes the first president of the United States.

**1848**
Gold is discovered at Sutter's Fort, California, attracting over 200,000 prospectors over the next three years.

**1861**
Confederates open fire on Fort Sumter, in the first hostilities of the Civil War.

**1865**
The Civil War ends. Abraham Lincoln is assassinated only a few days later.

**1929**
Wall Street crashes, and with it comes the beginning of the Great Depression.

**1941**
Japan attacks Pearl Harbor and the United States enters World War II.

**1945**
The first atomic bomb is detonated in New Mexico; bombs are dropped on Hiroshima and Nagasaki to end the war with Japan.

**1955**
Dr Martin Luther King, Jr, leads the Montgomery (Alabama) bus boycott.

**1963**
President John F. Kennedy is assassinated in Dallas, Texas.

**1968**
Dr Martin Luther King, Jr, and Robert F. Kennedy are assassinated.

**1969**
*Apollo 11* takes two men to the surface of the Moon.

**1973–4**
A world oil crisis plunges the US into economic crisis.

**1989**
An earthquake, 7.1 on the Richter scale, collapses a freeway and causes chaos in the San Francisco area.

**1991**
American-led forces liberate Kuwait in the first Gulf War.

**2000**
The presidential election is undecided by counting votes, and the Supreme Court gives the presidency to George W. Bush.

**2001**
Hijackers fly passenger airliners into New York's World Trade Center and the Pentagon. A 'war on terrorism' is declared.

**2005**
Hurricane Katrina hits the Gulf Coast states, killing thousands.

**2008**
The government injects billions of dollars into the economy after the 'credit crunch'.

**2009**
The US's first African-American president, Barack Obama, takes office.

**2011**
In Pakistan, Osama bin Laden is found and killed by American soldiers.

History

# Culture

Although the US offers up some of the world's greatest sights, sounds, and flavors, one aspect that often impresses visitors is the galloping pace of newness. 'Hey, what's new?' chimes from coast to coast. People jump on new technology, experiment with trends, and keep an eye trained on every stock price and newsflash. Bloggers leap to report everything from restaurant openings to political gaffes, while everyone else scatters personal updates across the latest social media. Audiences rush to see movies on opening weekends, making or breaking a film in the span of 48 hours.

This speed and flexibility has its up- and downside. Do Americans have a short attention span? Do they miss a bigger picture in pursuit of a quick decision, a quick laugh, or a quick buck? Sometimes, yes. Still, those same traits mean that Americans can often adopt fresh thinking, see new possibilities, and tackle opportunities with alacrity.

## THE NEXT BIG THING

Change and progress are more than embraced here; they are craved and pursued. They go hand in hand with the ideal of the self-made individual, someone who overcomes difficult beginnings to succeed. This principle inspired the early settlers seeking a fresh start, the Horatio Alger stories of the 19th-century Gilded Age, and even today's entrepreneurs.

Yet, there is also a deep-rooted appreciation for history and authenticity. Old buildings in urban centers are being 'repurposed' while being prized for their patina. The diners and main streets of small-town USA can seem to be in a time warp, until you notice that everybody is tapping on smartphones. Twentysomethings are increasingly interested in the innovations, design, and 'heritage brands' of previous generations.

## GEOGRAPHY

Let's start with some raw material. The United States claims some of the world's oldest and most impressive natural phenomena, including the vast Grand Canyon, the lush Everglades, Yellowstone's geothermal hotspot, and 'Old Man River', the

Western wear is a popular fashion

According to a 2010 census, 12.6 percent of the US population is African-American

mighty Mississippi, one of the longest rivers in the world, that traverses most of the country from north to south.

With an area of approximately 3,717,700 sq miles (9,629,000 sq km), including Alaska and Hawaii, the US is the fourth-largest country in the world, at nearly 40 times the size of the UK. Mainland USA (excluding Alaska and Hawaii) – called the 48 contiguous states – stretches for about 3,000 miles (4,800km) from the Atlantic to the Pacific, and for some 1,200 miles (1,900km) from the Canadian border to the Gulf of Mexico.

The largest state in the union is Alaska, at nearly 152,000 sq miles (1.4m sq km). The most populous state is California, with over 37 million people recorded in the 2010 federal census. Hawaii, the 50th state, is in the Pacific Ocean, some 2,500 miles (4,000km) to the southwest. The country's highest point is the summit of Mt McKinley (Alaska), at 20,320ft (6,194m). The lowest point is 282ft (86m) below sea level, in Death Valley (California), the second-lowest point on dry land anywhere in the world.

## GOVERNMENT AND POPULATION

The US is a federal republic consisting of 50 states and one federal district, Washington, DC. There is a primarily two-party political system, dominated by the Democrats and the Republicans. The system of government is based on the Constitution of 1787. The president is elected for a

four-year term and can be re-elected once. Congress is composed of the Senate, with two senators per state, and the House of Representatives, fixed at 435 members, proportionately drawn from each state according to its population. Each state has its own semi-autonomous government and local laws, headed by an elected governor. Americans can vote in local and federal elections from the age of 18.

The country's highest court is the Supreme Court, also based in Washington, DC. Eight associate justices and one chief justice preside over crucial cases, debating issues that reach into every level of American society. Sitting presidents nominate justices; the Senate must then approve the nominations. Justices are not endorsed by a political party. Once sworn in, justices have tenure for life, often far outlasting the presidents who appointed them.

The US is the third-most-populous country in the world, behind China and India. The population of nearly 309 million, according to the 2010 federal census, is made up of 72.4 percent whites, 12.6 percent African-Americans, 4.8 percent Asians, 0.9 percent Native Americans, and a small percentage of other races. Sixteen percent of the total population is Hispanic. More than half the population growth between 2000 and 2010 related to the boom in the Hispanic community. Of all the states, California has the biggest minority populace.

Religious affiliation is estimated at 81.2 percent Christian (Protestant, Catholic, evangelical, etc.), 12.8 percent none or unaffiliated, 1.65 percent Jewish, 1.51 percent Mormon, 1.27 Buddhist, and 2.18 percent other.

There is no official religion in the US. The separation of church and state, a principle endorsed by Founding Father Thomas Jefferson, was established in the First Amendment of the Constitution. This helped to ensure a secular government. That said, nearly all American presidents are considered to have been Christian, although some of the early leaders did not officially belong to a specific church. The reference to God in the federal motto, 'In God We Trust,' seen on American currency, started to appear in the 19th century.

The US does not specify an official language but, unofficially, it is English. In some neighborhoods with a strong immigrant population, the predominant language may switch, and most everyday transactions and even public signage can appear in other languages.

Several non-English newspapers are also published in the US.

## NATIONAL CULTURE

Other countries display their glorious past in museums, cathedrals, temples, and palaces. America has its share of renowned museums, too, but it best shares its exuberant character in its public life, from the streets to the beach. Other countries showcase their culture; America draws visitors into its way of life. In fields such as literature, classical music, and the visual arts, the United States has made great contributions.

## THE ARTS

America's performing arts continue to flourish. Seven world-famous symphony orchestras and opera companies reside in Chicago, New York, Los Angeles, Philadelphia,

The Guggenheim Museum in New York is an architectural masterpiece

Cleveland, Washington, DC, and Boston. New York City's Broadway theater district nurtures new playwrights and regularly mounts world-renowned revivals of classic works. In the 1940s, the Russian-born choreographer George Balanchine founded a company in Manhattan and created a new form of ballet. His steps are still expertly performed by his namesake troupe today.

Several of the past century's most influential popular-music styles were strummed into life in the US, fed by the traditions of various immigrant communities. Country, bluegrass, zydeco, gospel, and folk ballads are all quintessentially American. The experiences of African-Americans found expression in jazz and blues, which in turn morphed into rock and soul (*see also pages 132–3*). More recently, the street rhymes of hip-hop and rap have emerged from the country's tough urban neighborhoods.

Manhattan and California have spawned several leading art movements of the 20th and 21st centuries, from New York's Pop Art to California's explicitly political feminist art. These days, gallery owners watch the streets themselves, seizing on muralists and graffiti artists as the next wave.

The great museums of New York, Washington, Boston and Chicago stand among the world's finest for their collections of Old Masters, groundbreaking modern art, and crafts from all over the world. But the US has also devoted museums to home-grown treasures and collectibles, from vintage cars to mechanical toys.

Chicago's Millenium Park

The idea of the 'great American novel' has haunted writers for decades – the dream of somehow capturing the essence of the American character in a uniquely American language. Some consider Mark Twain's *The Adventures of Huckleberry Finn* to be the apogee. The early-20th-century authors F. Scott Fitzgerald and Ernest Hemingway also have their champions, as does the Chicago writer Saul Bellow. Perhaps the most essential aspect of the great American novel is that it has not been written yet, that it is always on the horizon, a glory to come.

A spate of dramatic buildings has put a spotlight on architecture over the last couple of decades. Many cities have built new homes for major museums and cultural institutions. Examples include Frank Gehry's swooping concert hall in Los Angeles and Rem Koolhaas's angular public library in Seattle. At the time of writing, a new World Trade Center is rising up in New York. And for a backward glance at architectural innovation, seek out one of the buildings designed by the 20th-century Modernist Frank Lloyd Wright (*see also pages 162–3*).

Film straddles the line between entertainment and high art. While Hollywood churns out hundreds of popcorn flicks a year, memorable movies have also been made, with globally adored characters and catchphrases that enjoy currency for generations. Cinema techniques invented by the French have taken off in the hands of US directors and star actors. Popular hits can occasionally become a branding goldmine – just think of *King Kong, The Wizard of Oz, Citizen Kane*, or *The Godfather*.

Out and about on horseback in arid country

## THE GREAT OUTDOORS

Americans are clearly spoiled when it comes to scenery; there is fantastic diversity in the landscapes. The country's environmental reawakening started just in time to preserve much of the natural beauty of the continent's wide-open spaces.

For fishermen, sailors, and anyone who likes the sea, there are the wild Atlantic coasts of Maine and Florida, as well as their Pacific counterparts in northern California, Oregon, and Washington state. In between are the Great Lakes of the Midwest, which might easily qualify as seas anywhere else in the world. Beach fiends gravitate to southern California and the Gulf Coast.

Throughout the country are vast national parks and nature reserves, attracting visitors to take a hike around the swamps of Florida's Everglades, climb in the Rockies of Colorado, or see the geysers in Yellowstone National Park. Even the deserts – the Petrified Forest southeast of the Grand Canyon, or Death Valley in California's Mojave – grant an enriching respite from civilization.

## CITY LIFE

America's cities are just too much fun to stay away from for too long. Each of the major hubs offers its own brand of adventure. The street life of New York is a carnival – endless movement, color, noise, taste, and aroma – sometimes hair-raising, always stimulating. Boston, Washington, and Philadelphia are metropolitan pillars of American history, proud and dignified towns that, even so, don't take themselves too seriously.

New Orleans offers a potent mix of old elegance and decadence, part-Gallic, part-Deep South, but always vibrant and musical. Santa Fe is its Spanish counterpart, but quieter, more the culture of fine arts than the vibrant energy of jazz. There's nothing quiet or delicate about big, boisterous Chicago, however. The town never fails to surprise visitors with the beauty of its lakefront architecture, or the breadth and vitality of its musical heritage.

Dallas and Houston are the bumptious concrete realizations of the Texan dream, ranchers gone oil-rich urban. These same ranchers fly to chic, sun-drenched Miami to realize yet more dreams (and to spend some of those riches in South Beach's upscale stores and restaurants). Sprawling, star-mad Los Angeles and gorgeous, nonconformist San Francisco are the last but not least points on the map in America's big push to the western coast. Big and small, America's cities are both playgrounds and workshops displaying the best, as well as doubtless some of the worst, aspects of a century of tireless urban development.

Pedestrians on 5th Ave, New York

## FANTASY PLAYGROUNDS

If you're exhausted from taking in the wonders of the real world, you can revel in the fantasy realms of Universal Studios and the Walt Disney World Resort, or else the decadent glamour of Las Vegas and the gaming areas that have sprouted across the country. The thrills and excitement are designed not to create too much stress, and usually stick to good clean family fun.(Apart from Las Vegas, of course; Sin City obeys few rules.) Children have an important place in American life, and it has long been understood in the US that all of us, some of the time – perhaps more often than we are willing to admit – are kids at heart.

## AMERICAN SPORTS

Americans love to play. They have their own versions of old European sports, such as baseball (derived from English cricket and rounders), as well as what they call football, but which looks to foreign eyes like a contest that might have been invented for Roman gladiators. In addition to spectator sports, you can participate in countless activities around the beaches of Florida, California, and Hawaii, including surfing and kite-boarding. Then, on winter slopes, snowboarders join skiers, risking their necks in curls and jumps. All come and go with the swift arc of a Frisbee (another American invention).

## DIVERSITY

In a country as vast and varied as the United States, it is hazardous

The US thrives as a melting pot of cultures

to try to define the catch-all moniker of 'Americans.' White Anglo-Saxon Protestants (WASPs)? Irish Catholics? Hispanics, Poles, Italians, Germans, Greeks, Arabs, Scandinavians, Russians, Jews, Czechs, Africans, Chinese, Japanese, Vietnamese? Or Sioux, Navajo, Cherokee, and Cheyenne? Or, for that matter, New Yorkers and New Englanders, Southerners and Texans, Midwesterners and hillbillies? Hippies, capitalists, political refugees, or evangelicals? And again, to confound all generalizations, Californians?

And then you realize that this is the answer. Endless lists and open-ended groups are fundamental to the American nation. Their culture is characterized by boundless variety. Somehow, people from every far-flung corner of the earth have ended up living together – not always peacefully, by any means – but despite revolution and civil war and riots, with such astounding success. Indeed, it is now part of what it means to be an American to be able to say that some of your family's roots are elsewhere.

Since the 1990s, the public has become increasingly aware of political correctness, an effort to reduce friction between genders, races, religions and other groups. By adopting 'PC' language and behavior, many in the public and private spheres tried to be more sensitive or positive towards vastly diverse communities. Some aspects were absorbed relatively easily, such as using 'developmentally disabled' for people suffering from mental disadvantages. Inevitably, there is a certain amount of backlash, especially in the form of politically incorrect humor. It's all part of the promise of free speech, one of the most treasured aspects of American life.

Perhaps the greatest part of a visit to America is to encounter such a wide range of different people. No generalization stands up to more than five minutes' scrutiny here. Pop culture and new media may make certain things more readily accessible, but this is far from a homogeneous nation of lookalikes, talk-alikes, and laugh-alikes.

The metaphor of America as a melting pot, bringing different elements together, has been around since its earliest days. In the more self-consciously multicultural present, people are more likely to think of the US as a mosaic, where various identities retain their distinctive qualities yet fit together so well.

# Food and drink

## NATIONAL CUISINE

America's range of cuisines is as diverse as its ethnic groups. Some areas with distinct immigrant and cultural identities have strongly defined local cuisines to match. Still, from Maine to California there are also basic dishes that have been claimed as generically American, such as steak and potatoes, hamburgers, chocolate-chip cookies, jaw-stretching sandwiches, and US-style pizza. And of course, nothing is more American than apple pie.

A note for Europeans: genetically modified food is very common in the US and is not labeled. Foods that are not labeled as organic, especially fast foods, are often GM. On the other hand, Americans are increasingly attentive to 'locavore' cooking, meaning dishes made with locally sourced ingredients that are usually organic to boot.

Americans are also sensitive to those with specialty diets and allergies. In large cities and vacation spots, it is easy to find vegetarian, vegan, and nut-, gluten-, or dairy-free options.

### New York and New England

New York City's contribution to the world of gastronomy begins with the hot dog, which you can have with either sauerkraut or fried onions, but never, authentically, without mustard. The deli sandwich is a special Broadway institution, with various permutations involving corned beef, pastrami, mustard, and rye bread. Although cheesecake may have come from Central Europe originally, it has never tasted better than in the Jewish delis and in Brooklyn.

New York City's ethnic neighborhoods are excellent places to explore various world cuisines. Some foods are longstanding traditions, such as dim sum or steamed pork buns in Chinatown. Pizza, thanks to over a century of Italian immigration, is a fiercely debated local favorite – nothing compares to a late-night slice. Others specialties are new trends, such as the rash of Korean-style fried-chicken restaurants that has popped up recently in 'K-town' on West 32nd Street. Food trucks and street vendors are increasingly competitive and inventive, with midtown falafel carts jockeying for space with roaming

It's not all dogs and burgers – a chef proudly displays his upmarket creation

Food and drink

**Meal times**

Americans eat weekday breakfast before 9am, but take their time over leisurely weekend brunches between 10am and 2pm. Lunch is generally eaten between noon and 1.30pm. In major coastal cities, dinner gets underway at 8pm; elsewhere, people tend to eat earlier, around 7pm.

cupcake sellers. On Sunday mornings, thousands upon thousands of New Yorkers nosh on bagels with lox (smoked salmon) and cream cheese.

Seafood is a strong suit in both New York and New England. Manhattan clam chowder has tomato in it, in contrast to the creamy New England type. Oysters are a treat, whether Long Island Blue Points or plump Wellfleets from Cape Cod. Lobsters, meanwhile, are the tasty symbol of Maine.

### The Mid-Atlantic region

Philadelphia notches its belt with several gut-busting local specialties. The Philly cheesesteak sandwich, for example, heaps a hoagie roll with shaved, grilled beef and melted provolone cheese. Other treats, such as the oversized pretzels, have their roots in the region's German heritage. Further south, near Chesapeake Bay, look out for soft-shell and steamer crabs.

### The South

More and more chefs are researching and championing true Southern cooking. It's a wide spectrum, but one quality runs throughout: richly flavored, substantial dishes, often turning humble ingredients into something special. Barbecue is a kingdom of its own, a realm where you'll be in awe of the pit masters. *See p.129 for details of the various regional barbecue styles.*

The coastal cooking of the Carolinas makes the most of locally available fresh fish and shrimp, and is often served with a side of hush puppies (fried cornmeal batter). 'Lowcountry cooking' refers to the seafood, grits, and rice dishes commonly found in Georgia and South Carolina.

Down in the Sunshine State, 'Floribbean' blends the Florida, Caribbean, and Latin flavors popular in Miami. Straight-up Cuban food is available everywhere, too, including *carne asada* (roasted beef) with earthy Cuban black beans and yucca, a starchy root vegetable.

New Orleans prides itself on some of the most distinctive cooking traditions in America. Its two signature styles are Creole and Cajun.

A classic Colorado Buffalo burger is served with sliced mango

The Creole tradition combines the French love of sauces; the Spanish penchant for mixing fish, meat, and vegetables with rice; and a taste for liberal seasoning with hot peppers that was developed in the West Indies and Africa.

Gumbo, a West African word for okra, is the basic ingredient in and the generic name for thick soups of chicken or seafood. Crayfish, pronounced and often spelled in Louisiana as 'crawfish,' is a favorite springtime shellfish best served boiled. Oysters here are plentiful and relatively inexpensive, encouraging New Orleans chefs to prepare them in many and marvelous ways: fried, in sandwiches or stews, or skewered and wrapped in bacon, for example

Cajun cooking is country-style cuisine, traditionally favored among the fishermen and farmers of the bayou, the descendants of French-Canadians. Spicy sausages and the world-famous jambalaya are classic Cajun dishes. Jambalaya is a colorful paella-like dish of rice and chicken, and crab or shrimp with bits of sausage or ham, pepper, and tomato.

The local variation on the submarine sandwich is the 'po-boy' (long) or muffuletta (round) – bread stuffed with cold meats, oysters, or other seafood, cheese, and salad.

Soul food is often conflated with Southern cooking and while it is related, it has its own unique identity. Developed during the time of slavery, soul food reflects the basic ingredients allotted to African-Americans, such as ham hock, offal, and collard greens.

Chicago is famous for its deep-dish pizza, which you'll need to eat with knife and fork

### The Heartland

The Midwest has far more than steak to tempt you with – but tucking into a rib-eye is certainly a pleasure. Chicago remains the foodie magnet for both casual and fine dining. One guilty pleasure is deep-dish pizza, its high crust stuffed with oozing cheesy toppings. *See p.166 for details on that other Chicago fast-food icon, the hot dog.*

At the other end of the dining spectrum, restaurateur Rick Bayless and his chefs have brought outstanding Mexican cuisine to Chicago. Molecular gastronomists and other high-flying experimental chefs have also gravitated here, most notably Grant Achatz, who cooks at the restaurant Alinea.

### Texas and the Southwest

Cooking in Texas and the Southwest draws on Mexican, Spanish, and Native American traditions, using all

Chimichangas, hand-rolled Sopapilla Mesa served enchilada-style

overstuffed burritos are now their own tradition.

As a Pacific Rim destination, California also boasts excellent Japanese, Chinese, and Thai restaurants. The Los Angeles area in particular has a wealth of Chinese restaurants with rarely seen regional treats – Szechuan, Taiwanese, Shanghai, and Cantonese.

'Fusion cuisine' started fizzing here, matching up styles from Asian to European and Mexican to Korean. Even pizza gets oddball twists, with toppings such as pineapple. Roll with it and you may be happily surprised.

### The Pacific Northwest

The Pacific Northwest has an abundance of superb fresh ingredients, as well as the sense to keep the cooking simple. Everywhere you turn are tempting seafood choices, including Copper River salmon, smoked or grilled on a cedar plank. Other notable regional flavors are mushrooms (all that rain is good for something), stone fruits, berries, and Washington's renowned apples.

kinds of chilis. One question you'll hear everywhere is 'red or green?', meaning which chili sauce you'd like.

Tex-Mex is a type of unique take on Mexican food, but has grown into its own styles and tastes. Eye-wateringly spicy chili comes under that banner. Texas-style barbecue, meanwhile, involves beef brisket or massive ribs, slathered in tangy sauce.

### California

Forget those old jokes about the West Coast's super-picky or holier-than-thou eating habits. Californian cooking is an astoundingly varied field, with a wealth of local produce and plenty of indulgences. The term 'California cuisine' still stands for fresh, simple dishes influenced by the melting pot of California's culture.

Mexican and Central American traditions have seeped across California's southern border, spreading tacos, mole sauce, and other specialties throughout the state. San Francisco's

---

#### Seasonal foods

Spring kicks off a produce rush, with asparagus and artichokes leading the way, followed by the season's first peas and carrots, which are often incorporated into Easter meals. In summer, farmers' markets bloom with tomatoes, squash, corn, melons, and waves of berries and stone fruits. In autumn, apples and root vegetables come to the fore. Southern states send grapefruit, oranges, and other citrus fruits north to brighten winter.

## WHERE TO EAT

Places to eat in the US range from the classic fluorescent-lit, 24-hour diners (think of the paintings of Edward Hopper) to clubby steakhouses to extravagant fine-dining restaurants.

Fast-food branches pop up throughout the country. Cafés offering simple meals or snacks are almost as widespread. In some cities, street vendors are particularly popular (*see p.267*) and locals make it a point of pride to seek out holes-in-the-wall.

## DRINKS

Seattle – the birthplace of Starbucks – was the town that redefined the coffee ritual the world over. Typically, Portland claims to have pioneered the way in the artisanal coffee business, but that could just be an example of an old Portland-Seattle rivalry. Either way, both towns have innumerable small independent cafés and roasters, such as Stumptown and Caffè Umbria. San Francisco and New York are also notable for their large numbers of coffee bars, with local roasters

The American bar is typically quite comfy

and several specialty drinks. But these days, virtually every town in the US has some kind of dedicated coffee shop.

Cold drinks are invariably served iced. If you want a good serving of soda or lemonade in the coffee shops and fast-food places, specify 'little ice.' Southerners cut the heat with chilled glasses of sweet tea. Beer is served frosty-cold, but without ice.

Wines from California put American vintages on the map and have continued to dazzle critics the world over. The days are long past when a Napa, Sonoma, or Anderson Valley winery was considered an upstart by French sommeliers.

For some drinkers, however, a few ounces of whiskey is all that's needed. America's home-grown version is bourbon, a mellow whiskey from Kentucky made of corn, malt, and rye. Drink the brown spirits straight, on the rocks, or with soda. If, on the other hand, it is horse-racing season, then it's time for a mint julep, a mix of bourbon, sugar, water, and fresh spearmint, often served in silver cups.

American beers have also risen above the gassy, industrial, canned brews of old. Brewpubs and microbreweries have sprung up all over the country, and there are now over 1,700 breweries nationwide.

Many bars promote late-afternoon and early evening 'happy hours,' with discounted drinks, extra snacks, or both. A particular attraction for spirit-drinkers is that American bartenders often serve very generous measures. Each state dictates when its bars close.

Food and drink

# Index

**315**

Index

Index

# Accommodations Index

**319**

Index

## Credits for Berlitz Handbook USA

**Written by:** Jennifer Paull and Annika Hipple
**Series Editor:** Tom Stainer
**Commissioning Editor:** Astrid deRidder
**Map Production:** Stephen Ramsay and Apa Cartography Department
**Production:** Linton Donaldson, Rebeka Ellam
**Picture Manager:** Steven Lawrence
**Picture & Design Editor:** Tom Smyth
**Photography:** All photography Abraham, Daniella and Richard Nowitz/APA except: Ace Hotels 268; Alamy 129; Alize 216; ARAMARK Parks and Destinations 206, 221; AWL Images 4TL, 65, 82, 99, 147; Boston Symphony Orchestra 93; Paul Brown/Rex Features 137; California Travel and Tourism Commission 6CR, 7TR&CR, 16, 223, 226, 227T&B, 228, 230, 231, 233, 234, 237, 239, 244, 246, 253, 254, 280; Colorado Tourism Office 37; Corbis 264, 298; Country Music Hall of Fame 135; David Dunai/APA 2R, 6TR, 50, 159, 160, 161, 162, 163T&B, 164, 165, 166, 167, 171, 172, 174, 289, 291, 302, 305, 311; Jack Edinger/Lollapalooza 175; Fotolia 5BL, 204, 205, 265; The Franklin Institute 103; Gasparilla Pirate Festival 14; Getty Images 67, 104, 141, 300; Glenwood Hot Springs 56; Greater Houston Convention and Visitors Bureau 178, 179; Greater Portland Convention & Visitors Bureau 87; Martyn Goddard/APA 7TL, 10/11, 28, 41, 43, 46, 47, 242, 247; Robert Harding World Imagery 168; Heeb/laif/Camerapress 4TR; Hilton Hotels & Resorts 170; Hotel del Coronado 249; Hotel Erwin 248; Hotel Palomar 116; Image Source/Rex Features 136; iStockphoto.com 6BL, 7B, 9TL, TR&BL, 17, 76, 77, 98, 127, 134, 156, 180, 201, 203, 207, 212, 283, 286, 290; Britta Jaschinski/APA 2L, 5TR, 6BR, 69, 70, 285; B. Krist for GPTMC 119, 122; Lake Placid/Essex County Visitors Bureau 72; Library of Congress 32, 296; Memphis Convention & Visitors Bureau 154; Mount Washington Cog Railway 84; Museum Associates/LACMA 229; NASA 144, 145, 299; The New York Times/Redux/Eyevine 211; Niagara Falls Tourism & Convention Corporation 73; North Carolina Division of Tourism 9CL, 126, 128; NYC GO 15, 92, 95; Le Petite Retreat 57; Photolibrary 102, 263T, 266; Portland Rose Festival Foundation and SCi 3.2 272; Norman Rockwell Museum 83; Royal Palms Resort and Spa 193; San Antonio CVB 9BR, 183, 194; Sanderling Inn 149; Snowbird Ski and Summer Resort 220; Sonoma County Tourism Bureau 255; South Dakota Department of Tourism 169; Starwood Hotels & Resorts 88, 269; Stowe Mountain Resort 85; Superstock 8T, 81, 262; Texas Tourism 177, 182, 184; Tim Thompson/APA 8BL, 259, 261, 271, 287, 313; Travel Portland 267; Mark Vancleave/Guthrie Theater 173; Virginia Tourism Corporation 30, 31, 33, 114, 115, 117, 133T; Visit Savannah 131; The Wauwinet 89; WDW News 5CL, 139, 140, 152; West Hollywood Marketing and Visitors Bureau 252; G. Widman for GPTMC 101, 118, 120; Zazzle Bay to Breakers 257

**Front cover:** CORBIS
**Back cover:** Fotolia (all)
**Printed by:** CTPS-China

**Contacting Us**

At Berlitz we strive to keep our guides as accurate and up to date as possible, but if you find anything that has changed, or if you have any suggestions on ways to improve this guide, then we would be delighted to hear from you. Write to Berlitz Publishing, PO Box 7910, London SE1 1WE, UK or email: berlitz@apaguide.co.uk
**Worldwide:** APA Publications GmbH & Co. Verlag KG (Singapore branch), 7030 Ang Mo Kio Ave 5, 08-65 Northstar @ AMK, Singapore 569880; tel: (65) 570 1051; email: apasin@singnet.com.sg
**UK and Ireland:** Dorling Kindersley Ltd, a Penguin Group company 80 Strand, London, WC2R 0RL, UK; email: customerservice@dk.com
**United States:** Ingram Publisher Services, 1 Ingram Boulevard, PO Box 3006, La Vergne, TN 37086-1986; email: customer.service@ingrampublisherservices.com
**Australia:** Universal Publishers, 1 Waterloo Road, Macquarie Park, NSW 2113; tel: (61) 2-9857 3700; email: sales@universalpublishers.com.au
**www.berlitzpublishing.com**